ADVANCE PRAISE

The historian Lord Acton once remarked that "history is not a burden on the memory but an illumination of the soul." It's important to add that illumination can happen only when history is told openly. Memory often places an intolerable burden—including a burden of silence—on those who endure injustice. The period of antisemitism in the Emory University dental school, for example, derailed the lives and scarred the memories of scores of Jewish students who studied there from 1948 to 1961. Fortunately, for the illumination of our own souls many years later, Perry Brickman has brought this history to light through dogged research and a gift for good storytelling. He has "extracted" the festering truth from the historical records like an abscessed tooth. Emory University and, one hopes, the former students who experienced that history are better because of his wise heart and his search for knowledge.

Gary Hauk
official historian of Emory University

My father, Gerald H. Greene (1925-1988), used to quip: "I was rejected by the best colleges in America!" Only once did he ever hint that it had anything to do with being a penniless Jewish kid from Brooklyn. Instead of enrolling in university, he enlisted in the Army Air Corps, served as the nation's youngest P-38 reconnaissance pilot, survived the War in the Pacific, and, after Japan's surrender, returned to civilian life. He was proudly self-taught, became a successful financial planner, made certain my brother and I attended excellent colleges, and concealed—beyond his mild witticism—whatever he may have felt about all the rejections. Not till reading Dr. Perry Brickman's remarkable book did I pause to consider what those rejections must have cost my father, and how—without the bird's-eye view of history available in *Extracted*—he must have taken it personally, just as Perry Brickman did as a young man, just as all the rejected, expelled, flunked-out, and "extracted" bright young Jewish dental school students did, unaware that they were part of cruelly biased social manipulation. This book is remarkable in so many ways: who knew that this highly-esteemed, retired oral surgeon concealed a storytelling knack rivaling that of his popular wife Shirley, an investigative gene akin to Bob Woodward's, and a writing flair that enlivens every sort of statistical and archival finding? The book is a treasure, a rare document created by an individual who suffered through the events of history himself and then returned to the scene of the crime as an investigative journalist and historian.

Melissa Fay Greene
author of *Praying for Sheetrock*
and *The Temple Bombing*

Perry Brickman provides us with an engaging and important addition to the history of antisemitism in American health professional education. Equal parts autobiography, the sleuthing of a history detective, and a compilation of the testimony of witnesses and victims, Brickman chronicles a notorious episode of bigotry at the Emory University dental school which resulted, decades later, in a public apology from the university.

Edward C. Halperin, MD MA
Chancellor/CEO New York Medical College/
Touro College and University System

When leaders of the Anti-Defamation League exposed a pattern of antisemitism at the Emory University School of Dentistry in 1961, they relied primarily on statistics to make their case. Nothing, however, was ever known about the real-life victims of the discrimination they uncovered. Now, over a half-century later, Dr. Perry Brickman, himself one of the students who was unfairly flunked out of the school, has told the human side of the story. Based on countless hours of painstaking research and original interviews, Brickman's book, *Extracted,* reveals the debilitating impact that bias in higher education has on the personal and professional lives of those it touches. It also provides an inspiring portrait of the resilience that victims can muster in rebuilding their lives, coming to terms with their experience, and working to reform the system. Seamlessly framing the Emory story and his own personal memories within a larger national context, Brickman's work will be certain to interest a wide audience.

Eric L. Goldstein, Judith London Evans
Director of the Tam Institute for Jewish Studies
at Emory University, and author of *The Price*
of Whiteness: Jews, Race, and American Identity

This book provides a significant contribution to the study of our country's history of prejudice and discrimination. Dr. Brickman's quest to understand what led to his dismissal from dental school in the early 1960s took him on a decade-long journey that unmasked systemic antisemitism at an esteemed academic institution and that ultimately led to an extraordinary apology to the victims. While the ADL provided the initial statistics that documented the discrimination, Dr. Brickman, through rigorous archival research and interviews, has woven here a fascinating tale of the long-term impact of bigotry and prejudice on him and his fellow students, and has demonstrated the importance and power of truth and reconciliation. His tenacity in pursuing this story and in seeking justice is inspiring.

Deborah Lauter
Anti-Defamation League, former Senior Vice

President (2015-17), National Civil Rights Director
(2006-2015), SE Region Director (2001-2006)

Dr. Brickman's extensive research over many years reveals how antisemitism took place in a major U.S. university dental school. Not only was it one of the worst cases of proven anti-Semitism in university history, but the author examines the diabolical plans to exclude Jewish dental students from becoming dentists. It is also a personal statement, in great detail, of what happens when one is persecuted because of religion.

Dr. Ronald Goldstein
Atlanta cosmetic dentist and author of
Change Your Smile **and** ***Esthetics in***
***Dentistry*; former International President of**
Alpha Omega Dental Fraternity

In writing this book, Perry Brickman has brought to life a history of the former institutionalized anti-Semitic bigotry intentionally, although unofficially, incorporated into the administration of the Emory University dental school, a direct conflict with the mission of developing knowledge and skills of its students. This well researched and documented account not only records the sordid actions of the incident, but it also brings to light the trauma, degradation, and psychological impact on the subsequent lives of the students so impacted.

In 2012, Dr. James Wagner, president of Emory University, on behalf of the university, publicly acknowledged and apologized for these grievous actions and provided a platform for the victims to be recognized and vindicated.

Marvin Botnick
Editor and Publisher of *The Jewish Georgian*

Extracted

E⚹tracted

*Unmasking Rampant Antisemitism in
America's Higher Education*

S. Perry Brickman, D.D.S.

NEW YORK

LONDON • NASHVILLE • MELBOURNE • VANCOUVER

Extracted

Unmasking Rampant Antisemitism in America's Higher Education

Published in New York, New York, by Morgan James Publishing. Morgan James is a trademark of Morgan James, LLC. www.MorganJamesPublishing.com

Photographs and Materials from the Emory University School of Dentistry and Atlanta-Southern Dental College courtesy of the Stuart A. Rose Manuscript, Archives, and Rare Book Library, Emory University. Emory event photographs courtesy of Emory Photo/Videos.

"American Dental Association Expected To Reject Report Urging Racial Quotas," *The Southern Israelite*, February 11, 1945, courtesy of the Jewish Telegraphic Agency, JTA.org. This story may not be reproduced without the written permission of JTA.

The University of Tennessee College of Dentistry graduation photograph, June 1956, courtesy of The University of Tennessee.

Excerpts from "Some of My Best Friends," © 1962 by the Anti-Defamation League of B'nai B'rith, 1962, courtesy of the Anti-Defamation League.

"Shining Light on Emory school's past anti-Semitism prompts healing—and, for one man, questions," Jessica Ravitz, October 13, 2012, courtesy of CNN. This story may not be reproduced without the written permission of CNN.

Materials from the Atlanta Jewish Community Relations Committee and Community Relations Council, courtesy of the Cuba Family Archives for Southern Jewish History at the Breman Museum.

"I've graphed my bad behavior for you," October 12, 2012, Susan McCarthy, courtesy of SorryWatch.com

Photographs from *The Journal of the American Dental Association* (JADA), courtesy of Elselvier.

ISBN 9781642792942 paperback
ISBN 9781642792959 ebook
Library of Congress Control Number: 2018911540

Cover Design by:	Interior Design by:
Rachel Lopez	Chris Treccani
www.r2cdesign.com	www.3dogcreative.net

Morgan James is a proud partner of Habitat for Humanity Peninsula and Greater Williamsburg. Partners in building since 2006.

Get involved today! Visit
MorganJamesPublishing.com/giving-back

For my dad, Paul Myer Brickman.
His determination and encouragement made a second chance
possible for me.

I am grateful to all my dental school classmates. After years of anguish, they were willing to open their hearts and souls and share their long-suppressed stories. Most of them had successfully responded to the financial, social, and emotional challenges they experienced at the Emory dental school. Yet they were relieved to be able to finally shed what for many of them was a life-long burden.

TABLE OF CONTENTS

A Remarkable Story

As a baby boomer, I knew, from stories around the Shabbat table and later from my own training in American Jewish history, that through to the mid-1960s bright American Jews had faced terrible obstacles in their professional advancement. I knew that schools such as Brandeis University and the Albert Einstein Medical School had been created to give young Jewish people who found the doors of other institutions barred to them a path to success.

Later in my professional life, I met brilliant scientists and researchers who had been in graduate school in the two decades after World War II. They knew that, in order to succeed, "they had to be gold to be considered silver," simply because they were Jews. I met men and women who had attended Ivy League schools in the 1950s and into the 1960s. They treasured their education and the opportunities it afforded them, but they recalled, not without a measure of bitterness, how they had encountered overt antisemitism in the classroom, lab, dining hall and dormitory. One woman who attended Wellesley in the early 1960s, described walking down the hall of her dorm for the first time, as she made her way to her assigned room. The names on the doors were all Goldberg, Epstein, Jacobs and the like. "I thought that strange. Were there so many Jews at Wellesley that virtually every room should be occupied by a Jew?" Even her roommate was Jewish. She quickly realized that all the Jews had been sequestered in one living and dining area. To those in the "outside" world she had made it. She had reached the academic stratosphere. But she and the other Jews "inside" that world knew that they were seen as "different." They were separate but certainly not equal.

I knew these stories, but these experiences came alive in an unprecedented fashion in these pages. These former Emory dental school students describe humiliation that makes one's skin crawl. The loneliness and sense of abandonment they experienced is palpable. When one mother, upon being told by her son—the one who had caused her such *nachas,* such parental pride- that he had been expelled, wails, "What have you done to me?" I relived the young man's horror.

Perry Brickman discovered, in an almost serendipitous fashion, that what had been done to him and to so many others was part of a much larger pattern. Perry and his wife Shirley were at Emory's Woodruff Library in the Manuscripts and Archives division, attending the opening of an exhibit on Jewish life at Emory. I happened, also serendipitously, to be standing next to them. We were in front of a graph showing the pattern of antisemitism that had prevailed at the dental school. I saw him blanch and then jab Shirley to make sure she had seen the chart. At that point I had no idea of his personal connection to that impersonal graph.

Other people might have been relieved to know that what happened to them and to others was part of something far bigger. They might have felt that the burden of personal shame they had carried at having been "failures" had been lifted. After decades of embarrassed silence, they might have told their story to family and friends. They might have said: "It wasn't *just* me. It was 65% of all Jewish dental students."

But Perry Brickman did far more than that. And here too is among the most remarkable aspects of this whole story. He remade himself. He went from being a retired oral surgeon to an amateur historian, and a sleuth. He followed every lead. He learned how to mine archives and spent hours in libraries reading histories, yearbooks, and phonebooks. He left no stone unturned. He took computer courses and hired a personal tutor to learn how to organize his documents on his laptop. (In that regard he surpasses most professional historians. They either work in chaos or leave to others—graduate students—to do that for them.) He read the literature, finding every book that might, somehow, shed light on the episode.

And most importantly, he personally tracked down every individual who was personally connected to this unpleasant saga. He schlepped all over the United States, with his amazing helpmate at his side, to probe, ask, discover, learn, and document. At first he had to chase people down. Some, unwilling to open these painful wounds, turned him away. Then, as word reached them from their friends of the remarkable job Perry was doing, they came back ready to participate. Even some of the "antagonists," the people who might have facilitated this travesty, reached out to him, anxious to present "their side" of the story.

And in the course of so doing, something else happened. He began to heal. The pain remained. How could it not, when he recalled his mother's plaintive cries? But the shame began to dissipate. How could it not, when he recognized that he had been an innocent victim in a scheme of age-old hatred and discrimination?

And then, possibly the most remarkable thing took place. Perry, at the urging of my colleagues and me, brought the story to Emory University. He expected push back and defensiveness. And why not? That is what Emory had displayed in the past. But we assured him that today was not then. And he found an open door. In fact, he found more than that. He found an institution ready to say the only words possible in a situation such as this: "We are sorry."

And they did not say them in an impersonal way, e.g. by issuing a statement or press release. No, they did it in the way that the great Jewish scholar, philosopher and teacher, Maimonides, says one must act for an apology to be real: face to face. They gathered the men who had been so scarred and, in the presence of their spouses, children, and grandchildren, they looked them in the eye and said, with no explanations (e.g. "Everybody did it, it was the 1950s") or justifications (e.g. "It was one dean of the dental school who was responsible, Emory University wasn't really like that"), they acknowledged: "We were wrong."

Other universities, including Emory, have apologized for legacies of discrimination and slavery. Rarely, however, have they had or sought the opportunity to do it face to face. Those of us who witnessed that moment will never forget it. Some of our recollections may be a bit blurred, because our eyes were brimming with tears.

A few years ago, while hiking high in the Colorado mountains, I was standing on a bridge over an exceptional mountain stream. A young couple nearby was trying to pose so that both they and the rushing waters were clearly visible. Try as they might they could not get the scenery to cooperate. I offered to help. As I returned their camera to them, the young girl said: "Aren't you Deborah Lipstadt?" I laughed at the lack of anonymity and acknowledged that I was. When she identified herself as Perry and Shirley Brickman's granddaughter, I insisted we take and send them a picture of the three of us. After repeatedly remarking at just how much I admired her grandfather and his accomplishments, I proceeded on my way. My hiking partners, intrigued by my encounter, wanted to know "Who is this Perry Brickman?" It was not the place to tell the important story in all its detail, so I promised a fuller account later and just said: "He did something *really* remarkable."

Here's that fuller account.

Deborah E. Lipstadt
Dorot Professor of Modern Jewish History and Holocaust Studies
Emory University
Atlanta, GA
August 2018

ACKNOWLEDGMENTS

Professor Eric Goldstein, Miles Alexander, Esq., Professor Deborah Lipstadt, Professor David Blumenthal, and Deborah Lauter, Esq.: There is just no way I could have penetrated barriers, uncovered facts, and told this story without their guidance and support.

Arthur J. (Art) Levin and Dr. Marvin Goldstein: These two men are the heroes of this historical tragedy/triumph. They shared a common fervor for honesty, fairness and equal opportunity, and withstood efforts to bury the truth.

Dr. Gerald Reed, Mrs. Charlotte Wilen, and Dr. Ronald Goldstein: Unconventional and insurmountable. Their unwillingness to bow to political pressure is preserved in their memoirs and their testimony.

My fellow schoolmates: Strong, dignified, and grateful. Your long silence was finally rewarded. A special thanks to Dr. Arthur S. Burns who initially spurred me to action.

President James Wagner, and Vice President Gary Hauk, Emory University: You are courageous and gracious. You have selflessly demonstrated the virtue of apology. By validating our side of the story, you have brought happiness to our hearts.

Librarians and archivists: Unequalled in their devotion to preserving recorded history. Great allies in my search for hidden clues and crumbs of evidence.

Many thanks to my publisher, Morgan James for their confidence and professional support.

A special expression of gratitude to Justin Spizman, my talented coach and developmental editor. You were a master hand-holder and cheerleader, and skillfully motivated me to achieve my long-sought goal.

Finally, my love, devotion, and thanks to my girlfriend, sweetheart, and incredible wife, Shirley, who has been my steady and exciting companion throughout my life. And to our amazing children, Lori Freeman and her husband Joe, Teresa Finer and her husband Paul, and Jeffrey Brickman and his wife Susan, for their love and untiring support. We are confident that our dear grandchildren Jason and Jessica Morse, Elena, Talia, and Anna Finer, and Joseph Brickman will serve as faithful storytellers in the future.

INTRODUCTION

It never occurred to me that I had an unusual story to tell until 2006, when I was almost 74 years old. To explain why it took me so long requires providing the background of a very fortunate first-generation Jewish-American youngster. I would now add an additional adjective, naive.

All four of my grandparents and my father emigrated from Lithuania to the United States. I was born in Chattanooga, Tennessee in 1932 toward the end of the Great Depression. I was spoken to only in English, and I learned to read and write only English during my formative years. I identified as an American.

Growing up Jewish in the South, I never felt that I was inconvenienced or discriminated against. I attended public schools, as did fellow students from a variety of ethnic and religious backgrounds. I don't recall a single uncomfortable moment in school from the first to twelfth grade. Of course, there were private clubs that our parents and others couldn't join and probably some restricted neighborhoods, but we understood that as "just the way it was."

My bar mitzvah in 1945 was certainly a personal milestone. But as a teenager, I was mostly animated by a sense of national relief that World War II was winding down. The newsreels showed Americans of all races and nationalities fighting for our country. It was a national effort, and in many ways, Americans were united as never before.

The slogans proclaimed, "Together We Can Do It." "Do Your Bit, Save Food." "Work To Win." We collected tin cans for the scrap drive, bought US saving stamps, and were "proud to be an American."

When the war ended, there were still inequities in America, but there was promise that better times were coming for all. I understood that to mean that there would be better opportunities for black Americans and for those others who were illiterate or uneducated. I honestly was unaware that there were religious barriers in America, or that I would personally encounter obstacles in a famous institution of higher education.

The year 1945 is the springboard for my story. *Extracted* rescues a long-forgotten article in the February 7, 1945 *New York Times* that foreshadowed the antisemitism unleashed on America's dental schools. It referenced a 14-page report by Dr. Harlan H. Horner, a top executive of the American Dental Association, and head of a committee appointed to upgrade dental schools throughout the US. The "Horner Report" appeared in the Journal of Dental Education and read in part: "The racial and geographical imbalance in the entire enrollment in the dental schools ... presents a more difficult problem." "[F]our states ... furnish 36% of the dental students." "These students are largely of foreign extraction and belong mainly to one racial group." "The Council believes that determined effort should be made on a national scale to counteract the trend ...."

The story reached a handful of Jewish communities via the Jewish Telegraphic Agency but was either unread or not given sufficient importance to warrant a response. The Anti-Defamation League (ADL) New York office expressed outrage, but officials of the American Dental Association brought the matter under control by vehemently insisting that the Horner Committee report was not endorsed by the ADA.

When three of my Jewish friends and I applied in 1951 to Emory University School of Dentistry, we were oblivious to the antisemitic culture of the school. By 1953, all four of us would be gone— flunked out of the school. We were embarrassed and humiliated. Our innocence disappeared. Individually, we went our separate ways and deliberately cut off contact with each other. We had no idea what happened to those who followed us. My wife labeled us a "fraternity of silence."

So, it was on a late summer day, September 10, 2006, that I was astonished to come face-to-face with 1962 ADL documents that strongly suggested my friends and I had been failed out of Emory's dental school in May 1952 because we were Jewish. The authenticity of the documents was bolstered by the fact that they were part of a public exhibit sponsored by the Tam Institute of Jewish Studies at Emory University and curated by Emory Professor Eric Goldstein.

The ADL statistics had first appeared in the Atlanta Journal-Constitution on March 26, 1962. They indicated that during the 1948-1962 tenure of Dean John Buhler, 65% of the Jewish dental students were flunked out or were made to repeat one or more years. On March 27, 1962, Emory's president publicly denied the ADL allegation, and sent a delegation of the Emory Board of Visitors to suppress the sentiments of an angry Jewish community. The matter then lay dormant for forty-four years.

Six years of research turned up all the living victims, most of whom agreed to record their stories. Like me, they had also remained silent through the years, unaware that they were targeted simply because they were Jews. A one-hour documentary was produced and screened for Emory University officials. After announcing their intention to apologize in an October 7, 2012 *New York Times* article, an official apology by Emory's President James Wagner was made on October 10, 2012 at a public gathering in Atlanta.

The historical apology of Emory cleared the air about a controversial issue which had been suppressed for over a half century. It was a rare instance in which a powerful university announced in the nation's "newspaper of record," its intention to apologize for a long history of antisemitism, then granted a public platform for its victims to be recognized and vindicated.

The apology cannot be underestimated. For this courageous action, Emory University deserves our praise and gratitude.

The Horner Committee's antisemitic quota policies originated in the early 1940s and went unchallenged for twenty five years. Even though formal quotas have not survived legal challenges and are gone, Jewish students in America's colleges and universities are now being aggressively and openly targeted by organized and well-funded groups whose policies are more deeply entrenched than quotas ever were, and whose impact goes far beyond the job market. Boston University professor Michael Kort recently asserted that the economic threat to American Jewry has been superseded by a far more dangerous political and cultural threat, that reaches much further and deeper into our society. Surveys of what Jewish students, especially those who attempt to defend Israel, currently experience on so many college campuses makes this clear. The lessons of the past remain as urgent and timely as ever.

CHAPTER 1

A Glimpse into the Past

Sunday, September 10, 2006, changed my life. On that day, my wife Shirley and I were invited guests at the premier of an exhibit: "Jews at Emory: Faces of a Changing University." The exhibit was created as part of an upcoming community event at Emory University entitled "30 Years of Jewish Studies at Emory," celebrating the phenomenal growth of the Jewish Studies program there. Back in 1976, Emory University had established the first Chair of Judaic Studies—a chair funded principally by Atlanta attorney I.T. Cohen and his wife in memory of Jay and Leslie Cohen, their son and daughter-in-law who perished in a tragic hotel fire in Jacksonville, Florida on December 29, 1963. The program was sponsored by the Rabbi Donald A. Tam Institute for Jewish Studies, the Emory University Archives, and the Manuscript, Archives, and Rare Book Library at Emory University.

Our invitation to the exhibit premier announced, "… the attendees will be escorted by Professor Eric Goldstein to the Manuscript, Archives and Rare Book Library (MARBL) on the 10th floor of the Woodruff Library to view the Exhibition which Dr. Goldstein had curated." The reader was reminded that, "since the earliest days of Emory University's history in Atlanta, Jews have been a significant presence at Emory where they have served as important symbols of change during the university's transformation from a regional Methodist college into a national research institution. This ongoing exhibit features photographs, documents and artifacts."

It was only a ten-minute drive from our home to the Emory campus for the event. We were nostalgic, having attended the inauguration thirty years before. It was also a romantic reminder that Shirley and I met at a fraternity event in 1950 on the same campus to which we were headed. Although the Jewish New Year autumn holiday was only 10 days away, it was still a warm 85 degrees in Atlanta on September 10. The slight easterly breeze was hardly noticeable as we walked the three blocks from the Fishburne parking deck to the Joseph A. Jones Room on Level 3 of the Woodruff Library where the event was scheduled. The Jones Room was a popular venue for small to midsize gatherings situated adjacent to the larger Schatten Gallery, where the Jewish Federation had previously hosted several large exhibits.

When we arrived, we noticed the academic community and representatives of the organized Atlanta Jewish community, many of them Emory alumni in their own right, enthusiastically mingling. The university had invited attendees to hear faculty members speak proudly about their renowned Jewish Studies program, which had achieved national status since its inception thirty years before. Emory alumni were represented by speakers who would be invited to share experiences of Jewish life at Emory during their respective eras.

Dr. David Blumenthal, the first recipient of the Chair of Judaic Studies, offered warm words of welcome. He acknowledged Dr. James Wagner, president of Emory University, as well as the president of the Atlanta Jewish Federation, and numerous other Jewish community leaders. The program proceeded in well-planned order, combining the scholarly precision of the Emory academy and the lively exuberance of the Jewish community leaders. The tone was properly set for the esteemed panelists to express their lavish praise for their alma mater. As a former Emory undergraduate, I could certainly relate to the warm feeling they all had for the university. But even after so many years, it was still difficult for me to restrain my silent resentment of the same university that tolerated such uncivilized behavior in one of its graduate schools.

Sensing my discomfort, Shirley squeezed my hand, and I managed as always to bring my emotions under control.

As a dramatic conclusion to the program, Professor Eric Goldstein led the large crowd from the Jones Room to the 10th floor of the Woodruff Library to view the exhibit he had curated on Emory's Jewish history. Before we headed for the elevators leading to the 10th floor of the library, Professor Goldstein described his long interest in the history of Jewish life at Emory. He reminded the crowd that Emory had a rich Jewish history, which had evolved in many ways over the years. He told us that he would be available for questions but had designed the exhibit to be self-explanatory.

The MARBL library had been reserved that evening for our group. The excitement of the crowd, as it spilled out from the ascending elevators into the narrow vestibule leading to the exhibition space, momentarily interrupted the normally decorous air of the library. Once inside, the visitors quickly adjusted their behavior and quietly followed Professor Goldstein to the first of five sections.

Shirley, a veteran docent at Atlanta's Breman Jewish Museum, was impressed with the quality and scope of the exhibit. For the most part, the exhibit was celebratory, demonstrating the remarkable presence of the Jewish people at Emory throughout the years, and highlighting the many accomplishments of Jewish alumni. The exhibit was meticulously categorized into five sections: 1) Emory's first Jewish students 2) Jewish fraternities 3) Jewish organizations 4) Jewish professors 5) Quotas and Anti-Semitism.*

*Throughout, I have chosen to spell antisemitism without a hyphen because doing otherwise distorts its essential meaning and historical origins. It is not hatred of "Semitic" peoples (an erroneous historical concept itself inasmuch as there are Semitic languages, but no Semitic peoples). It is Jew-hatred. Such was the meaning given to it by its originator, Wilhelm Marr. Such was the meaning of the term when used by the Nazis and scores of other Jew-hating antisemites. The hyphen, therefore, acts as a linguistic *distraction from the plain meaning of the word: hatred of Jews (Judenhass). I have chosen to write it in lower case as a personal attempt to belittle its practitioners and lessen their significance. I do this knowing, full well, that it played the pivotal role in the story I tell.*

Up to the final section, neither Shirley nor I encountered any historical surprises. But when we reached the section titled "Quotas and Anti-Semitism," we were blown away. We suddenly faced, head-on, three large panels dramatically recalling the alleged history of antisemitism at Emory's dental school a half-century before. I was shocked to see that the panels included a chronological and pictorial exposé of the "Jewish problem" at Emory's dental school from 1948 to 1961.

The first panel highlighted the Anti-Defamation League's (ADL) 1960-1961 charges against Emory. **A bar graph from an out-of-print 1962 ADL book,** *Some of My Best Friends* **showed that the dental professors failed 65% of Jewish students over a ten-year period, contrasted with 15% of non-Jewish students over the same ten-year period.** The second panel showed Emory's denial of these claims, while the third panel showed the dental school resignation letter Dean John Buhler sent the university on April 12, 1961.

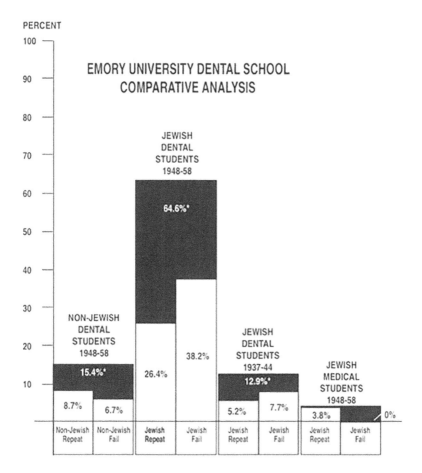

ADL bar graph showing 65% failure rate of
Jewish dental students at Emory

I couldn't believe my eyes. My head was swimming, my heart racing. I was taken back in time to 1952, reliving that dark period at Emory when, after completing my freshman year at Emory dental school and returning home to Chattanooga for the summer, I received a letter of dismissal from that very dean. The document was cold and brief and offered no option for a return to the program. I was left feeling helpless, confused, and upset.

"What have you done to me?" my mother wailed. I still remembered hanging my head, unable to answer her question. I had no idea how it happened, and it came as more of a shock to me than to my parents. Though shamed and humiliated, I refused to let this destroy my dream, and I went on to apply and gain acceptance to dental school at The University of Tennessee, where I ultimately graduated fourth in my class. I never looked back. In the ensuing years, I had no desire to know what was going on at Emory, or why I was so abruptly asked to leave.

Returning to reality, I looked to see if we were obstructing the flow of the crowd, and to observe the reaction of the rest of the group to the controversial fifth section. The visitors filed by smoothly, seemingly unfazed or perhaps uninterested in the shocking revelation facing them. The people, still excited by the first four sections, were expecting to view more familiar facts and faces. This information, however, just didn't resonate. Out of respect, they lingered a few requisite moments. Then, unimpressed, they moved on, having concluded an otherwise enjoyable afternoon. But I just couldn't believe what I was seeing. It was like a flashback to one of the most challenging and difficult times in my life.

My eyes returned to the panels before me. The statistics on the bar graph were telling, but they were only numbers. There were no faces of the former students, including me, whose hopes and dreams had been shattered. Who were they? How many were there? Were they still alive? Question after question jolted through my mind.

I reexamined the panels, seeking details, hoping for answers. The captions under the bar graph delineated the ADL's charges of antisemitism. Dean Buhler's resignation, signed and dated, was displayed in its entirety. An article from the *Atlanta Journal-Constitution* quoted the Emory administration: "It was the Dean's decision to leave. He could have remained if he had wanted to." The article continued, "When further questioned by the press, Emory denied the charges and said they had no validity or credibility." It concluded, "Emory officials said they were sorry if there were any misunderstandings."

I quietly called Professor Goldstein to the side and asked him how and why he had seen fit to highlight the event. He told me he thought Emory had reached the point where they were prepared to confront the issue, and they had given him clearance to proceed with the exhibit. I didn't respond. I thought to myself, *I only know my story. Could it really be that so many others shared a similar experience? What a strange way to confront an issue. Are they testing the waters? If no one responds, will they feel they have done their part and just drop it? If there is a response, will they be willing to talk about it?*

I was overwhelmed and nervously turned to Shirley. "I know this is my story, but I had no idea so many others shared my experience. There must be other news articles I should look for, and other stories I should hear." Clearly, it would be a major undertaking if I chose to pursue the matter further.

The ride home was unsettling. The questions in my head offered no answers. For years I had remained clueless regarding the situation at the Emory dental school while attending, and in the subsequent years to come. With the exception of my wife, very few people knew my story of antisemitism and hurt. Neither my children, nor my professional partners and colleagues, nor my neighbors and friends were aware of my past experience at Emory. The bombshell of history I had just encountered dared not be discarded, but I wasn't sure I was up to the task. Quickly rejecting that notion, I asked myself, "Where do I start?"

A Past Not Soon Forgotten

It was not difficult for me to enter my own personal time machine. Once I made the commitment to revisit the past, visual images flooded my brain. Names and dates competed for my attention. I recorded them all. I highlighted each one with very specific detail. If this story were to be told, it had to focus on my classmates, my colleagues, and my fellow dentists.

My memories of this time in my life were mostly positive and reassuring up to a point. I had come to Atlanta in 1949, well prepared to pursue a career in dentistry. My family, who had worked so hard on my behalf, was proud of my scholastic achievements at Emory. I had a B+ average, as did most of my AEPi fraternity brothers. I had every reason to believe that would carry over into dental school.

I was just 19 years old when I was flunked out of the Emory dental school. Back then, I was told I was a failure. Now, armed with new information, I knew that it wasn't just me. Sixty-five percent of the Jewish dental students were failed during the tenure of Dean John E. Buhler. This wasn't poor studying habits or grades. Rather, this was widespread racism, calculated and targeted antisemitism.

Intellectually, that was a difficult and serious concept to embrace. I resisted the victim mentality. But there it was. As the 1962 ADL bar graph illustrated, we were kicked out because we were Jews. Many of us smart Jews at that.

After the event at Emory, I began making regular visits to the Emory campus. The Woodruff Library was imposing, requiring security clearance to access MARBL, the Manuscript, Archives, and Rare Book Library, located on the tenth floor. I combed the *Campus* yearbooks, with special focus on the dental and medical schools. I was able to determine with accuracy the matriculation of the Jewish students, and how many graduated and at what rate. I became intimately involved with each of them, although I had never personally known many of them. I concentrated on the decade between 1950 and 1960. The failure rate of the Jewish dental students during that period was astonishing. We simply vanished. There was no explanation. There was no rhyme. There was no reason. As much as I fought this notion, there was only one logical explanation.

My initial intention was to confine my search to the years between 1948 to 1961, but it was like an archaeological dig. I was able to identify the full 579 Jewish dental students who attended Emory University and its predecessor, Atlanta- Southern Dental College, from 1913 to 1988, the year Emory dental school closed its doors. I was disappointed to learn that all the records of the school were destroyed. But the MARBL archives at the Woodruff Library preserved all the personal papers of former Emory President Goodrich C. White.

I read that President White engineered Emory's purchase of the Atlanta-Southern Dental College in 1944 and learned of his increasing friendship with Dean Ralph R. Byrnes, and his reliance on Byrnes to keep the troubled dental school running in the present and post-WWII years. White convinced the aging Byrnes to remain as dean until together they could identify and hire his successor. An extended correspondence between Dr. White and Dr. John Buhler, who was hired in 1948, revealed a close personal relationship. Unfriendly references to Jewish dentists were clues that a sinister story awaited full disclosure. Something poisonous was brewing between these two men, and only time would tell its full impact.

Dean Ralph Byrnes Atlanta Southern Dental College 1925-1948	Emory President Goodrich C. White 1942-1957	Dean John E. Buhler Emory U. Dental School 1948-1961
1	2	3

I eagerly sought Dr. Buhler's papers. The Emory librarian informed me that Buhler's papers, if they ever existed, were never held in the Emory collection. Based on evidence of the dean's outsized ego, I maintained a certain confidence that he would leave breadcrumbs of the legacy of his career. I was sure of it. It was my job to find his papers.

I began this journey almost 50 years after my time at Emory. I was 74 years old, healthy, and had a loving and supporting wife and family by my side. I was retired and had the luxury of time to continue my investigation. When I began my search for answers, I knew that uncovering and extracting evidence should be a natural talent for an oral surgeon who had forty-four years of similar experience with embedded and impacted teeth. But little did I know this extraction would be much more complicated and involved.

Live Testimony

In the early days of my research at the Emory Library, I increasingly felt a burden, a responsibility to those other students who like me, had lived in doubt and uncertainty for all those years. I knew that I had to record each of their stories—their testimonies belonged to history. But first, I would have to locate the students, now in their 70s and 80s. And then I would have to decide how to initiate the interviews. I wasn't even sure if anyone would speak to me, as I assumed many of them had the same open wounds I had maintained over the years.

Destiny soon crossed my path, providing an opportunity for me to speak with a former college classmate, prominent Atlanta attorney Miles Alexander. We were attending a community event and were seated next to each other. Prior to the program, Miles asked me what I had been up to lately, which led to a discussion of the Emory University School of Dentistry. Miles was an undergraduate at Emory University from 1948-1952. With total recall, he recited the names and whereabouts of many of the Jewish students impacted by the events that occurred at the dental and medical schools during the late 1940s and early 1950s. Miles urged me to continue my research, but agreed that a priority must be placed on personally interviewing those Jewish dentists who were around during the Buhler years. He insisted that I obtain written permission of all recorded interviews. He also suggested that I have each oral interview transcribed by an outside source to verify the authenticity of the recorded accounts.

Dr. Theodore C. Levitas, a native Atlantan and a Navy veteran, was already a third-year dental student at Emory dental school when

John Buhler assumed his deanship in the fall of 1948. When I returned to Atlanta in 1962, Ted was well established in his practice limited to children's dentistry. He was active in the local dental society and was one of the leaders of the Atlanta chapter of Alpha Omega, the Jewish dental fraternity.

Ted agreed to meet me at a deli in suburban Atlanta. When I called him, he had insisted on knowing why I wanted to meet. I told him that I had recently attended an exhibit on Jewish Atlanta curated by one of Emory's Jewish faculty members. A section of the exhibit included the controversy at the dental school. I wanted him to fill in some of the gaps.

So we met. I told him that I had seen things in the exhibit of which I was not aware. I shared the data and statistics compiled by the ADL, the denial of the accusations by Emory President Martin, and a facsimile of Dean Buhler's resignation on April 12, 1961. I asked Ted if he would fill me in, based on his experience and memory, on what transpired in the dental school during Dean Buhler's 13-year tenure, and what Alpha Omega's role was during that time. I also wanted to know more about the reaction by the Jewish community, if any, to the circumstances.

With a cold face and angry tone, Ted upbraided me. "Are you trying to hurt Emory?" I immediately answered no. He followed, "At this point, what difference does it make?" The conversation was almost over before it started. After a few moments of silence, Ted decided to talk. He told me how his plans to enter the dental school after graduation from college were interrupted by service in the Navy in 1943. Shortly before his discharge from the Navy in 1945, he applied to and was accepted for the 1946 dental school class. Soon after he was discharged, the school notified him that his acceptance to dental school was withdrawn.

Ted's cousin, Dr. Irving Goldstein, had a faculty friend who said he would try to help get Ted into the dental school. The first day of school in the fall of 1946, a freshman student dropped out. Ted was selected to be her replacement.

Ted acknowledged the dental school problem. He said that he and others had approached the Emory University administration, asking them to investigate the "Jewish" situation. Despite the Jewish efforts, Emory denied the allegations, and nothing changed. I recall that the meeting ended on a somber note. Both of us got up and politely left the restaurant. His defensive attitude made it clear to me that I was on to something. The more pushback I received, the more confident I was in the course I was taking. But I saw the need to proceed quietly and cautiously. Even though it was now April 2007 and decades after this travesty, I sensed an unexplainable wall of resistance to my inquiries.

Ron Goldstein had been a friend of mine since college days. A native Atlantan, Ron followed his father Irving Goldstein and his uncle Marvin Goldstein into dentistry. He was one of the few Jewish dental students during the Buhler era who was able to make it through school in four years. He graduated in 1957 and had already established himself as an international authority on esthetic dentistry.

I phoned Ron and told him I wanted to talk with him about the project that I was working on. He was currently writing another book on esthetic dentistry and found the privacy he needed in his home office. He readily agreed to be interviewed and invited me to meet with him at his home the following Friday afternoon. We sat in his study, and I placed my recorder on a long table covered by several of his publications and press reviews.

Ron showed me a 1983 article in which he was prominently featured in the magazine section of the *Atlanta Journal-Constitution*, an article in which he shared personal insights into his life and dental practice. In the article, one of his celebrity patients, comedian Phyllis Diller, enthusiastically offered her praises.

Goldstein, then 49, informed the reporter that his road to success was not achieved without many unpleasant moments. "At the end of my first year of dental school, Dean Buhler called me into his office, and I sat down, and he said, 'Ronald, I flunked nineteen from your class. You're the twentieth. I can either flunk you or pass you.' Then he says, **'but why, why do you Jews want to go into dentistry? You don't**

have it in the hands,' and he repeated himself. He says, 'you need to go into other professions, you don't have it in your hands.'"

Ron paused to interject a long-held thought. "The dean's smear about Jews and their lack of digital skills was a pure out-and-out lie. But it was contagious and was repeated by some of the faculty and actually by several of the students. I remember thinking how outrageous the accusation was. The long list of Jews with extraordinary manual dexterity was unquestionable. Yascha Heifetz, Arthur Rubenstein, George Gershwin, Benny Goodman, Marc Chagall. And what about the Jewish diamond cutters in Antwerp, Tel Aviv, and New York City?

"In the end," Goldstein said, "the dean told me he was going to pass me because my father and my uncle were giving him a hard time. But he unfairly flunked other Jewish boys that year."

And he gave me names and examples.

Soon after Goldstein appeared in the *Journal-Constitution* article, he was summoned by the local dental society to face ethics charges based on his statements. Ron told me that the charges had been brought by one of his dental school instructors, and that all members of the ethics committee were Emory graduates. He said that the chairman of the committee refused to hear the case against him, and told the committee, "I was a student at the school at the same time. Everything he said in the newspaper article about the dean and other members of the faculty is true."

I narrowed the recorded session to Goldstein's four years at Emory dental school. Ron cited graphic examples of religious discrimination at the school under Dean Buhler. He said that when Buhler left his faculty post at Temple dental school in 1948 to become dean at Emory, his reputation preceded him. "How do you know that?" I asked. He hastened to reply, "Because the Alpha Omegans at Temple called my father and my uncle and told them. Write that down," he said.

Seven years would pass before a personal visit to the Temple University dental archives in Philadelphia would convert this unsubstantiated rumor into a documented and disgusting reality.

******

My interview with Ron Goldstein was a much-needed boost. I had a strong feeling that it would open previously unopened doors. And it did. Again, and again, I heard some variation of the following statement: "Ron told you that? Wow. Tell me when you want to hear what I have to say. It's been a long time, but there are things that I will never forget."

I was now hot on a scent that just couldn't be ignored. I knew I had to put a plan in place to get to the bottom of this riveting time in history. Obviously, I had to make a list of people I wished to locate, visit, and interview. Then I had to prioritize my investigative work, taking into account age, geography, and probable importance of that individual's testimony.

With these criteria in mind, I located William Book, a native of North Carolina and a 1940 graduate of Atlanta-Southern Dental College. Dr. Book, a 94-year-old widower, lived with his daughter Rosalyn in a trendy subdivision in Woodstock, 30 miles north of Atlanta. He had lost his vision but retained a keen memory. He provided amazing insights that could only have been obtained in a live interview.

In the course of our conversation, Dr. Book happened to recall that soon after he opened his dental office in Knoxville, Tennessee, he attended a dental school classmate's wedding in Valdosta, Georgia. He remembered the approximate date but couldn't remember the bride's name. Sensing his frustration, I assured Dr. Book that I would do my best to dig up the information. It wasn't on my bucket list and had nothing to do with my dental school research, but it was small recompense for the valuable history he had provided me.

The Southern Israelite newspaper was founded in 1925 in Augusta, Georgia. Under new ownership, it moved to Atlanta in the 1930s and became a popular weekly source for Jewish business and social news in the Southeast. The newspaper received its national news from the Jewish Telegraphic Agency (JTA). I had recently learned that digitized copies of *The Southern Israelite* were available. As soon as I returned home, I went online to the newspaper's website to see if I could find the wedding announcement.

Finding the wedding announcement would require considerable browsing, because Dr. Book's memory of the wedding date was several months off the mark. But Lady Luck was on my side. By chance, or perhaps by divine intervention, I pulled up the front page of the February 16, 1945 issue.

Just as I was prepared to scroll to the wedding section, however, my attention was drawn to the bold headlines of a two-column article acquired from the Jewish Telegraphic Agency's New York office: *"American Dental Association Expected To Reject Report Urging Racial Quotas."* A high-ranking member of the Dental Educational Council of the American Dental Association (ADA), Dr. Harlan H. Horner, was being accused of proposing restrictive "racial quotas" in U.S. dental colleges. Columbia and New York University (NYU) were specifically mentioned as Horner's targets.

American Dental Association Expected To Reject Report Urging Racial Quotas

New York (JTA)—Dr. Sterling Nead, president-elect of the American Dental Association, disavowed the reports by Dr. Harlan H. Horner, head of the Dental Education Council of the ADA, advocating "racial quotas" in dental colleges, and declared that Dr. Horner's statements did not reflect the sentiments of the ADA.

Dr. Spear's statement climaxed a nation-wide controversy aroused by the revelation that Dr. Horner, in reports to the House Committee on Education, Columbia University and the New York University had criticized the racial "imbalance" in the last two institutions and suggested that a quota policy be adopted for students based on racial origin.

Dr. Nead predicated that the trustees of the ADA would reject the Horner recommendations and other sources declared that Horner, himself, was likely to be relieved of his post.

The first inkling of Horner's activities was the publication in the Journal of Dental Education of an article embodying his recommendations. Further investigation disclosed that he had studied the composition of the student body at the Columbia School of Dental and Oral Surgery and recommended that racial quotas be established, and that he had submitted a similar recommendation for all dental schools throughout the country to the House Committee on Education.

The Anti-Defamation League of B'nai B'rith then revealed that a similar report had been made to New York University. Officers of both institutions denied that they were planning to accept the Horner proposals and pointed out that they were bound by charter to accept students without consideration of race or religion. Students in both colleges protested against introduction of a quota system.

Even today, I remember wondering why the racial quota issue was considered newsworthy in a southern Jewish newspaper. In the South in 1945, racial quotas were absolutely not an issue. Black students were not accepted at Emory, Loyola of New Orleans, or The University of Tennessee at Memphis. They were accepted only at Nashville's Meharry dental school, one of two predominately black schools in the United States. My curiosity was rewarded in the last paragraph of the article, which indicated that the Anti-Defamation League (ADL) was investigating charges of racial and religious quotas at NYU and Columbia dental schools. I reasoned that the story was publicized in *The Southern Israelite* because of the religious aspect of the alleged quotas. I also knew, of course, that Jews were considered in certain circles to be a separate race. The charges were serious but seemed to be focused on the New York area.

I did a Google search on Dr. Horner, but came up empty. In retrospect, I should have gone to the public library and checked out later issues of the *New York Times* and other Eastern newspapers. Assuming that it was an isolated matter, I didn't follow up any further.

But the Horner story lingered in the back of my mind. As my investigative skills improved and I learned how to access national databases, I discovered that the Horner Report was a major story with far-reaching repercussions. I no longer wondered if anyone had ever heard of Dr. Harlan H. Horner and the Horner Report. I found abundant evidence that he had a dark and scheming objective.

My research work was exciting and productive. Highlights included finding and interviewing ninety-three-year old Arthur J. (Art) Levin, the hero of this story. Levin, in the 1950s, was the Southeast Director of the Anti-Defamation League (ADL), headquartered in Atlanta. Against all odds, and almost single-handedly, he exposed the virulent antisemitism at the Emory dental school. And then there was the drama of finding Dr. John Buhler's complete papers at the Medical School of South Carolina Waring Library in Charleston.

My journey through the history books would take me all over the country, including trips to Florida, Alabama, Tennessee, Mississippi, South Carolina, New York, Illinois, Michigan, Massachusetts, and of course all over Georgia to gather and interview valuable witnesses. Teary-eyed, they allowed their wives and grown children to hear, for the first time, the stories of the tremendous antisemitism they had experienced.

Through this discovery process, I gradually accumulated a large collection of books describing anti-Jewish hatred in Europe and America. This was not just a manifestation of nativism and xenophobia prevalent in the lower classes of society. Numerus clausus ("closed numbers"- the quota system), took root in the colleges of Hungary, Austria, and Germany and was implemented to exclude Jews from their universities. "Too many Jewish lawyers, too many Jewish doctors."

The system was adopted and implemented by the finest American universities. Harvard's president, A. Lawrence Lowell, was the most prominent American educator to openly propose a quota on the number of Jews gaining admission to universities. Lowell was convinced that Harvard could only survive if the majority of its students came from old American stock. He didn't operate secretly. It was front and center, out in the great wide open. His proposal appeared on the front page of the June 17, 1922, issue of the *New York Times*, perhaps the most respected newspaper in the world. All the Ivy League schools fell in line with his proposal. It became extremely difficult for Jewish students to be accepted to medical schools. Even those few who succeeded found it extremely difficult to find top-rate residencies.

Dentistry was soon to follow a similar dark and sinister path. Sixty-two-year-old Harlan H. Horner was an educator and demographer who retired after a forty-year career in the New York State Department of Education. The American Dental Association hired him, and he assumed his position as the Executive Secretary of the Council on Dental Education (CODE) on July 1, 1940. Horner's stated goal was to elevate the criteria for admission to the thirty-nine US dental schools and standardize their curricula.

Between 1942 and 1943, Horner and his committee members conducted a national survey. According to reports in the *Journal of the American Dental Association*, a third of the dental schools, including Atlanta-Southern Dental College and Temple University, did not receive full approval from the Horner committee. I discovered documents threatening loss of accreditation if the schools didn't comply with the suggestions of the committee.

After Horner had his way with the vulnerable deans, he felt emboldened to publicly demand a quota system for the nation's dental schools. When unveiled in the New York Times, Horner did not change his position. The public reacted with anger and shock.

Eager reporters located Dr. William J. Gies, the non-Jewish Columbia University professor who was chosen by the Carnegie Foundation in

1922 to conduct the first comprehensive study of dental education in the US and Canada. The 650-page Gies report was the blueprint for the formation years later of the Council on Dental Education.

Outraged over the council's suggestion that students be admitted on the basis of the ratio of their "racial group" to the general population, Dr. Gies said, "It is shameful to stress, or even take notice of any racial or religious differences between students seeking common careers in the colleges of a democratic country.... The university is the last place where religious or racial background should be considered." He concluded, What's the difference if a dentist is Jewish or Gentile? Are we going to come to the point where an Englishman's decayed teeth can only be extracted by a Spaniard? The whole proposition is as absurd as it is bigoted."[4]

The ADA denied knowledge of the Horner report. While they repudiated the recommendations of the committee, the ADA spokesmen accused the Jews of deliberately misinterpreting the report and intentionally besmirching the character of their "highly respected" secretary. This was just one example of a widespread and concerning process of outright antisemitism, a common practice in the 1940s and 1950s.

As I stood in front of those three large panels in Atlanta on September 10, 2006, little did I know I was about to begin an investigative journey spanning the next ten years of my life and almost 100 years of history. This is the story of my journey and the journey of my brothers. Decades ago, we stood in the face of antisemitism that threatened to derail our lives, careers, and sense of purpose. Even though many of us were victims of Emory University, we were not victims of circumstance. We were targeted, compartmentalized, and decisively removed from an academic institution that was supposed to stand for higher learning and greater morals.

Some of us went on to be successful dentists with remarkable practices all over the world. In fact, some of my fellow classmates ended up changing the way dentistry is now practiced. The bigoted leaders at Emory University tried to flush us out of dentistry, but only made us fall more in love with it. Today we remain strong and proud of all that we accomplished in the face of what seemed like an insurmountable opponent.

I am one story, a singular example living within the history books of academic America. As I stood in shock in September of 2006, I sensed a higher calling. Someone, anyone, had to tell this story. I hadn't intended for it to be me, but my curiosity and hobby turned into an introspective and extraordinary account that seemed lost in the history books.

I would eventually approach the Emory administration in 2011 to show them my findings. After much research and interviews, I knew for certain Emory had denied and even covered up a decade of overt antisemitism at their dental school. My journey proved that I had not only uncovered a tremendous stain on the history of Emory University, but also on the dental profession as a whole.

A Forgotten History

CHAPTER 2

A Forgotten History

A t 8 p.m. on Wednesday, October 10, 2012, the President of Emory University, Dr. James W. Wagner, proclaimed to an overflow audience at Dobbs Hall on the Emory campus, "I am sorry. We are sorry. Sorry for the decade of antisemitism at the dental school, and sorry for Emory's having deliberately delayed this very apology for over fifty years."

Richard Arnold, a 1958 Emory dental school graduate, was the first of the crowd to respond. Accompanied by his wife and children, who had traveled with him from Miami, Florida, Arnold spoke in a clear and defiant voice that tempered his emotions. "I never for a moment doubted that I was qualified, even when I was told I would have to repeat a year. But, over the years, I never told my story to my children. Why? Because they weren't raised in an environment like this. It would have been too much to expect them to understand this type of behavior. But now that the President has spoken up, that validates our stories."

All the major networks covered the event live. For three weeks, it was the second most visited news article on *The New York Times* website. Surprisingly, not one dissenting voice emerged. On the contrary, there were letters and articles posted that exposed long-festering tales of discrimination and antisemitism in the nation's professional schools.

When I presented my story to audiences throughout the country, attendees queued up to show me wrinkled documents, yellowed by time. The indignities they suffered mirrored my own painful experiences.

21

Gradually, I was convinced that this was not exclusively an Emory phenomenon. It was widespread, and not confined just to the dental profession. I needed to widen my horizon. The obvious questions haunted me. What was this all about? How far back did this all begin? How did this even happen?

I recalled and re-read the controversial information I had uncovered on Dr. Harlan H. Horner. Horner was an educator and demographer who retired in December 1938 after a 40-year career in the New York State Department of Education. In 1940, the ADA hired him to conduct a survey of the nation's thirty-nine dental schools. The stated goal was to elevate the status of the schools and its students. From his Chicago office, Horner sent questionnaires to the thirty-nine deans. How many students do you graduate annually? What is the status of research in your institution? How many full-time faculty members do you employ? How far is your school from its target population? Are you associated with a university? Provide a physical description of your school.

Horner and his committee members then performed site visits between October 1942 and June 1943. Thirteen of the schools received the lowest rank, that of provisional approval. The deans of the schools were privately informed of their deficiencies. The schools faced loss of their credentials if they didn't comply with the recommendations of the committee. They shared no further details, as the work of the Horner committee was deemed confidential information.

Excerpts of the Horner report appeared in the *New York Times* on February 7, 1945, sharing headlines that morning with the alarming reports of Nazi death camps. The rumors were now facts. Millions of Europe's Jews had been murdered. Yet now the American public was being informed that the immediate and overriding concern of Dr. Harlan H. Horner, one of the ADA's top executive officers, was that 36% of the nation's dental students were Jewish. With total disregard for the world crisis and no pretense of sensitivity, he proposed that quotas be imposed in American dental schools to ensure equitable racial and geographic distribution.[5]

Were principles of fair play and decency meaningless to Horner and his committee? Had Horner taken the pulse of the American public and found it sympathetic to his sense of priorities? Just who was this Dr. Horner, and who were his associates and collaborators? What was the history of the Council on Dental Education? Where did it derive its purpose and goals? Was Horner merely engaging in social engineering, or was this undisguised antisemitism? What had Jews as a group done to earn the enmity of these distinguished educators? In the aftermath of this targeted assault on fellow Americans, how did the public and the press respond?

I would soon find the answers. Dr. Horner was a native of Moravia, Iowa, considered the heart of America's farmland. He was a graduate of the University of Illinois. While there, he served as an aide to Dr. Samuel Draper, the president of that institution. He continued serving his mentor, who in 1904 was appointed as the first Commissioner of Education of New York State.

Horner's adult life in Albany, New York encompassed the breadth of professional education in the advanced society of New York State educational circles. He was well read, well-traveled, and had professional contact with policymakers. He earned an honorary PhD degree. He was a skillful orator and a polished administrator.

I researched the nine members of Horner's committee. They represented the highest echelons of dental educators. Their pedigree was remarkably similar. They were the Protestant princes of their profession. They were self-selecting intellectuals of old stock similar to the New England Brahmins described by Barbara Miller Solomon in *Ancestors and Immigrants: A Changing New England Tradition.*[6]

Michael Dobkowski, in *The Tarnished Dream: The Basis of American Anti-Semitism*, portrayed the Brahmins in similar terms: "They had served as the rudder of the ship of state since its inception and for good reason, since they were certain they were the best America had to offer." They saw themselves being "gradually eclipsed by the immigrant populations." Ultimately, "it drove them down the path of scapegoating, intolerance and intellectual isolation."[7]

There had to be more to the story. I was at a distinct disadvantage because I had never studied the subject of Jews in America in high school or college. It was obvious that I lacked historical context. But I did know that a review of antisemitism in America would be the springboard for a better understanding of the issue.

****

Historian Michael Dobkowski, in his introduction to *The Tarnished Dream*, states that not until 1920 did American scholars recognize the existence of antisemitism as a significant development in American history. Continued scholarly discussion of antisemitism in America was mostly delayed until after World War II.[8]

Author David A. Gerber cites early opinions that tended to dispel the notion that hostility toward Jews was a unique practice. They asserted that it was a function of ethnocentrism or "nativism," the hostility of native-born white Americans toward all foreigners. During the colonial period, they commented that Jews suffered civil, political, and religious penalties as did such non-Jews as deists, atheists, and members of dissenting churches. They added that during the mass immigrations from the 1820s to the 1920s, Jews were certainly not the only immigrant people subject to prejudice, hostility, and discrimination. Gerber strongly disagreed. He said that Jews were unique among foreigners,[9] and quotes Oscar Handlin who wrote that the Jews were "the most prominent and the most vulnerable of all immigrant minorities discriminated against."[10]

David Gerber commented that the nativist argument strangely neglected an important reality of Jewish-Gentile relations in America: the Christian belief concerning the guilt of the Jews as a people for the crucifixion that had led to centuries of persecution in the Old World, and which vigorously followed them to the New. Also omitted was that immigration restrictionists demonstrated deeply antisemitic feelings toward Jewish immigrants, and less focused hostility to other groups such as southern Italians. They found Jews not only alien and different, but also pernicious and disgusting, insisting that Jews must give up their ancient traits before they could be recognized as Americans.[11]

American History professor Leonard Dinnerstein[12] and Michael Dobkowski[13] present hundreds of pages chronicling virulent antisemitism as it appeared in legal documents, novels, literary journals, newspapers, theatre, and movies. The bibliographies are exceptional. Dinnerstein states emphatically, "All aspects of American antisemitism are built on the foundation of Christian hostility toward Jews."[14]

For Jews in America, the thrust of restrictive provisions and antisemitic attitudes was clear. The young nation thought of itself as Christian. Full legal and religious equality would come only after a long and difficult struggle. That it did was as much a result of Jewish effort, skill, and endurance as of a native spirit of American tolerance.

It is apparent that, in many circles, Judaism as a faith and way of life was not positively viewed. Judaism was perceived as a backward religion, and to many presented a direct and serious challenge to the American spirit and character. It went beyond a matter of misunderstanding. The Jews' very nature and religious essence were interpreted in literature and by social commentators as being anathema to America's Christian heritage.

The view of the Jews as Christ killers, rejected by God and justly punished for their sins, was widely taught in American Sunday schools in the early nineteenth century[15] and echoed by religious publications. They spoke of the "conspiracy of the Jewish rulers against Jesus Christ." Popular novelists of the time reminded their readers that "Jews nailed Jesus to the cross and reviled Him." As early as 1812, Hannah Adams, the first professional woman writer in the United States wrote, "The history of the Jews exhibits a melancholy picture of human wretchedness and depravity."[16]

An Illustrated History of the Holy Bible contains a great deal about "perverse Jews" who murdered Christ, concluding that Jewish suffering is just retribution for their heinous sin.[17] In the historical novels of the nineteenth century, we see these themes reiterated. Jews are a narrow people, bigoted by nature and proscribed by their faith from accepting a more humane and compassionate way of life—Christianity. These preachings of Christianity, reinforced by historical fiction, offer justification for prejudice. The only Jewish characters sympathetically portrayed were those who found their savior and converted to Christianity. The Jews could find little comfort in their tenuous security as Christians continued to upbraid their character and faith.

Non-theologians equally shared the criticism. Professor John Huston Finley, president of Knox College and later City College of New York, emphasized in 1888 his belief that there is a danger in Jewish unflinching loyalty to ancient customs and incomprehensible Talmudic obligations. Persecution has "engendered in them a morbid, revengeful and isolated disposition" that prevents them "from grasping the kind hand of Christianity."[18] Noted historian James Hosmer, who wrote a treatise on Jewish history in 1893, concurred. "The heart of the Jew can be very unamiable," he wrote. "His heart has lost none of its contempt for Christians."[19]

Thus, in the nineteenth century, Judaism became associated in the minds of many Americans with formalistic adherence to foolish ritual, narrow racial identity, Christian hatred, and delusions of grandeur. The "Chosen People" were often portrayed as intolerant and insensitive, conceited and aggressive, and not averse to subverting the ideals of Christian society.

Some historians have downplayed the significance and impact of the well-documented assault on the Jew and his religion in early American history. Comments in the American Jewish press suggest that this was not the case. As early as the 1850s, Rabbi Isaac M. Wise, the spiritual leader of Reform Jewry, stated that one reason for publishing his magazine, *The American Israelite*, was to counteract the current stream of abusive stereotypes. "A rascally Jew," he explains, "figured in every cheap novel, every newspaper printed some stale jokes about Jews to fill up space, and every backwoodsman had a few jokes on hand to use in public addresses; and all this called forth not one word of protest from any source."[20]

Professor Dobkowski writes, "The pervasiveness of this negative imagery is one more indication that America was not as tolerant in this fluid and turbulent age as some of its apologists would believe; it is one more index of the continued presence of anti-Semitism in American society. Despite all professions of equality, prejudice persisted, and it was expressed, consciously or unconsciously, through the stereotyping of the American Jew."[21]

At the time of the first census in 1790, there were only about 2,000 Jews in the United States in a population of 2 million. The American Jewish population of about 4,500 in 1830 rose to 40,000 in 1845, and leaped to 150,000 by the time of the Civil War. From this figure the number increased to about 250,000 in 1880. This increase was largely made up of German Jews who had been discouraged by the wave of reaction engulfing Europe in the wake of the Napoleonic Wars. Swept immediately into the current of westward expansion, the German Jews were carried far from their points of entry.

In the rapidly growing communities of the Middle West, the Far West, and the South, many of these immigrants made the transition from peddler to prosperous merchant with extraordinary swiftness. In such cities as Cincinnati, Chicago, Louisville, St. Paul, Dallas, San Francisco, and Los Angeles, German Jews were accorded a high status based on priority of settlement—they were among the "first families"—and the wealth and distinction they had achieved. The mention of such names as Straus, Rosenwald, Seligman, Warburg, Schiff, and Morgenthau is alone sufficient to indicate this amazing upward mobility.[22]

On the eve of the Civil War, Jews were already being blamed for the fears and anxieties that the upcoming war was generating. Antisemitic charges erupted on both sides of the Mason-Dixon line. People were wary of merchants who, in their minds, were taking advantage of the hardships brought on by the war. At one point, General Grant issued an order expelling "Jews as a class" from his lines. Although President Lincoln rescinded the order, the general-in-chief of the Army informed Grant "the President has no objection to you expelling traitors and Jew peddlers."[23]

The country was exploding in growth during this same time. It was a period Charles Beard termed "The Second Revolution." It was the revolution that assured the triumph of the business enterprise. It had been fought and largely won by 1877. From 1865 to 1977, writes Matthew Josephson, "three-quarters of the American people set to work, instinctively, planlessly, to build a heavy industry where there had been almost nothing of the sort, and to produce twice as much goods, food, and wealth of all kinds, as they had produced in 1860."[24]

The tycoons that rose to power with the triumph of the second American Revolution were, as Charles Beard has pointed out, largely of North European stock, mainly English and Scotch-Irish and of Protestant background, as the following names will readily confirm: Gould, Vanderbilt, Huntington, Harriman, Rockefeller, Carnegie, Cooke, Morgan, Armour. The first threat to the unchallenged dominance of these industrial tycoons came from German-Jewish immigrants in the United States. As mentioned above, these included the Straus, Rosenwald, Seligman, Warburg, Schiff, and Morgenthau families.[25]

On Wednesday, June 13, 1877, Joseph Seligman was bluntly and noisily refused accommodations for himself and his family at the Grand Hotel in Saratoga Springs, New York.[26] Although not a unique event, it was notable as Seligman was a banker of great prominence and a friend of the late Presidents Abraham Lincoln and Ulysses S. Grant. Therefore, the affair made headlines in places as distant as New York City, Philadelphia, Cleveland, Chicago, and San Francisco. Many chroniclers consider this incident the defining moment of antisemitism in America. Within a decade, gentlemen's clubs, exclusive resorts, and private schools began to bar Jews. By the early 1880s, social discrimination against Jews was obvious whenever prominent members of Gentile society gathered in cities of all sizes—from New York and Boston to Mobile and New

Orleans. Shortly thereafter, exclusive boys' schools such as Groton as well as other secondary institutions designed for the male offspring of the nation's elite were founded.

Overt antisemitism increased as the percentage of European Jewish immigration grew from 0.9% of the total annual influx in 1881 to 6.5% of the gross in 1887. Across America, Protestants became even more outspoken on this question, opposing Catholics as well as Jews. Boston led the assault, and young scions of patricians banded together to form the Immigration Restriction League (IRL). The nucleus of the new group consisted of recent Harvard graduates concerned about maintaining America's Anglo-Saxon heritage and traditions. The IRL attracted some of the most prestigious names in the Boston community, including A. Lawrence Lowell, who would assume the presidency of Harvard University in 1909. In 1922, he would openly advocate for Jewish quotas at Harvard.[27] Within the next two decades, the IRL gathered support from similar clubs in New York, Albany, and Chicago.[28]

Jews were attracting enemies on all sides. They were bitterly attacked by the Catholic Church and Catholic communities in New York, Baltimore, and Boston. In 1889, *The Catholic World*, a reputable journal to that date, published a malevolent essay titled *The Anti-Semitic Movement in Europe,* recounting how Jews had rejected Jesus and how their concern with "money, money, money" reverberated in every century. The Baltimore Catholic newspapers reported that "there was probably no way of being a member of the German-Catholic milieu without being anti-Semitic."[29]

Farmers in the Midwest, who had seen the prices of their crops drop on the world market, formed alliances. Antisemitism was endemic in the rural areas as the prairie farmers saw the Jews with the merchants and the financiers. Antisemitism simultaneously flourished in urban America. On April 3, 1893, a, fierce debate ensued on the editorial pages of the *Detroit Evening News*: "Why is the Jew Hated?"[30]

Jews desperately tried to prove that they were loyal Americans. No matter what Jews did or said, they were always regarded as a group apart.

As the century grew to a close, humorist Mark Twain wrote a piece about the Jews. "Will it ever come to an end? Will a Jew be permitted to live honestly, decently, and peaceably like the rest of mankind?" He added, "He is not a burden on public charities, he is not a beggar. In benevolence he is above the reach of competition."[31]

A correspondent asked Twain if there was hope for change. Was there anything that Jews could do to change their image? Twain thought not. "You will always be by ways and habit and predilections substantially strangers—foreigners—wherever you are, and that will probably keep the race prejudice against you alive."

Although Twain offered no encouragement for Jews to think that things could get better for them, American Jews had difficulty accepting his assessment. They prayed that the twentieth century would see their full integration into American life.[32]

The 1910s

The Gilded Age in United States history is the late nineteenth century, from the 1870s to about 1900. The term was derived from Twain's 1873 work, *The Gilded Age: A Tale of Today*, which satirized an era of serious social problems masked by a thin gold gilding. Nor did the medical and dental services available to the rich and the poor in the United States approach the standards in Europe. This was a national embarrassment that attracted the attention of two of America's wealthiest families, the Carnegies and the Rockefellers. They allocated large sums of money to address the needs of education in general, and medicine and dentistry in particular.

In early 1900, Henry S. Pritchett was appointed president of the new Carnegie Foundation for the Advancement of Teaching. In 1908, the American Medical Association's Council on Medical Education commissioned the Foundation to perform a detailed study of American medical schools. A pilot study had revealed uniformly low educational standards, especially in the large number of proprietary schools, and the Foundation was selected as a neutral party. Pritchett took note of a recent book on education by a progressive young Louisville school principal, Abraham Flexner.

The Carnegie Foundation appointed Flexner to their research staff, and between January 1909 and April 1910, he personally visited all 155 medical schools throughout the United States and Canada. When Flexner's findings were published in June 1910, they caused a sensation.[33] He reported an overproduction of ill-trained men due mainly to the existence of a very large number of commercial schools sustained in many cases by advertising methods attracting ill-prepared youth. His assessments were scathing. He noted that Johns Hopkins School of Medicine was the only medical school to require an undergraduate degree for entrance. Flexner recommended approval of only 31 schools. He was not completely successful, but by 1922 only 81 schools survived.

Flexner's 389-page report was followed by a second report in 1912, also commissioned by the Carnegie Foundation. It was based on a whirlwind survey of medical education in England, France, and Germany. The writings of Theodor Billroth, the famous German/ Austrian physician, greatly influenced Flexner. Billroth's 1876 book on the history and future of medical education at the German universities was an important source on the German tradition of medical education. At the same time, it heralded the rise of antisemitism in the Austrian public sphere.

The 1926 English translation does not omit Billroth's enmity to Jews. Beginning on page 105, Billroth devotes six pages to disparaging Jewish students. **"They are untalented and stupid and will never accomplish anything...."** "There is an entire lack of breeding at home...." "Most of them possess meager talent for the natural sciences, and the majority are utterly unfitted for the career of medicine."[34]

Flexner, himself a Jew, chose to overlook Billroth's racial and religious remarks. But it is clear that he was greatly influenced by Billroth's approach to medical education and used it as a model for his report. In Flexner's report to the Carnegie Foundation he wrote, "...I venture to declare, without fear of contradiction, that in point of scholarship and trained capacity, the American college graduate is sadly inferior to the German student some three years younger."[35]

We will soon see that Harlan H. Horner, Secretary of the Council on Dental Education of the American Dental Association, whose survey was likewise underwritten by the Carnegie Foundation, would use the Flexner report (based on the Billroth model) as the template for his 1944 report.[36] Unlike Flexner, Horner chose to openly target Jewish students.

The 1920s

Aware and mindful of the publicity surrounding the Flexner report, the Dental Educational Council of America (DECA) was formed in 1910 to improve dental education, and to classify and accredit all dental schools, including the proprietary schools. They were eventually joined by the Dental Faculties Association of American Universities (DFAAU), which did not recognize proprietary schools. The latter group's approach would predominate.

By 1922, one year of pre-dental schooling and four years of dental school were required. Dental curricula were standardized among the member schools. Scientific research was encouraged, and new courses were established. Meanwhile, dentistry continued its efforts to interest the Carnegie Foundation in surveying dental education. The 1910 Carnegie-sponsored Flexner report on medical education had been an immense force in upgrading and standardizing medical schools. A comparable report on dental education could show where and how the preparation of future dentists must be improved.[37] Resolutions adopted in 1913 and again in 1920 urged such a survey. Finally, the campaign was successful, and a study of dental education in the United States and Canada was begun in 1922. Dr. William J. Gies, a Columbia University biochemistry professor interested in dental education, science, and clinical applications, had been chosen for the monumental job by the Carnegie Foundation for the Advancement of Teaching.

The Gies report, *Dental Education in the United States and Canada*, took five years to research and write. It consisted of 250 pages of text and more than 400 pages of appendices, including lengthy descriptions and evaluations. The 650-page Gies report was methodically developed at Gies's office at Columbia University in New York City.

In the report, Dr. Gies praised the profession for "advancing dentistry toward its full possibilities in health service." One historian, in summing up the effects of the Gies report, said that it "will always stand as an accurate and dependable sourcebook in the history and evolution of dental education in America, and awakened the public to the significance of dental care as a health measure. It also emphasized the fundamental obligation of society to give dental education and research adequate financial support."[38]

Prior to the completion of his report, Dr. Gies suggested that the four associations of dental educators should merge for the benefit of dental education. That merger was the first tangible result of the Gies study. The new body was the American Association of Dental Schools, created in 1923.

The profession did not favorably receive every proposal made by Dr. Gies. There were too many conflicting and overlapping interests. For example, when Dr. Gies suggested the establishment of a joint agency to devise and administer a standard national examination, controversy over the method of choosing members took place. Ten long years would pass before the first national examination was administered in 1933.

At approximately the same time, Nicholas Murray Butler, the president of the same Columbia University, announced deep cuts in Jewish admissions at the university. Butler described an explosion of Jewish students at Columbia, which was causing a "Jewish problem." The fear was that Jewish enrollment would reach a tipping point, causing the Anglo-Saxon establishment to withhold financial support and send their sons elsewhere for their education. Butler was particularly concerned because of his institution's location in New York City, with its large Jewish population. He took drastic measures to reverse the trend. As early as 1917, in his annual report, Butler was quoted in the *Brooklyn Eagle* as saying: "... that while existing examinations and preliminary requirements be retained, they be used merely to form an eligible list from which the university faculty shall select, on grounds of previous record, personality and promise, those students upon which it thinks it worthwhile to expend the resources of the university."[39]

Other Ivy League schools followed suit. Worried that it was enrolling too many mediocre young men from elite prep schools, Harvard adopted the College Entrance Examination Board as its key basis for admission in 1905 in order to attract and enroll higher-caliber students. But there was one big problem: too many of those higher-caliber students turned out to be Jews. By 1908, the percentage of Jews in Harvard's freshman class jumped from almost zero to 7%; in 1915, the proportion was 15.1%, and by the spring of 1922, the figure had reached 21.5%. It became clear that a system of selection based solely on scholastic performance would lead to the admission of increasing numbers of Jewish students, most of them of Eastern-European background. That was too much for A. Lawrence Lowell, Harvard's president. He worried that "clannishness" would drive away white Protestant applicants—and eventually even qualified Jewish applicants.[40]

President Lowell decided to implement a new plan. The Harvard admission application began to require each student to identify his mother's maiden name. It even asked, "What change, if any, has been made since birth in your own name or that of your father? (Explain fully)." Using this data, Harvard's admissions office devised a labeling system in the 1920s. An applicant designated "j1" was "conclusively Jewish," "j2" indicated a "preponderance of evidence" in that direction, and "j3" meant that it was a "possibility."[41]

On June 17, 1922, page 1 headlines in the New York Times read: "LOWELL TELLS JEWS LIMIT AT COLLEGES MIGHT HELP THEM." The subtitles followed: "Says It Might Tend To Combat The Increasing Tendency to Anti-Semitism." "Favors Direct Action Instead of Indirect Methods Adopted By Other Institutions."

From his Albany, New York, administrative offices in the Department of Education, Dr. Harlan H. Horner had a bird's-eye view of the sinister changes developing in higher education. But this was just the beginning. His time would eventually come.

The 1930s

In many ways, the 1930s showed marked improvement and rising standards in US medical and dental schools. The breakthrough in dentistry occurred when, at its annual meeting in 1935, the American Dental Association (ADA) created a committee on dental education at its annual meeting. This committee was instructed to conduct a survey of the educational status of the profession, with a view to fulfilling the provision of the constitution and bylaws of the ADA, which declares as one of its purposes the obligation "to elevate and sustain the professional character and education of dentists"—a purpose and an obligation that had from the origin of the dental school been delegated almost entirely to the educational institutions. This led to the formation of the Council on Dental Education (CODE) in 1937. Their first formal meeting was held in May 1938. An ADA statement was issued: "We believe that such a council on dental education created by and responsible to the American Dental Association can become an effective agency in promoting high standards among the dental educational schools of the country."[42] This injected the dental world with greater hope that progress was being made. In a few short years, however, CODE would endorse a report that indicated a growing sentiment against Jews.

The 1940s

In April 1940, the ADA hired Harlan Hoyt Horner to be the full-time secretary of the Council on Dental Education (CODE). The 62-year-old Horner had a 35-year career in administration in the New York State educational system, preceded by five years as an assistant to New York State's first Commissioner of Education, Dr. Samuel Draper. In the final decade of his career, Horner had served as Associate Commissioner of Education in charge of higher and professional education.

Horner's primary charge was to develop a plan to elevate the status of dentistry in America. This would include organizing and administering criteria for accreditation of the nation's dental schools.

Horner began his work at the Chicago headquarters of the ADA on July 1, 1940, quickly immersing himself in his new job. Horner was welcomed by Dr. Gerald D. Timmons, who had assumed the position of secretary of the ADA on March 1, 1940. Timmons came from the Indiana University School of Dentistry, where he taught for 15 years.

Wasting no time, Horner sought confidential information from Timmons concerning Indiana's dental school. Timmons declined to get personally involved in the politics of his alma mater. However, in a letter of July 12, 1940, Timmons referred Horner to a former protégé, Dr. John Buhler, a young part-time Indiana dental faculty member. How the nascent Timmons-Horner-Buhler alliance would affect Emory dental school is described in detail in Chapter 12.

Dr. John E. Buhler	Dr. Harlan H. Horner	Dr. Gerald D.Timmons
Dean-Emory U. Dental School	Executive Director-Council on	Dean-Temple U. Dental School
1948-1961	Dental Education-1940-1948	1942-1963
43	44	45

Under Horner's guidance, detailed questionnaires were developed and sent to every dental school, requiring technical information about the schools' property, and personal information about each of the 9,014 students in the US dental schools. These forms covered 10 separate areas of operation, all of which had a direct bearing on the operation of a dental school as it pertained to the "Requirements for Accreditation" published by CODE.

CODE began its visitations to the schools in October 1942. During 1942 and 1943, Horner and his committee members traveled to all 39 dental schools for onsite inspections and evaluations. They completed this work by the third week in June 1943. Horner took the opportunity during the visitations to point out glaring deficiencies to the school officials.

Following the method employed by Flexner in 1910, Horner made it clear to the schools that they would risk loss of their accreditation if they remained unaffiliated. Graduates of unaccredited schools would not be eligible to take state board examinations and would thus be ineligible to practice dentistry. We will soon see the effect Horner had in Georgia.

The eight years Dr. Horner worked in Chicago for the ADA were spent with a singular purpose. He was first and foremost a demographer. With charts, tables, and graphs, he plied his trade. Having toiled so long in academia, with rigid and unbending rules, he was highly disciplined. For the first time, he had no one supervising him. He was in control of a vast system and used the power of his office to enforce his agenda.

Horner's age and vocation allowed him to avoid service in World War I, and he was too old to be drafted for World War II. He had no children, so was spared the anxiety and concern of most American parents as the country prepared itself for war. In Horner's correspondence there was seldom any mention of the tumultuous events engulfing the world.

While Horner and his committee members were crisscrossing America on comfortable passenger trains, Nazis were transporting innocent Jews in cattle cars to the death camps of Auschwitz, Treblinka, and Majdanek.

Horner seemed to have lived in an academic cocoon. Of course, he lived in an era when there was great animosity toward immigrants, including Jews. He lived in the country's most populated state, with the largest percentage of immigrants. During his time, the Ivy League schools imposed strict quotas on Jews and other minorities.[46] His mentor, Andrew Sloan Draper, was president of the University of Illinois and later appointed the first Commissioner of Education of the State of

New York. As Draper's full-time assistant, young Horner was in close contact at the beginning of his career with Nicholas Murray Butler.

Butler was the president of Columbia University and a senior member of the NY Board of Regents. Butler is said to be the one who initially recommended that his colleague Draper be offered the New York commissioner of education position.

In 1922, Butler severely curtailed Jewish matriculation at Columbia University, leading to similar action by many of his colleagues at other universities. They simply copied the numerus clausus quota system policy adopted by Hungary, Poland, and other Eastern European countries in 1920 to exclude Jews from its universities.[47]

Many mainstream thinkers in higher education advocated for the discrimination against Jews in the guise of keeping "the national ratio correct." That meant if Jews were about 3-4% of the overall population in the United States, they should be similarly represented in the professions.[48] It is not much of a leap to argue that Horner bought into the views of President Butler of Columbia and President Lowell of Harvard on this issue.

During the 1930s, Horner doubtless read articles by Charles Lindbergh and Henry Ford[49], as well as other isolationists and nativists in the daily newspapers he received in Albany. He would have been very familiar with American novelists Nathaniel Hawthorne, Edgar Allan Poe, F. Scott Fitzgerald, and T.S. Eliot, whose novels include antisemitic material. In Hawthorne's novel *The Marble Faun*, Jews are described as "the ugliest, most evil-minded people" who resemble "maggots when they overpopulate a decaying cheese."

Dr. Horner was certainly aware of the eugenics movement, which had its headquarters in New York State. Many of the intellectuals in our country were involved in that movement, as well as the movement to impose birth control on the poor masses. Financial support for eugenics research and policy development came primarily from the Harriman, Carnegie, and Rockefeller Foundations, with whom Horner was quite familiar. These movements worked hand in hand with the anti-immigration proponents. Influenced by this pseudoscience, in 1924 Congress enacted immigration quotas against nations of "inferior stock," in effect closing America's "golden door." A decade later this would cut off an escape route for millions of Europeans, most of whom were Jews.

The fortunate few who made their way to America hoped to become productive citizens. Many were talented and refined, and fluent in several languages. Harlan Hoyt Horner was not sympathetic to their dreams and aspirations, and certainly not fond of their "racial" derivation.

On June 21, 1948, Dr. Horner, on the occasion of his retirement, was the honoree at the 25th anniversary meeting of the American Association of Dental Schools in Buffalo, New York. John Buhler, Secretary of the Association, was asked to introduce the guests at the speaker's table.

As Horner was winding down his career, his young friend and colleague Dr. Buhler was embarking on the third stage of his academic career. The day following the dinner, Buhler (along with his wife and two children) drove to Atlanta, where he assumed the deanship of the Emory University School of Dentistry.

The following year, in the fall of 1949, my mother would drive me down from Chattanooga, Tennessee, to Emory University, where I had been accepted as a freshman student. I would enjoy two idyllic undergraduate years before entering my freshman year at Emory dental school in 1951. Dean Buhler spent less than two minutes addressing my class. I don't remember ever seeing him again.

CHAPTER 3

In the Beginning

T hank God that many of my early childhood friends in Chattanooga are still alive. A few years back, 23 of us (who started school together in the first grade) posed for a group photo. We attended the same grade school, junior high school, and high school. We have moved seamlessly along our individual paths, never forgetting those formative years.

As a child, I lived two separate lives. Until three o'clock each day, I attended public school, where I was often the only Jewish student in my entire class. When the final bell sounded, I collected my homework and, without looking back, walked down the front steps of the school and into a vehicle parked across the street. Years later, a former classmate confided in me that he and others thought that was my family chauffeur. But the truth is that four days a week, the driver would then pick up six or seven more Jewish students at other schools and take us all to Hebrew school. When Hebrew school ended at 5:30 p.m., I would walk the six blocks to my parents' coal yard and drive home with them.

I attended synagogue on Saturday mornings. On Sunday mornings, my dad would drive my sister and me to Sunday school. In the afternoons, we would enjoy youth activities at the Jewish Community Center to round out the week of Jewish events.

I lived in a mixed neighborhood, which included Protestant, Catholic, and Jewish families. Early on, I sensed the hostility between the Protestants and Catholics. In fact, the Catholic kids attended their own

41

parochial schools. But I never personally experienced any discrimination or antisemitism. My maternal grandfather, a native of Lithuania, moved to America with an older brother in the late 1890s. He did so presumably for religious reasons. My mother was four years old when her dad was murdered in his grocery store in south Chattanooga. We were told that it was a bungled robbery. Newspaper accounts did not cite a religious motive.

During the war, I saw my uncles enter the armed forces. My father had a serious head injury and received a medical deferment. Even then, my mother was active as a Red Cross volunteer. We generally knew about the war in Europe and in the Pacific but were unaware of the fate of our fellow Jews. In my December 1945 bar mitzvah speech, probably written by our rabbi, I hinted at a Jewish homeland in Palestine. Time was passing by so quickly. In just three more years I would be off to college.

Looking back, it's hard to believe I never applied to any college other than Emory University. My mother was determined that I should become a dentist, and a friend in Atlanta recommended Emory dental school. Her friend also told her that my chances of acceptance to the dental school would be enhanced if I took my pre-dental requirements at the undergraduate division.

We sought advice from our trusted family dentist, Dr. Ewing B. Connell. Dr. Connell was a graduate of Vanderbilt dental school, but the school had closed in 1926 and was no longer an option. He agreed that Emory would be a good choice for my pre-dental studies. After that, he suggested that I add The University of Tennessee dental school in Memphis to my list as well.

My friends and classmates were applying to three schools: The University of Chattanooga, The University of Tennessee in Knoxville, and Vanderbilt University in Nashville. My mother, who dropped out of high school to help support her widowed mother, wanted something different for me. There was no discussion. I was going to Emory.

I did my part in high school, studying hard and making good grades. During my senior year at a local private military high school, the entire school was forced to close due to an outbreak of polio. We received our assignments at home via mail and mailed back our completed homework. This helped to sharpen my study skills. When they lifted the quarantine, I returned to school with increased confidence in my newly acquired self-starting ability.

My high school, sometimes referred to as Baylor School for Boys, was eager to place its graduating seniors in good colleges. Long before the now popular standardized tests became universal, we were tested to determine our personal and professional aptitude. I was told I tested well in science, math, and languages. The school made these scores available to the colleges to which we applied.

Before being accepted by Emory, counselors told me it would be advisable to make myself available for a personal interview with an Emory alumnus. My uncle, Ted Brickman, identified a fellow Chattanooga attorney, Mr. Aubrey F. Folts, who served on the Emory University Board of Trustees. We scheduled a time to meet, and he conducted the interview at his impressive law offices in a high-rise office building in downtown Chattanooga.

Mr. Folts was very cordial and made me feel comfortable. He had already reviewed my school records and other personal information that was on his desk. He gave me the opportunity to explain why I had chosen Emory. "It wasn't complicated," I told him. "Emory appears to be the best school in the area for pre-dental studies, and my parents are offering to support me in my career path."

Mr. Folts told me that he was impressed with my resumé. He was pleased to say that he knew most of the people who had endorsed my application, including relatives, friends, and my uncle who was a legal colleague. He would let the folks at Emory know that he supported my application. He walked me to the reception room and had kind words to offer my parents, who were waiting there for my return.

I soon received my official acceptance letter from Emory, accompanied by all the academic, financial, and social information and requirements necessary to enroll in the college.

The summer passed quickly as I prepared to begin college. I had been wearing a military uniform throughout the past year, and my mother offered to take me to town to purchase some suitable college clothes.

That year, Labor Day fell on Monday, September 5, 1949. The Emanon Club, a Jewish social group my parents belonged to, held their annual outing at the 1,200-acre Harrison Bay State Park, adjacent to 40 miles of Chickamauga Lake shoreline, originally developed as a Tennessee Valley Authority recreation area. It was an opportunity for hardworking folks to relax after a hot summer. It was also the perfect opportunity for their teenagers to gather and share plans for the upcoming year. We weren't all that eager to explain details to the adults, so we told them what we thought they should know. To be truthful, I had never visited a college campus, and I didn't know any more than they did.

On Sunday, September 18, 1949, we made our customary weekly visit to my grandparents, this time to say goodbye. I was their first grandchild, and their pride in my continued development was obvious. I assured them that I would keep them in mind and write often. My grandfather surprised me with three silver dollars, two weeks earlier than his usual Rosh Hashanah gift.

The following day, Monday, September 19, my father's alarm clock rang at 4:30 a.m., his usual time to get up and go to work at his coal yard in downtown Chattanooga. But on that day, he delayed his departure until my mother, sister, and I awoke at 7 a.m. My mother would drive me to college that day.

My parents, my sister, and me

My 13-year-old sister, with tears in her eyes, gave me a hug goodbye. My dad proudly voiced his confidence in me, and Evelyn, the family maid, beamed as the "little boy" she had raised since he was six weeks old headed to college. She surprised me with some homemade fried pies to enjoy on my long road trip.

My dad would be taking the bus to work that day. The family car, a 1939 Oldsmobile, would provide our transportation to Atlanta on historic US Highway 41, a two-lane highway with multiple curves that offered few opportunities to pass the slow-moving cars and trucks in front of us. It took four hours to complete the 120-mile road trip. I-75 wasn't completed until December 21, 1977, with its final segment opening between Marietta, Georgia, and Cartersville, Georgia. Bypassing Atlanta, we took a series of narrow neighborhood streets to reach our destination. Emory had a northeast suburban address, located six miles from downtown Atlanta.

We reached the Emory University campus in the early afternoon. Our destination was Alabama Hall, the centrally located dormitory to which I had been assigned. My mother was ready to leave as soon as I transferred my belongings to my third-floor room. Noting a pay phone in the vestibule, she used her last opportunity to urge me to keep in touch.

My two roommates arrived early in the afternoon, about the same time I did. Pete Sotus from Miami Beach, Florida, was of Greek heritage. Johnny Maloof's parents had immigrated from the Middle East, and owned a dry-goods store in Cartersville, Georgia, just 30 miles north of Atlanta. Pete and Johnny were both pre-med students. The three of us grew up with first-generation parents who spoke more than one language. Though we pledged different social fraternities and different religious student organizations, we enjoyed a strong ethnic bond.

The five-day orientation process began on Wednesday, September 21st, and was well-planned. We were assigned our first-quarter classes and reminded that weekly chapel attendance was mandatory. This came as a surprise to some of my classmates. I just smiled and thought, *What's new? That's the way it was back home.*

Emory's culture did not include interscholastic football, so we came to appreciate the importance of fraternity involvement. There were 967 students in the college, and practically everyone joined a fraternity.

In 1949, the 12 non-Jewish fraternities were located on Fraternity Row and featured large antebellum houses. The two Jewish fraternities, AEPi and TEP, had a 30-year history at Emory, but both were located off-campus in rented homes. I don't recall our being told that we Jewish boys could not walk down Fraternity Row and join one of the Christian fraternities. We just knew it, and no one lost any sleep over it. On the other hand, our fraternities were included in all the intramural sporting contests, and to my knowledge there was never a disparaging word spoken on the playing field. During my two undergraduate years at Emory, I did not encounter any antisemitic behavior.

Two statistics stand out in my mind. First, each year the school conducted an "Ugly Man Contest," and recognized the fraternity that raised the most money for charitable causes. My fraternity won the award annually without interruption. Second, a scholastic award was presented each year to the fraternity with the highest scholastic average.

Alpha Epsilon Pi and Tau Epsilon Phi shared the honor every year. No one ever claimed that Jewish students were graded differently than our counterparts. If that were so, we couldn't have placed first and second each year. We would learn much later that there were quotas restricting the number of Jewish students into the college. A review of the yearbooks indicates that about 7% of the students in the college were Jewish. There is no way to determine how many were turned away. However, it appears that once you made the cut, you were graded equally.

Emory was founded as a Methodist school and was still nominally Methodist. The Emory Christian Association (ECA) was the official religious student organization. The Catholic students were few in number, while Hillel, the national Jewish student organization, attracted more members than any of the other religious cohorts. Curiously, Hillel was still considered a member of the Emory Christian Association.

During my first year at Emory, the first day of Rosh Hashanah, the Jewish New Year, began on Friday night, September 23. Having recently arrived in Atlanta, most of the Jewish boys chose to go to services downtown at one of the five synagogues. Fortunately, we didn't have to skip classes, as the services fell on Friday night, Saturday, and Sunday. I was impressed with the large attendance at the Ahavath Achim Synagogue. I certainly felt at home. It was a great way to start my first year in college.

In summary, almost everyone loved his undergraduate experience at Emory. We were treated equally in the classroom. Year after year, the Jewish fraternities were first and second in scholastic standing. The students, the faculty, and the school were warm and welcoming. Was it different being Jewish? Was there discrimination? Well, we certainly knew, and the university knew that we would not be invited to join a non-Jewish fraternity. And looking back—although we didn't realize it at the time—there were no Jewish faculty members and no Jews in the Emory administration office. But again, it was a Methodist school, a private school, and at that time that was the accepted norm. Bottom line: we were comfortable, and we really enjoyed the Southern hospitality. We had no reason to believe it would be different in a graduate school of the same university.

Peers

The majority of the students I met in my classes and in the freshman dormitory were good ol' Southern boys. You couldn't let the accents fool you. They were naturally friendly, smart, and ambitious. Most of them were well rounded and eager to get involved in multiple extracurricular activities. They had been told that grades alone would not get them into graduate school. Emory was seen to be the proving ground for future lawyers, businessmen, physicians, and dentists.

During fraternity rush week, I came in close contact with Jewish boys because we were limited to attending AEPi and TEP events. Several Atlanta boys were day students, and there was a sizable contingent from South Georgia. But the majority were Floridians and New Yorkers. They were a bit intimidating inasmuch as they tended to hang together; yet they seemed willing to accept the lone Tennessee boy into their group. I was drawn by the warm welcome from the AEPi fraternity advisor, Arnold Hoffman, and the AEPi president, Norman Trieger. Miles Alexander and Elliott Levitas were my favorite TEPs. When it came time to decide which fraternity to join, it was difficult to break the bonds I had made with them both.

At that time, there was no way to know that in two years fellow freshmen Art Burns, Allen Shaw, Herman Levin, and I would be freshmen at Emory dental school. And we certainly had no idea that by the end of our second year in the dentistry program, all of us would be flunked out. Or, perhaps most surprising, that destiny would bring us back together 56 years later to resume our friendships.

I also had no idea then that I would return to Atlanta 12 years later and settle in the same neighborhood as Miles Alexander and Elliott Levitas, now prominent Atlanta attorneys with strong ties to Emory. Miles never forgot what happened to his frat brothers at the Emory dental school and devoted countless hours to showing me how to rectify the injustices. I had the additional fortune of reconnecting with so many other AEPi and TEP fraternity comrades, who would become lifelong friends. Destiny has a way of intertwining and intersecting again and again. All of our worlds would continue to crisscross and intermingle, a pleasant yet unexpected twist.

Polite Antisemitism

The predominant culture at Emory exuded white Southern pride and superiority throughout the university. While the collegial atmosphere developed over the past hundred years did not allow overt expressions of discrimination, it was easy to detect.

If you were a student walking down Fraternity Row, you could see and feel it. If you picked up a copy of the *Campus* yearbook, you could read it. When an article on the members of the Board of Trustees appeared in the weekly *Emory Wheel,* you didn't have to read the names or look at the faces to know that we were not represented. Although it never occurred to me to inquire or dive deeper into this phenomenon, I would have discovered that there was not a single Jewish member on the Emory faculty. For a Jewish boy from nearby Tennessee who had never had a Jewish teacher in public or private school, it was not all that offensive, but it was a familiar reminder of the barrier that remained in place.

When our Atlanta alumni visited the fraternity house, we were impressed by their affluence and their notable accomplishments in the business world. This allowed us to overlook the obvious fact that very few Jewish students were being accepted to the Emory medical and dental schools, and the opportunities to join law firms, banking institutions, and hospital staffs were almost nonexistent at that time.

When my freshman class arrived at Emory in 1949, America was recovering rapidly from a costly war. The veterans had paid their price and were focused on reentering society and discovering life as civilians. Atlanta was emerging as the capital of the South. Although closely situated geographically, Emory was relatively immune to outside forces as she ambitiously and independently planned her future growth. There was a huge town-and-gown divide.

Growth actually had begun five years earlier. On September 1, 1944, President Goodrich C. White, on behalf of Emory University, purchased the assets of the historic Atlanta-Southern Dental College (ASDC). This fire sale was occasioned by a 1943 survey of dental schools by the Council on Dental Education (CODE) of the ADA. ASDC was ranked at the bottom of the nation's 39 dental schools and received "provisionally approved" status. If its deficiencies were not addressed, ASDC would lose its accreditation and its graduates would not be able to practice dentistry. What were those deficiencies?

Prior to the sale, Atlanta-Southern Dental College, a proprietary school, apparently did not employ a quota system. Their Jewish students came from as many as 13 states, including New York and New Jersey. After the 1944 transition to Emory, Jewish students were restricted to three states—Georgia, South Carolina, and Florida. Non-Jewish students continued to be accepted from 21 states. This policy continued until 1962, a period of 18 years.

After the sale, President White convinced Dean Ralph R. Byrnes to remain as dean until a successor could be identified and hired. Dr. John Buhler arrived from Philadelphia in the fall of 1948 to assume the deanship. Buhler was the protégé of and assistant to Dr. Gerald Timmons, dean of the Temple University dental school. The record shows that, like Atlanta-Southern Dental College, CODE also visited Temple in 1943. Temple was ranked #38 of the 39 dental schools and also received "provisionally approved" status. We will document in Chapter 12 how Dean Timmons and his administrative assistant Dr. Buhler corrected Temple's "deficiencies" and thereafter acquired full approval of CODE.

John Buhler came to Emory in the fall of 1948. Upon his arrival, he was fully aware of the unofficial quota system that had been imposed on the nation's dental schools, and to which Emory had already complied. With his mentor Dr. Timmons' approval, Dr. Buhler brought with him a recent Temple dental school graduate, Dr. John Bartholomew, to help him implement his plans and practices. A number of the existing staff at Emory were already sympathetic, and easily brought under his sway. Buhler could have been satisfied with the status quo, but that was not enough for him. According to Ron Goldstein, "My dad and uncle, Drs. Irving and Marvin Goldstein, were warned by Temple faculty members that Buhler was an antisemite."

It took Buhler less than two years to accelerate his plan. And freshmen students Brickman, Burns, Levin, and Shaw were about to step into his trap.

┌─────────────────┐
│   **CHAPTER 4** │
└─────────────────┘

Calm Before the Storm

A s far as I was concerned, Emory was the perfect match for me. I experienced a seamless adjustment to college life from that early September day when my mother dropped me off at the Alabama Hall dormitory.

My roommates, Pete and Johnny, were friendly and courteous. We couldn't have been more compatible with each other. They were pre-med and I was pre-dent, so we shared many of the same classes together. We often had the same professors, which made studying for exams much easier than had we gone it alone. Pete and I would become colleagues 15 years later, as our career paths took us to nearby DeKalb County, Georgia, to practice our respective specialties of general surgery and oral surgery.

Fraternity rush week began soon after we arrived at school. As I mentioned earlier, my roommate Pete came from Miami Beach, Florida. Pete was Greek, and practically all his high school friends at Miami Beach High School were Jewish. More than a few came with him to Emory. Pete didn't think twice about which fraternity he wanted to join. He wanted to pledge AEPi, one of the two Jewish fraternities on campus. Hushed discussions were going on at the fraternity house about Pete's announced preference. Carefully and with much sensitivity, the AEPi upperclassmen told Pete that his future was of prime importance, and that his chances to gain acceptance to Emory medical school would be lowered if he was affiliated with a Jewish fraternity. They felt obligated to insist that it would be in his best interest to join a non-Jewish fraternity.

For the first time while on campus, that unanticipated event made me aware that an inequality of opportunity existed at Emory. I suddenly learned what everyone knew or would eventually know—that there was a Jewish quota in the medical and dental schools. What we wouldn't know for years was that there was also a Jewish quota in the college. This was not apparent because once you were accepted to the college, you were treated exactly as were all other students. The policy was set many years before, and no one seemed uncomfortable with the way things were going.

We were also unaware that there was a policy of not having Jewish faculty members in the college. Apparently, this long-standing policy was also not a concern for the Jewish community or the many Emory Jewish alumni. Thus, we students became accustomed to a system that limited our numbers but provided a level playing field for those of us who were chosen to be members of the Emory family.

The whole idea of fraternity rush week was both strange and exhilarating. How different it was from the social and religious life to which I was accustomed. Coming from a relatively small Jewish community in Chattanooga, I never had a choice of what youth group I would join. The Jewish boys belonged to AZA and the girls joined BBG, the youth groups of B'nai B'rith, a national Jewish organization. We were a homogenous group. Our numbers were small, and we shared similar ethnic, religious, and socio-economic backgrounds. We all belonged to the same orthodox synagogue and had known each other all our lives.

I found myself immersed in a nonstop frenzy of fraternity rush parties, rotating between the AEPi fraternity house and the rival TEP house. I don't remember being informed by the university that Jewish boys were limited to visiting those two fraternities. Unknowingly, a few of the Jewish boys joined the long lines of freshmen walking down Fraternity Row to present themselves to the members of the 12 non-

Jewish fraternities. Their efforts would go unreciprocated, as they would soon find out.

The Jewish fraternity houses were not located on Fraternity Row. In fact, they were both situated off campus, about one mile from each other. They had not yet been allowed to be part of the Fraternity Row community, even though both fraternities had been around for decades. The TEP house was west of the campus on a quiet street showing no signs of a university atmosphere. The AEPi house had a North Decatur Road address, set back just a few feet from a busy thoroughfare east of the campus. The Jewish houses looked like houses. The non-Jewish houses looked like mansions.

The lack of parking facilities was irrelevant. None of us had cars, and we reached our destinations in the old-fashioned way—by foot. Once inside the frat houses, we encountered a whirlwind of introductions, refreshments, and entertainment. Each group claimed dominance over the other fraternities in athletics, social activities, and scholarships. Some of the members were veterans of WWII and were more mature and less boisterous. I was impressed as they pointed out their filing systems containing years of past tests in biology, chemistry, and all the other essential subjects. We would have access to the files, we were told, if we joined their fraternity. We were reminded that it was important to maintain good grades. It was seldom mentioned, but we were all aware of the clouds of war developing in the Korean peninsula.

Less than a year later, the conflict escalated into open warfare when North Korean forces—supported by the Soviet Union and China—moved into South Korea on June 25, 1950. On June 27, the United Nations Security Council authorized the formation and dispatch of UN forces to Korea to repel what was recognized as a North Korean invasion. Twenty-one countries within the United Nations eventually contributed to the UN force, with the United States providing 88% of the UN's military personnel. College students in good standing were granted deferments from the draft. Medical and dental students would continue to maintain their deferments. One of my AEPi fraternity brothers, Irwin Goldberg from New York City, received a commission in the Air Force following graduation in 1950. He was killed in action over Korea on May 3, 1954. A memorial plaque bearing Irwin's name is prominently displayed at the Emory Alumni Memorial Building.

During rush proceedings, AEPi played their trump card. They announced that they had received permission to build a house at 11 Fraternity Row, and that it would be completed and available for occupancy for the upcoming 1950 school year. After 30 continuous years at Emory, AEPi would finally take its place alongside the non-Jewish fraternities with a prestigious Fraternity Row address.

I proudly remember the groundbreaking ceremony. Norman Trieger, our chapter master, in coat and tie, surrounded by the 55 members of the fraternity, unearthed the rocky soil with the ceremonial shovel. Local and national dignitaries in attendance included past national officers David Goldwasser and Max Rittenbaum, both prominent Atlanta AEPi alumni. We will hear about them later in a distinctly different role.

A few months later, even before the house construction was completed, AEPi competed with all other fraternities in the annual Dooley's Frolics weekend. It would mark our entry into the classic event. Dooley's Frolics began in 1941, the same year the Emory trustees allowed dancing on the campus.

Based on a selected theme, each fraternity combined its imagination and manual labor to construct a Hollywood-like set on its front lawn. The 1950 theme was "Popular Songs," and the AEPi entry was "The Bowery." Our front yard featured a life-size facsimile of the street and neighborhood in lower Manhattan, a familiar sight to a large number of our New York frat members.

I was the lone Tennessean in my rush class. My fellow freshmen came from Florida, New York, and Atlanta. They seemed quite at ease, as the members we were meeting from both fraternities shared similar backgrounds. I felt more at home with the few members from small and midsized Georgia towns, whose accents sounded like music to me. I made many friends over the course of just a few days, and I was eager to enter the fraternity life at Emory. In the end, I chose AEPi, but throughout my two years in the college, I maintained friendships with the guys I met in both fraternities.

I was pleased to find that there was a newly formed Hillel chapter at Emory. There were fifty-six members in 1950, making it Emory's largest undergraduate religious organization. Members of both fraternities attended services there. Active members included TEPs Elliott Levitas, Miles Alexander, Arthur Burns, Herman Levin, and Barry Garber. Hillel President Leon Eplan, along with Allen Shaw, Dick Bloch, Bernard Palay, Ted Wolff, and Donny Rosenberg, represented AEPi.

One of our members, Elliott Levitas, became a 1956 Rhodes Scholar, receiving a master's of law degree from Oxford University, England, in 1958. In 1964 he was elected to the 94th US Congress and to the four succeeding Congresses. Miles Alexander, after graduating with honors from Emory, received his JD from Harvard Law School. Miles would become a lifelong friend, and our relationship extends to our children, who maintain close personal and professional ties. Miles, one of Emory's outstanding alumni, stands out as the prime force guiding and encouraging me in uncovering and revealing the Emory dental school story.

I soon realized that my high school had prepared me well, and I was able to start several of my subjects at an advanced level. As such, I met a new group of students and increased my circle of friends. I made time to join the college orchestra and enjoyed playing in the woodwind section.

As I was preparing to come to college, I'd had a flare-up of a chronic medical problem, necessitating surgery. Because of a delayed recovery, I took the round-trip Greyhound bus to Chattanooga every weekend to have my dressings changed. At school, I had to be excused from swimming, exercise, and contact sports. I fully recovered in due time and was happy to get back into action.

At Emory, inter-fraternity athletics was a long-established tradition. I had always enjoyed sports, and was competitive in baseball, basketball and football in high school. Until I fully recovered, I would have to be a spectator. One fall afternoon, October 24, 1950, I joined friends giving vocal support to our fraternity tag-football team. The upper athletic field was in the center of the campus and was easily accessible to Emory students as well as to Atlanta high school girls who had an open invitation to attend our games. Today's game, AEPi vs. TEP, a natural rivalry, drew an unusually large crowd.

In 1950, there were no co-eds at Emory, and it was customary for college students to date high school girls. I recognized two of the three young ladies slowly strolling across the athletic field toward the sidelines. As the trio grew nearer, I remembered the third girl. The previous fall, a few of my friends and I crashed a dance at the Georgian Terrace hotel in downtown Atlanta. The mystery lady was the sweetheart of the high school boys' youth group hosting the party. All the members of the group broke in for a dance with her. She was clearly the belle of the ball. Somehow, I got the feeling that she was unapproachable. Besides, she was at least three years younger than I. So, I didn't follow through at the time.

But now we were face-to-face. I was speechless. She wasn't. "Where did you get that vest?" she asked. Actually, it was a fake leopard vest my mother had selected for my college wardrobe. "My uncle got it on a recent safari to Africa," I replied. That smart-aleck answer drew an even smarter retort, but divine intervention had taken over. Five years later, on June 26, 1955, Shirley Berkowitz and I would exchange vows at the Progressive Club in Atlanta.

The Application Process

The motivation to study and to excel in my courses was ever-present. Each member of the fraternity was expected to do his part to maintain our standing. We were proud when our fraternity placed first or second in the school competition each quarter.

By now I didn't need the encouragement. My goal was to get into dental school. I had a girlfriend, and I definitely wanted to stay in Atlanta, but I knew the odds of a Jewish student getting into Emory dental school were slim. It became obvious that I would be competing with two cohorts—the general pool of applicants and my Jewish friends.

I had an unwavering desire to become a dentist. It's true that I was pre-programmed, but nothing had influenced me otherwise. At that time, the options weren't as boundless as now, and we didn't have the luxury of spending extra time and money to explore other professional opportunities. It was like a racehorse with blinders, moving as fast as possible in one direction to the finish line. And there were lots of horses. As it turned out, to continue the equine metaphor, some of us had extra handicaps.

The summer between my first and second academic years passed quickly. I spent the summer months at home working odd jobs. I visited my family dentist for my annual cleaning and examination and received his compliments on my progress. Dr. Connell advised me to move quickly in the dental school application process, and to apply to more than one school. He was active in Tennessee state dental affairs and didn't conceal his hope that I would consider the University of Tennessee as my first choice.

Sunday morning men's softball at Warner Park was a ritual in Chattanooga. A sizable group always attended early morning minyan at the synagogue, but by ten o'clock the crowd had assembled, and team selection began. I arrived early with glove, uniform, and cleats. The old-timers were chatting it up, and the other regulars were ready to go. My college friends and I had been away for a year and were hoping to make the cut. Nothing had changed. Everybody would have a chance to play.

In the dugout, I was expecting to hear questions about my first year at school. I was already accustomed to the incessant banter in the fraternity house. The New York and Florida boys would talk about anything and everything. Then I remembered that Southerners keep their thoughts to themselves. Just like playing poker, you keep your cards close to the chest.

By the end of the game, I did exchange a few words with boys who had been away at Vanderbilt University and The University of Tennessee, and we agreed to get together to compare our college experiences. When we finally met, I was not surprised to hear that they had not encountered religious barriers at school. The fact that they could only join a Jewish fraternity did not strike them as being anything other than customary social behavior.

When it came time for medical and dental school, practically every Jewish boy from Chattanooga, Knoxville, and Memphis and the majority from Nashville chose UT Memphis. The reasons were simple. It was relatively inexpensive, and there was no history of discrimination at UT dental or medical schools. I wished I could feel that positive. But I told myself, "If you can make it into Emory dental school, everything will be all right. It will be just like in the college. Once you're accepted, you'll be one of the boys."

The application process was simple and uneventful. I communicated with Emory dental school and with UT dental school in Memphis and received similar responses on how to initiate my application. I would have to submit my college grades and maintain my grade average in the upcoming year. I was further informed that applicants would have to take a chalk-carving dexterity test administered at listed regional locations.

I learned from an enclosed brochure that Emory was a four-year school located in downtown Atlanta, six miles from the college campus. The classes began in the fall of each year. The stationery bore the Atlanta-Southern Dental College heading. I had never heard of that school and was unaware that Emory had taken over the school in 1944. Looking back, I suppose they were trying to save money by using up all the old stationery. The letter did not state that Emory was only provisionally approved by the Council on Dental Education of the American Dental Association. As we will see later, they were judged to have serious deficiencies that required correction. The dean, John E. Buhler, signed the letter.

I was surprised to learn that Tennessee was a three-year school. During World War II, all dental and medical schools adopted an accelerated three-year program consisting of thirty-six months of nonstop learning. Tennessee was the lone school maintaining that model. There were 12 classes of three months' duration. Theoretically, if accepted after two years at Emory, I could begin my studies at Memphis in June 1951 and then graduate in May 1954. The UT dental school was located in downtown Memphis. Founded in 1878, it was promoted as being the oldest dental school in the South and one of the eight oldest dental schools in the country. Student dormitories were conveniently located across the street from the school. Tennessee was ranked as fully approved by the Council on Dental Education.

The Emory application form asked for the religion of the applicant. It also asked for the applicant's father's religion and birthplace. (I suppose it was important that they should know my father was born in Lithuania.) It also required three letters of reference, one of which was to be from the pastor of the church you attended. A few years later, Dr. Buhler amended the application form, adding RACE as an additional component. The applicant was provided three choices, CAUCASIAN, JEW, or OTHER. I was unable later to find a copy of the Tennessee application form.

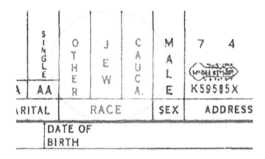

The 1960-1961 Buhler application form

I returned for my sophomore year at Emory ready to resume my academic studies and my fraternity activities. This year I would live in the new fraternity house with two roommates, pre-law freshmen Larry Goodrich from Tampa and Allan Davis from St. Petersburg, Florida.

I was elected scribe (secretary) at the first fraternity meeting. As an officer, I would come in frequent contact with our chapter advisor, Arnold ("A.B.") Hoffman, who was a graduate of the Emory Business

School. An outstanding athlete as an undergraduate, he was considered in his time a BMOC, Big Man on Campus. He was very well liked by the faculty and members of the Emory administration, particularly Dean of Students E.H. Rece, Dean of the College Judson (Jake) Ward, Director of Religious Affairs Sam Laird, and Dean of Administration Boisfeuillet Jones. A.B.'s day job was comptroller of Dwoskin's, a prominent manufacturer and retailer of fashionable drapes, wallpaper, and murals. However, his real love was the AEPi fraternity.

At the time, A.B. was still single and spent almost every evening at the fraternity house. He knew every one of our AEPi brothers, and through his advisor counterpart at the TEP house, Eli Kaplan, he was familiar with every TEP member. A.B. loved Emory and was a father figure for all the undergraduates. In July 1956, after five years of seeing suspicious things happening to "his boys," and hearing stories sifting through the rumor mill, Arnold Hoffman would be the initial whistleblower calling attention to the shameful activities occurring at the Emory dental school.

Admission Not Acceptance

The excitement of living, eating, shooting pool, and playing bridge at our new fraternity house was incredible. Today's students would say "amazing, crazy, awesome." The fraternity spirit was at its peak. Rosalyn Goldberg, the wife of past national master Sidney Goldberg, had decorated the house. We weren't allowed to hang out in the gorgeous first-floor living room. Only when we had dressy parties, were we and our dates allowed there.

We had a wonderful live-in housemother, Ma Poes, who knew how to keep us in line with both humor and love. There was absolutely no drinking allowed in the house. Not only could we not afford it, but there were so many other activities to occupy our time. We were a serious bunch, and spent a lot of time in the Asa Griggs Candler Library in the center of the campus.

There was only one car in the entire fraternity, and our trips to drink a beer at Moe's and Joe's and Harry's were infrequent. More often, we sent someone to get gallons of ice cream from the Miss Georgia ice cream store at the corner of Highland and Ponce de Leon Avenues. We occasionally splurged on Sunday evenings and ordered from the sensational downtown Leb's delicatessen, which had no minimum requirement. In retrospect, how could they afford to deliver only two corned-beef sandwiches?

Academically speaking, the second year was a bit more challenging than the first. My high school studies had not prepared me for organic chemistry, and that was my first serious challenge. The legendary fraternity filing system was a godsend. I learned to work backwards from the answer to the question, and soon learned the system. I finished the quarter with a B.

The minimum pre-dental requirement was two years. We knew that some students ended up taking three and even sometimes four years before acceptance. Money and pride motivated the desire to get in after only two years. This increased the pressure and intensified our self-concern. At that time, we were not prepared to see the situation as anything more than a numbers game. My anxiety was allayed by knowing that The University of Tennessee dental school was a reasonably certain backup option.

As close as we were, our camaraderie was now limited to fraternity involvement. We already regarded one another as competitors. We avoided talking to each other about our applications to dental school. We took our chalk tests on our own at different times and locations and didn't even discuss how we thought we had done. I found the carving test quite simple. Much easier than the model airplanes I carved from balsa wood during the war.

The dental school didn't send us a list of our future classmates or their hometowns. Even after being accepted, we were not invited for site visits nor encouraged to take any preparatory courses or shadow a practicing dentist. We had no contact with local dentists and absolutely no idea what awaited us.

Norman Trieger was one of my AEPi idols. During his junior year, he was inducted into Phi Beta Kappa. He was one of the boys from the Bronx who wanted to make the South his home. During his senior year he applied to Emory, NYU, Columbia, and Harvard dental schools. Emory turned him down, but the other three schools accepted him. Baffled by the rejection, Norman asked the dean of admissions what was the problem? Norman described the scene. "The dean leaned back and stretched his long legs over his desk. 'Don't take it puh-sun-ally, son. We just don't take any naw-thu-ners.'" Years later, Norman, by now a distinguished dental and medical educator, told me that it never occurred to him that the problem could be his being Jewish. "I did so well as an undergraduate at Emory, I couldn't consider that it would be different in the dental school."

Years later I heard the same account from fraternity brother Frank Fox, who settled for NYU dental school after Emory rejected him. Fox, a Brooklyn native, had a stellar academic record at Emory. His older sister and her family lived in nearby Cartersville, and she encouraged Frank to make his home in Georgia. With little hope for success, Frank made an extra effort to gain acceptance. He took a bus down to the dental school.

"Dean Buhler was disturbed when, without an appointment, I knocked on his door and entered his office at the dental school downtown on Courtland Avenue. I knew I wouldn't be allowed to stay very long, so I asked him directly if he had a Jewish problem. 'Who says we don't take Jews,' he quickly responded. Off the top of his head, he named the three or four Jewish students in the school and demanded that I leave."

My classmates Ross Stemer, Beryl Tenenbaum, and Ed Wolf, all excellent students, were likewise refused admission. This caused consternation among those of us who would be seeking admission the next year. Ross, whose father was a Savannah dentist, would become a successful advertising executive. Beryl was accepted to the University of Georgia medical school and practiced in Augusta, Georgia for many years. Ed, a native of Youngstown, Ohio, graduated from Western Reserve dental school and became an orthodontist.

When we finally received our acceptances or rejections during the spring quarter, we kept the news to ourselves. Inevitably, the news leaked, but we avoided public celebration. The school accepted four Jewish boys, and they all came from Emory. Art Burns and Herman Levin from the TEP fraternity, and Allen Shaw and me from AEPi. I have no idea how many non-Emory students were rejected or whether other schools accepted them.

I didn't stop to weigh the pros and cons. I made my decision with my heart. I would stay in Atlanta and go to Emory. It defies all rational thought that the four of us—Allen, Art, Herman, and I—were not in touch during the summer break. The separation continued when we entered dental school in the fall of 1951. Even though we were not eligible to join the three non-Jewish dental fraternities, we obviously decided that we would be better off if we weren't seen hanging out together. We should have heeded Benjamin Franklin: "We must, indeed, all hang together or, most assuredly, we shall all hang separately."

CHAPTER 5

Out of the Frying Pan,
into the Fire

As I entered Emory dental school in September 1951, little did I know that my three Jewish classmates and I had almost no chance at success, and that the majority of the Jewish boys who followed us over the next ten years would fare no better.

We can question now whether those of us who chose Emory dental school exercised due diligence in our selection process. The collective vision of the day appeared to present an unbridled opportunity for success. Boy were we mistaken.

On April 20, 1951, the national office of the Anti-Defamation League issued a three-year progress report on its "Crack the Quota" program. In an article titled "Barriers Down," it stated, "In the space of a year and a half—a single tick of the clock in the calendar of social change—there has been increasing evidence that the barriers of bigotry in higher education are breaking down."

In his nationally syndicated weekly column, which appeared in *The Southern Israelite*, Boris Smolar, a prominent American Jewish journalist, observed on May 4, 1951, "There will be greater opportunities for Jewish men to enter the medical profession because of the increasing need for more doctors." Not everyone agreed. For those less optimistic, there was sufficient background noise to trigger caution for Jews in Atlanta and throughout the world.

67

On March 16, 1951, the American Jewish Committee charged that, just six years following the end of the Second World War, antisemitism was growing in the Soviet Union and its satellite countries. Jews were being deported from mainland Russia to Siberia. A hundred thousand Hungarian Jews were being deported from Hungary. There was a purge of Jews in Czechoslovakia and mass imprisonment on treason charges. Romanian Jews were being arrested and displaced to salt mines and concentration camps. Even in the United States, Delray Beach, Florida, was a fortress for antisemitism.

By 1951, the Florida Ku Klux Klan was at a crossroads. The Jim Crow laws were being challenged, and an anti-mask ordinance was enacted by the 1951 Florida legislature. By the summer of 1951, the Klan began to roll back progress and initiated a series of 12 bombings throughout the state. The Northern press dubbed it "The Florida Terror." The principal targets were the NAACP, B'nai B'rith, and the Catholic Church. The Klan continued to respond violently to the freedom rides, sit-ins, and mass demonstrations. Florida remained a Klan stronghold, particularly in the Jacksonville area. On March 9, 1951, ADL Assistant Director and General Counsel Arnold Forster visited Jacksonville, Florida. While there, he ripped into the KKK.

Forster was a brilliant lawyer and tactician. Nevertheless, it never occurred to him that, to the Jews in Jacksonville, Miami, Tampa, and Pensacola who were about to send their sons to Emory dental school, there was a much more important story they should be aware of. If anyone should have made the connection, it was certainly Arnold Forster.

Six years earlier, in February 1945, Forster and his colleagues at the ADL had captured headlines in the *New York Times* when they revealed efforts by the Council on Dental Education (CODE) of the American Dental Association to impose Jewish quotas at Columbia and NYU dental schools. The controversy was short-lived. The New York newspaper PM courageously reported the covert effort to limit the presence of Jewish students in the nation's dental schools and urged its readers to speak out. The Jewish Telegraphic Agency (JTA) picked up the story and distributed the news to its regional subscribers. The story, in abbreviated form, appeared in less than a dozen Jewish community weeklies. The February 16,1945, *Southern Israelite*, based in Atlanta, included the JTA report, but there was no editorial comment.

Quite the opposite in Miami. George J. Talianoff, the new Executive Director of ADL in Florida, responded quickly to the JTA story. Talianoff wrote a spirited opinion piece in the February 16, 1945 *Floridian*, the widely-read Jewish weekly.

"Those who are concerned with the preservation of the basic American principle of freedom and equality of opportunity for all, must protest against this action… by repudiating Dr. Horner's reports as inconsistent with the educational traditions of our democracy and the record of the American Dental Association."

Talianoff was unaware of any problems at Emory or at any other dental schools not mentioned in the JTA article. His remarks were general in nature, not directed to any specific schools. Apparently, the national office was focused on the New York City area and didn't see the necessity of discussing the problem with its regional directors. In fact, when the American Dental Association vigorously claimed that they knew nothing of the CODE report and repudiated its content, ADL National Chairman Judge Meier Steinbrink graciously accepted their explanation and moved on to other more familiar battlegrounds.

At that time, Florida had no dental school, and there were no plans on the drawing board. They paid handsome subsidies ($1,500 per student, in addition to the tuition) to Atlanta -Southern Dental College (later Emory), Maryland, and possibly other dental schools to accept their pre-dental students. Despite Talianoff's strong stand, his warning presumably had little influence on his readers, as Jewish boys unknowingly continued to apply to Emory dental school for at least the next ten years.

It never occurred to Forster to stop in Atlanta on his way to Jacksonville, and make a few inquiries about the Emory dental school. With a few discreet questions, he would have discovered a quota system, in place since 1944, that was much more egregious than those uncovered by the ADL in New York in 1945. He would also have found that there was not a single Jewish faculty member on the dental school staff, and there had not been one since Samuel Lawrence Silverman, who died on October 6, 1934, at the age of 45. The current dean, Dr. Ralph R. Byrnes, had occupied his position since 1931.

One former faculty member whom I interviewed labeled Byrnes a vicious antisemite, "worse even than Buhler." I also interviewed Robert Bunnen who had just completed his sophomore year in June 1943. He described being summoned to Byrnes's office and being told to clear out his locker. "Your grades don't merit allowing you to return," he was told.

"But I am in the top third of my class," Bunnen replied.

"No, you are not. Now get out of here," the dean responded.

Bunnen, now 86 years old, with a trembling voice told me, "I was only 19 years old. What could I do? I could have killed that son-of-a-bitch."

He told me that he closed the door behind him and found himself in the vestibule, talking out loud to himself. At the same time, he became aware of the dean's secretary, busily typing a document. "Her name was Minnie Jackson. She wore her hair up in a bun."

Still talking aloud to himself, he declared, "I'm a good student. There's got to be more to this."

He continued to tell his story. "Mrs. Jackson looked up, narrowed her eyes, and without hesitation answered my undirected question. 'There is,' she offered, speaking for the dean and for herself. 'We all know this war we're in is a Hebrew war. You're a Hebrew. Now get out of here and go fight for your country.'

"There wasn't anything I could do. I just had to drive home and tell my parents."

If Forster had been given the opportunity to visit the Emory dental school library, he might have browsed the 1927 yearbook of the Atlanta-Southern Dental College (precursor to the Emory dental school), which included photographs of all the fraternities and social clubs. He would have gained additional insight into the culture of the time and learned more about the KKK's presence in Georgia.

Ku Klux Klan Club at Atlanta-Southern Dental College (1927)

Armed with this information, and still mindful of the events that occurred in New York only six years before, Forster could have intuited that the quotas were enforced by the same CODE committee (headed by Dr. Harlan H. Horner) that strong-armed the officials at Columbia and NYU. Perhaps he would have sought additional information but would have found it hard to come by. Without question, he would have met stubborn resistance not only from Emory dental school and Emory University but also, as we will later see, from the organized Jewish community. He was an outsider, and his counsel would have been unwelcomed. Fortunately, a decade later, his day would come.

In 1962, Forster and his colleague Benjamin Epstein would publish *Some of My Best Friends.* The book, which enjoyed multiple printings, summarized discrimination and antisemitism in the United States during the first 50 years of the 20th century. Ironically, the 11th chapter, titled "The Graduate School," documents the unparalleled antisemitism that occurred at the Emory dental school between 1944 and 1962. It presented irrefutable statistics showing that, under Dean John Buhler's tenure, 64.8% of the Jewish students were either flunked out or made to repeat one or more years.

But it was 1951 when Forster visited the South. The ADL was not alone in suffering tunnel vision. In 1951, no one in Atlanta envisioned the tragic events developing at Emory.

On March 23, 1951, Representative John Rankin of Mississippi attracted national attention when he sought to remove the portrait of the alien "Jewish Rabbi" Maimonides from the walls of the US House of Representatives. In 1945, this same Congressman Rankin, on the floor of the House, had defended the Council on Dental Education's attempt to impose Jewish quotas in the nation's dental schools. He viciously attacked his colleague Emanuel Celler of New York, who had introduced the matter to the floor. As Celler finished, Rankin jumped to his feet and shouted, "I am getting tired of the gentleman from New York raising the Jewish question in the House and then jumping on every man who says anything about it."

He continued: "Why attack the American Dental Association? That organization has done what it had the right to do. I wonder if the gentleman knew that 90 percent of the doctors who get on the civil service roll are Jews, and 60 per cent of the ones we are compelled to accept in our veterans' hospitals are Jews. Remember that the white gentiles of this country also have some rights."

On May 4, 1951, hate sheets smeared Jews for General Douglas MacArthur's ouster by President Truman. Thousands of Americans were swept into the Korean War, and many blamed the Jews for the US involvement in the war. On April 20, 1951, an article appeared in the *New York Post* about a whispering campaign against American Jews, which had as its origin the conviction of spies Julius and Ethel Rosenberg for providing the USSR the secret components of the atomic bomb. Many Americans had opposed America's entry into World War II, labeling it a "Hebrew war," and claimed that the Jews had dragged us into it. Now Senator Joseph McCarthy of Wisconsin charged that the cosmopolitan Jewish traitors were siding with their Russian communist comrades to overthrow America. All Jews were suspect. McCarthyism was rampant.

Our families were unwilling to acknowledge the signs, choosing to disregard the potential risk they foreshadowed. But the writing was on the wall. In the beginning, we concluded that the positive experience we enjoyed at the college would find equal expression at the Emory dental school. We were mistaken. Thomas Carlyle once said, "Our business is not only to see what lies dimly in the distance but to do what lies clearly at hand."[50]

A House of Hope

During my sophomore year at Emory, I met Lee Moscowitz from Manchester, Georgia. Lee transferred to Emory after two years at Vanderbilt, where he had joined ZBT fraternity. Though he was ineligible to join another fraternity, Lee had an open invitation to take his meals at our house. Our Southern connection led to a lifelong friendship.

Lee was on a business/law track and planned to be in Atlanta for at least five more years. He had a lead on a basement apartment on East Morningside Drive that would be available in the fall and was looking for someone to share the cost of the lease. The apartment was conveniently located halfway between the Emory campus and the downtown dental school. It was about a ten-minute drive to Shirley's house and a twenty-minute drive to the dental school.

During the summer, my dad bought me a black four-door 1939 Mercury that federal agents had confiscated from a convicted bootlegger. The vehicle had extra springs in the rear to conceal the weight of the illegal alcohol in the trunk. The rear end was raised conspicuously when the trunk was empty, so I kept baggage in the trunk to maintain a level appearance. The car cost $300, but it turned out not to be such a good bargain. It had a lousy radiator, and I had to stop every 30 miles on my way to Atlanta to add water. I was exhausted by the time I finally pulled up to my apartment. Lee had already taken occupancy and was there to help me get situated. I arrived a few days before school began, allowing plenty of time to familiarize myself with the neighborhood.

In 1951, Atlanta traffic was predictable. The school was situated on the corner of Forrest and Courtland Avenues, and I reached my destination with plenty of time to spare. I parked in the school lot on the Forrest Avenue side, walked across the busy two-lane thoroughfare, and entered the street-level entrance of the four-story dental school. I soon learned that we would spend the majority of our time in the basement laboratory, which housed the freshman dental anatomy and prosthetic labs.

A sign directed the incoming freshmen to the main floor where a student guide met us and led us to a nearby classroom. My eyes swept the room. There were ten rows with eight chairs in each row, and each chair was occupied. The wooden floors were dull, the ceilings quite high, and there was no air conditioning.

We were left alone for a few minutes, which gave each of us time to size up the classmates we hoped to work with over the next four years. There seemed to be an even mix of young college-age men and older, more mature men, probably war veterans. I spotted my three friends, whom I had not seen over the summer break. I sensed that they were just as apprehensive as I was.

The orientation began. Four or five different personnel briefed us, some of whom wore dental jackets with stripes over their shoulders, identifying them as faculty. We received a schedule of our classes for the first semester. Then we were assigned lockers for our materials and equipment. Finally, we were provided a manual of rules and regulations, dress code, and expected behavior. I only remember the names of two of the men who addressed us.

The first man, Park Englett, was the representative of Atlanta Southern Dental Supply Company, which would be selling us our dental supplies and equipment over the next four years. He was friendly and put us at ease. Of course, he wished us good luck because he wanted us to be customers for the rest of our professional careers.

The second, Dean John Buhler, was tall, neat and trim, and wore a business suit. He didn't even try to convey a pleasant demeanor. In military fashion, he gave us two orders: 1) we were expected to conduct ourselves in a professional manner and 2) we were told to look to our right and then to our left, followed by the prediction or admonition that it was highly likely that one of the three of us would not graduate. No one dared to ask any questions. He left abruptly. I don't think I ever saw Dr. Buhler again.

I left that day feeling less than comfortable. I didn't like the environment, and I felt as if I had relinquished control. Nevertheless, I resolved not to let that feeling get the best of me. I never once shared that negative feeling with my classmates, my friends, my girlfriend, or my family.

That was not the case with the men who sat in my section of the laboratory. We were seated alphabetically and were in close contact at least six to eight hours every day. Though no one overtly expressed his feeling, especially to an instructor, one became accustomed to the familiar banter up and down our section. The non-specific grumbling was incessant.

The greatest stress occurred in the dental anatomy lab. From a block of wax, you were expected to perfectly carve the crown and root of every tooth in the dental arch from the incisors to the molars. It wasn't horseshoes—close didn't count. The precise dimensions, as provided in the textbook, had to be perfect to the tenth of a millimeter. It might take three or four hours to carve a tooth.

The four instructors took turns sauntering down the aisles, peering over our shoulders to check our progress. From time to time they might offer constructive advice, but more often than not they'd just ridicule us. We seldom asked for help because it was an invitation for an insulting comment.

The instructors, when not moving about, sat on an elevated platform on the right side of the room. There was a certain protocol for calling students up to check their tooth carvings. They summoned us alphabetically. You rose from your bench and walked about 20 feet to the dais. It was like walking the gangplank. On arrival, the student looked up, waited for acknowledgement, and then submitted his wax tooth carving to the instructor.

You could witness the drama from anywhere in the room. "You call this a tooth?" Then you heard a pop as the instructor snapped the tooth in half and threw the two parts soaring into the air. "It looks like a plane to me. Look at it fly."

Some of our comrades were from small rural areas. Returning the rejected tooth to the student, the instructor would taunt him. "Boy, here's a nickel. Go call your daddy and tell him to get the tractor ready. You're comin' home to the farm."

When the day was over, the four Jewish boys went home separately. We didn't have a dental fraternity house. The others headed to their three respective fraternity houses to hang out. We learned from them that several of the instructors who had graduated only a few years before would join them at the frat house for a beer. Apparently, the badgering was a sham—a moment of clarity for us all.

Herman Levin left midway through the year. His departure was unexpected and had a sobering effect on the entire class. Herman's seat was to the far left of the room between classmates Lester and Lowery, just across from the plaster bin. The class had just returned to the lab from the noon break and were settling in for the remainder of the day.

The chaos began with the sound of equipment and instruments hitting the floor and sliding across the room. Then came Herman's voice, uncharacteristically loud and angry, and seeming to come out of a loudspeaker. "I'm not going to put up with any more of this *#*#," he announced. Within a few short minutes, he was gone.

None of us attempted to dissuade Herman, neither his classmates nor his instructors. He left without a word of consolation. One down, three to go.

Sixty years later, I located Herman in Jensen Beach, Florida. A retired clinical psychologist, he related the self-rehabilitation path he had taken after leaving Emory. It was all good. After departing Atlanta, Herman returned to his home in Pensacola to rejoin his family. Herman's younger brother Fred was always a "Gator," but any possible thoughts of following his brother to Emory were dashed.

Brother Fred attended the University of Florida in Gainesville and went on to attend law school there as well. Wikipedia cites the following: "The College of Law was renamed the Levin College of Law in 1999 after prominent Pensacola trial lawyer and alumnus Fredric G. Levin (JD '61), who donated $10 million to the college, a sum that was matched by a $10 million grant from the state of Florida to create a $20 million endowment. A new courtroom facility at the law school was completed in 2009. The facility was made possible by an additional $2 million donation from the Levin family."

I often wonder "What if?" What if Fred Levin had followed older brother Herman to Emory? The Levin Emory Law School?

One of our instructors, William Ashendorf, was an equal opportunity sadist. Standing barely 5'4", he took pleasure intimidating all students, especially those who were taller than he was. That included just about everyone. He must have been abused as a student and was doing a good job of paying it forward.

Ashendorf was a pacer. With an expressionless face, he moved up and down the aisles, barely lifting his feet from the floor. We never knew when the shoe was going to drop. One afternoon, my friend Allen Shaw threw caution to the wind. Art Burns and I were shocked to see Allen standing in the aisle next to our bench. Disregarding protocol, he had walked from his location in the back of the room to our section to share his frightening tale.

"I was sitting at my desk engrossed in my lab work when I felt a finger poking the front of my lab jacket. I looked up to see Ashendorf. He was scratching the name label just above the left upper pocket of my lab jacket. I stopped working and looked up to him for an explanation. 'A.J. Shaw?' he asked. 'What does that stand for, Abraham Jacob?'"

Another moment of clarity.

Years later, I interviewed 1959 graduate George Marholin in his Brooksville, Florida, retirement home in the Florida Panhandle. His wife of 50 years, Eleanor Nodvin Marholin, looked on as George recalled in detail his dental school experience.

"Ashendorf seemed to me like a German, a Nazi. When he was around, I felt like I was wearing a yellow star, like the Jews in Europe." He continued, "Ashendorf and Bartholomew. Both reminded me of Nazis."

My weekly schedule didn't vary: on the way home from school, the usual Swiss cheese sandwich on rye and draft beer at Atlanta Cracker baseball player Ted Cieslak's The Dugout, a popular neighbor pub at the corner of Piedmont and Morningside. I dropped by occasionally to catch up with my fraternity brothers. Advisor Arnold Hoffman was eager to hear how things were going at the dental school. He was a trusted friend, and in retrospect, I should have told him the truth. But I was determined to work my way through the mess I had gotten myself into.

Shirley was a junior at Grady High School, and our relationship was serious.

Occasionally, I would take lab work over to her house on Pasadena Avenue and cure the dentures with boiling water in her kitchen. We were not supposed to take work home, but everyone did. It was impossible to complete your work in the allotted time, so you exercised caution when bending the rules.

As my first year of dental school drew to a close, my attitude actually became more positive. There were so many times that I had faced deadlines, but I was always able to get my work in on time. I still was uncomfortable with the school itself, but I felt that I was no worse off than most of my classmates. I had never been publicly or privately humiliated like some of the guys. Furthermore, I had not been called in to any faculty member's office or the dean's office for counseling or probation.

During the last week, we took exams and turned in our completed lab work. Each student was assigned a number to attach to his lab work so the examiner could grade it objectively. They expected us to believe that. What a joke.

Which reminds me of the Emory dental school's Class of 1958's 55th class reunion meeting to which I was invited to speak by Dr. Ray Davis, a member of the class. The reunion was in conjunction with the hundredth anniversary of the Thomas P. Hinman dental meeting, which occasioned a large attendance. The dinner meeting was held at the meeting room of Le Giverny Restaurant on Saturday evening, March 24, 2012.

After my presentation, one of the surviving class members stood up as tall as he could and faced his classmates. In a pronounced South Georgia drawl, he recalled the last day of their freshman year. "Y'all remember we had to turn in our typodonts [an artificial model containing artificial teeth used for teaching technique exercises]. It was the one chance we had to see the quality of work of our classmates. 'Course we didn't know whose work was whose 'cause we'd each been assigned a number. But we could see how well our work stacked up against the others. I remember one of our classmates (I can't remember who) whispering to me, 'You want to see a Jewish typodont?'

"'How do you know?' I asked. He pointed to a gold foil filling and called my attention to the multiple scratches on the gold surface. That's where the instructor tried unsuccessfully to pull out his filling."

The two Jewish boys in that class were present that evening. The lanky Georgian looked their way, shook his head apologetically, and quietly sat down. The meeting adjourned without any further comment.

During my last week in school, Lee and I had a serious flood in our basement apartment. The landlady wasn't too happy, and neither were we. The last few days I lived out of my car. On my last day I drove by to say goodbye to Shirley, and headed home to Chattanooga to await my fate.

Castles Made of Sand

With the advantage of time and the benefit of hindsight, we can speculate about what attracted four young Jewish men from diverse backgrounds to Emory dental school in 1951. Three of the men were from Florida, and one from Tennessee.

There were only three dental schools in the Deep South at the time we were considering dentistry as a career. These included: Emory, Loyola (New Orleans), and Tennessee. Florida, with no dental school, was granting a subsidy of $1,500.00 to Emory dental school to take its students. Additionally, Emory dental school appeared to give Florida residents who attended Emory University preference when they applied to its dental school.

Jewish students from Florida who were attending Emory University for their pre-med and pre-dental studies were doing quite well in their academic and social lives, and were pleased with their acceptance into the Emory family. However, even with these economic advantages, not many Florida Jews were enrolled in the Emory dental school. Only a few were being accepted into the Emory medical school.

Without taking anything else into consideration, Emory appeared to be a reasonable option for the men from Florida. But Tennessee would have been a much more logical choice for me.

It is now clear that it was a bad decision for the four of us. We sailed into a storm that was already brewing. If we had done our homework, we would have quickly discovered that every Jewish boy who preceded us at the dental school since the arrival of the new dean had been flunked out or made to repeat at least one year. This should have at least made us suspicious. Taking it to the next step, we had only to check with the Alpha Omega national dental fraternity to confirm our suspicions about Dean Buhler. The Jewish dentists in Philadelphia who knew Dr. Buhler at Temple University had already sent word ahead to their Atlanta colleagues that Buhler was an antisemite.

Given the above information, none of us should have applied. But, having applied, why were we accepted? It didn't make any sense. Years later, Emory History Professor Eric Goldstein was able to access files that provided the answer.

When Emory University took over Atlanta-Southern Dental College (ASDC) on September 1, 1944, it knew the school was poorly ranked, receiving only provisional approval by the Council on Dental Education of the ADA. The school had been cited with numerous deficiencies, and Emory took measures to ensure a gradual upgrading of the school. Emory deemed it important to be involved in the admissions process of the dental school and placed representatives of the university on the admissions committee of the dental school. The new dean of the dental school would not have sole control over who would be accepted. That explains how we were accepted. Once they selected the applicants, however, the keys were turned over to Dean Buhler. That's how we were kicked out.

Even before Emory took it over, there was an antisemitic culture at the Atlanta-Southern Dental College. Being a proprietary school, the owners found it necessary to accept all students capable of paying tuition. Before Emory took over, the university accepted Jewish students from 12 states, including New York, New Jersey, and Connecticut. After Emory took over in 1944, Jews were restricted to three states: Georgia, Florida, and South Carolina.

When Dr. Buhler became dean in 1948, he was already aware of the change of policy at the dental school. It was just a matter of time before he would take the policy to another level. Buhler did not feel it necessary to conceal his antipathy for Jews. A Dean John Buhler letter dated January 31, 1952 to Dr. J.W. Douglass was published in the Journal of the South Carolina Dental Society. In the letter, Dean Buhler complains to Douglass that there are a few people in the Atlanta community who are critical of Emory's selection process. (Could he deny that there was an obvious Jewish quota?) He boldly asserts that this will not deter him from doing what is correct. Douglass, an Atlanta-Southern Dental College '28 alumnus, resurfaces in 1964, succeeding in getting Buhler appointed Dean of the new dental school in Charleston, S.C.

Soon after returning home, I would receive a formal letter of dismissal from Emory dental school. The letter was dated May 22, 1952 and signed by Dean John Buhler. Citing broad academic failure (which was totally false), the letter did not give me the opportunity to return and repeat the year. This devastated my parents, especially my mother, who revealed her deep disappointment and embarrassment. Perhaps I was one of the lucky ones spared the shame of walking out of Buhler's office with a scarlet letter on my shirt. Buhler extracted me from his university in a cold and informal manner—a simple letter with no plausible explanation or justification. At least not from my point of view.

For the first time, I blamed the school. My mother would have none of that. "Emory? That can't be." That was a sobering moment for me. I could no longer portray myself as a victim.

After several requests, Buhler agreed to allow my dad to come to Atlanta. After an hour, Buhler told my dad that he couldn't do anything. I would have to write the governing board, asking them to reconsider their decision. My appeal was denied.

My dad became reconciled to Emory's final decision, and began working on alternate solutions.

I resumed college studies at the local University of Chattanooga, resolving to maintain my dignity and move on with my life. When I called Shirley to tell her that I wouldn't be returning to Atlanta, she was incredulous and thoroughly confused, but her faith in me was unwavering. Her loyalty sustained me in my road to recovery.

I didn't call Art Burns or Allen Shaw to break the news to them. At that point, I had no idea how they had fared. I shut them out of my mind. They were no longer part of my life.

CHAPTER 6

Back Home

———————

My parents, both children of European immigrants, had much in common. Each suffered the sudden loss of a parent at an early age, and each was selfless in helping their single parent raise their younger siblings. They worked long and hard hours, taking great pride in their accomplishments.

But when it came to their moods and personalities, they could not have been more different. They were a living example of the quirk of nature that causes opposites to attract. Each was comfortable and confident in his or her own right, but never tried to influence the other to change and be like they were. That worked just fine for them. But their differences made it difficult for me to figure out just what it would take to please them. I found it easier to earn their approval by my accomplishments than by my words. From early childhood, I found refuge in my upstairs bedroom, assiduously attacking my homework while listening to my radio.

But now I was back home with my tail between my legs. This time I couldn't avoid the tension that confronted my family and me. After the initial shock subsided, we all got off the mat, brushed ourselves off, and discussed options. Together, we succeeded in rechanneling our tension into the energy I would need to redirect my path. My younger sister Rita, now 16, was very much like our dad. She maintained a sweet smile, asked no questions, and was always in my corner. Her upstairs bedroom was across the hall from mine, and we enjoyed being back together again. I was her big brother, and in her eyes, I could do no wrong.

At the time, it didn't occur to me that my experience was not unique. Years later, to my surprise and amazement, I listened to dozens of men who followed me at Emory describe how they suffered the same grief and disappointment. They had been suddenly cut loose after two, three, and sometimes four years of dental school. But they didn't have a safety net.

I listened to their stories with patience and understanding. After years of suppressing their emotions, they recalled the guilt their mothers (it was always the mothers) laid on them, refusing to even consider that they had been treated differently than their fellow students. Many of their families had limited financial resources and would find it difficult supporting them in pursuing an alternative career path. They would have to overcome the resistance inherent in making serious life changes. That these young men were able to escape the grip of despair is testimony to their resilience, courage, and unceasing determination.

My dad was charming. In the summer, sitting at the office desk of his mom-and-pop coal yard, the Dixie Coal Company, he would make phone calls to customers, convincing them of the wisdom of buying their winter fuel supply six months before they actually needed it. This enabled him to give full-time employment to his two drivers, Rob and Leonard, who would load the coal on the trucks and deliver their cargo to homes in the suburban neighborhoods. I knew Rob and Leonard from my early childhood. On rainy days, Dad would send one of them to pick my sister and me up and drive us to school in the coal truck.

There were several other nearby coal dealers who competed with my dad for the small but steady peddler traffic. My dad had a reputation for keeping "honest scales." The majority of the peddlers trusted Dad to honestly weigh them in before moving out to the coal yard to fill their empty wheelbarrows with the coal they would sell to their neighborhood customers. After weighing out with their load of coal, there was always the familiar "See ya' later, Mr. Dixie." They didn't leave until they heard a humorous response from my dad.

Before the concept of networking became popular, my dad cultivated a wide and diverse range of friends. His social activity began early each morning. Awakened at 4:30 a.m. by his Little Ben alarm clock, he drove downtown for breakfast with the morning regulars at the downtown S&W Cafeteria. After his second cup of coffee (he liked his coffee steaming hot), he drove the six blocks to the coal yard. He was always the first dealer to open his gates in the early morning.

So my dad found it natural to reach out to anyone who could help me regain my footing. He suggested that I walk across the street and talk to our neighbor Dr. Wilbur K. Butts, the longtime chairman of the biology department at The University of Chattanooga. "Tell him that you were a biology major at Emory, and you are transferring to UC and would appreciate his advice."

But this discomfited me. I don't remember having ever seen Dr. Butts or Mrs. Butts entering or leaving their house. It would be my first visit, and I would be shamelessly asking for a favor. I was reluctant to follow my dad's advice. Not able to resist the urging of my father, I soon found myself knocking at their front door. Before there was any human response, I heard an uninterrupted chorus of dogs, howling in unison.

Mrs. Butts, neatly dressed, opened the door, and before greeting me turned and in some private canine language silenced her boisterous pets. In that brief moment of noiseless calm, my eyes scanned the living room to her right. Gracefully perched on the chairs and the sofa were a menagerie of cats. The rest of the feline family was roaming the hallway behind her.

She read my mind. "We have 12 dogs and on any given day 14 to 16 cats." That explained the stifling odor infusing the room. I convinced myself that it was the appropriate time to state the purpose of my visit. "I'm transferring to UC, and I'd like to speak to the professor about majoring in biology."

Before she could respond, the professor, who was listening to our brief conversation from around the corner, moved to his wife's side. He had already shed his jacket and tie and lacked the formal appearance of a college professor. He put me at ease by quietly inviting me into his study. At least six of the cats followed.

I spared myself the anguish of recounting my whole story. I'm not certain the professor even knew that I had been in dental school. He was delighted that I would be studying in his department and agreed to offer advice after he had a chance to look at my transcripts from Emory. I expressed my gratitude and hastened home to take my first ever midday shower.

Back to the Drawing Board

Thus, began a much-welcomed return to a normal scholastic atmosphere. The University of Chattanooga offered more than a mental sanctuary from a year of dismal oppression. The school motto immediately inspired me. Inscribed in Latin on its coat of arms, it read *Faciemus*: "We shall achieve."

The university was located on a tree-lined campus of slightly less than 300 acres, about a mile from the center of downtown Chattanooga. I spent the first four years of my life in an apartment on nearby Houston Street, three blocks from the northwest boundary of UC. Our family synagogue, B'nai Zion Congregation, was still located on the corner of Vine and Maple Streets, just one block west of the university. My parents' coal yard was located at 236 E. 10th St., a 15-minute walk from the university. I was back on familiar ground.

Although I cut off contact with my former dental classmates, my Atlanta AEPi fraternity brothers maintained their support for me during this troubling time. Teddy Wolff, now master of the fraternity, wrote frequently. As did Allan Davis, Sandy Kimball, Larry Goodrich, Ed Zwig, and Lee Moscowitz. I still have every one of their letters. Ted's girlfriend Ellie was headed to dental hygiene school in Memphis, and Ted told me I had to get into school there so I could keep an eye on her.

Much to my surprise, I discovered there was a fledgling colony of AEPi fraternity at The University of Chattanooga. I affiliated with them. Half of them were local boys and half were Northerners who were mesmerized by the easy pace of a small Southern university. The fraternity provided a welcome social and religious environment for the growing number of Jewish students. Sixty years later, in October 2016, Chabad would purchase a 10,000-square-foot building in the historic Fort Wood neighborhood, minutes away from the UC campus.

I kept my eyes open for part-time job opportunities. I was living at home, but I strongly felt that I had to at least be able to cover my social expenses. In my letters to Shirley, I proudly reported a steady part-time job at Olshine's, a busy downtown retail men's store. I picked up another few bucks opening a jewelry store before the owner arrived each morning. In the evenings I knocked on doors taking orders for metal address plates I would affix to the tops of mailboxes. I worked at the coal yard when my mom took my dad to an increasing number of doctor's appointments. I felt that I was in some measure repaying my parents for all they were doing for me.

Shirley and I exchanged long and frequent letters. I described joining my friends for Sunday morning minyan (prayer services) at the synagogue, followed by the ritual softball game at Warner Park. I was doing my best to remain mentally and physically healthy.

Serving My Country

Uncle Sam was always on my mind. Between the Korean War's outbreak in June 1950 and the armistice agreement in 1953, the Selective Service inducted over 1.5 million men. They lowered the induction age to 18, and active-duty service commitment was extended to 24 months. Some 23,000 young men were drafted each month. Another 1.3 million volunteered, usually choosing the Navy or Air Force. The Army was to be avoided if at all possible. At war's end, 33,651 US battle deaths were recorded; 100,000 were wounded. Two of my friends lost their lives in aerial combat over Korea. We were all fearful of when "the shoe would drop." Some of my friends enlisted before being drafted, hoping for a better assignment.

I was classified 1A by the local Selective Service Board. Their unofficial policy was to grant deferments to full-time college students who maintained passing grades. During the 1952-53 year, I appeared twice before the local board for a status interview, and once in Knoxville for a physical examination.

I scheduled my studies unencumbered by pre-dental requirements. I already had those under my belt. Dr. Butts, true to his word, provided a list of the courses I would need to qualify for a major in biology. Even then, I decided to continue working toward a minor in Spanish. I was determined to earn a college degree, no matter what direction my future would lead me.

My courses were top-heavy with science-related subjects, which included qualitative and quantitative chemistry, comparative anatomy, and bacteriology. My schedule also included English literature, music appreciation, and challenging courses in Spanish.

Despite my dad's chronic infirmities, he began working behind the scenes. He took me aside one day and asked if I still wanted to be a dentist. This meant that he still wanted me to be a dentist. So, I replied yes. He then told me that he had arranged for me to get an afternoon job as a plaster boy at Mynatt's dental laboratory. It would be an unpaid job, but they would take my manual skills to a different level. No one would be able to question my digital dexterity in the future.

At the same time, my dad consulted friends and family who were active in Tennessee politics. They had contacts in Governor Gordon Browning's office in Nashville and Senator Estes Kefauver's office in Washington. He was encouraged by their interest in my case. Dad also had UT alumni friends who were working on my behalf. We were hoping for an interview at the dental school, with the possibility that I might be admitted in the July quarter of 1953.

Dr. David B. Karr, my dad's former high school classmate and lifelong friend, was our family doctor. He was a Dr. Welby-type old-fashioned

GP/surgeon whose waiting room was always packed. Since finishing medical school at UT Memphis, and completing his internship, he confined his life to his profession. He was never too busy to see another patient. He eluded marriage but was considered an eligible bachelor.

"Doc" Karr wasn't surprised to hear what had happened to me at Emory. He told my dad, "That kind of thing happens around here all the time. They play dirty."

Hoping to interest me in medicine, Doc invited me to accompany him as he made rounds in the hospital. One day he offered to fix me up with one of the student nurses. When I sheepishly declined, he told me he would ask her out himself.

These numerous offers of help were an initial source of encouragement. But they didn't seem to be materializing fast enough. In the end, the cumulative effect of their efforts influenced the outcome. However, for the present, I didn't feel that we were making progress.

Even though I was able to remove much of the negativity from my mind in just a few months, I couldn't selectively erase events of the past three years. In effect, I completely expunged memories of two happy years of college life and one year of miserable life at the Emory dental school. Thankfully, there was one major exception. I just couldn't keep Shirley out of my mind. Shirley and I were exchanging mail three or four times a week. Evelyn, our maid, would intercept the mail and secretly place many of Shirley's letters under my bedroom pillow. Both of us saved every letter, and they remain to this day as a faithful journal and account of our time together.

My mother, in her way, did her best to restore my confidence. She had always enjoyed playing rubber bridge with a few of her lady friends. She expanded the scope of her skill, and soon began competing in the local duplicate bridge league. She took me under her wing and tutored me to the point that she would occasionally take me with her to the evening game at the bridge club. She may have created a monster.

One evening, I opened the cards I had been dealt, and after seeing the vast array of high cards, I fought to keep my eyes from dilating. You're never supposed to tip your hand to your opponents.

I opened the bid with "one club," and we went unchallenged as my mother gradually took the bidding to "six clubs." When I responded, "seven clubs," the lady to my left, Bessie Payne, quietly but firmly "doubled," indicating that she was prepared to defeat me. The bid came back to me and I "redoubled," bragging to the world that I could take every one of the 13 tricks.

My opponents were somewhat taken aback at my brazen display, but not nearly as much as my mother. She was mortified. Of course, she wouldn't say anything, but her dark eyes launched a flame of anger across the bridge table.

Ms. Payne started the action. I took the trick and methodically took the next nine tricks. Having captured 10 tricks, I revealed my hand and with a flourish disclosed my three remaining winning cards. There was no question. I would win a "top" on that hand. No one in the room who played those same cards would reach a grand slam, doubled and redoubled.

As soon as we got up from the table, my mother said, "Don't you ever do that again. The minute Bessie Payne doubled you, you knew that you had a top. It wasn't necessary to redouble. Now when they tally the boards at the end of the evening, everyone will see what happened at our table. All you did was publicly embarrass her. I guess I never thought I would have to tell you that this is a gentleman's game. And, by the way," she added, "it's unethical to display your cards like you did. You're supposed to play out every card. You're lucky they didn't call over the director and report it. He could have penalized you."

I was both stunned and speechless. I was only trying to convince my mother that I was a winner, not a loser. She didn't belabor the issue. Despite my breach of etiquette, she was pleased to see that my spirit hadn't been broken.

In late May, I learned that our family dentist, Dr. Ewing Connell, was in line to soon become the next president of the Tennessee Dental Association. Two years earlier, Dr. Connell had strongly advised me to consider UT dental school. He told my mom, a lifelong patient of his, that he would see Dean Ginn at the upcoming state convention and would talk to him about me.

During that same time, Dr. Marvin Goldstein, in his role as a national officer of Alpha Omega, was also lobbying Dean Ginn on my behalf. Marvin's private papers, permanently maintained in the archives of Atlanta's Breman Jewish Heritage Museum, verify his early involvement in exposing the antisemitism at the Emory dental school. In 2006, soon after his papers became available to researchers, I would first learn of Marvin's courageous role in helping me and other Jewish dental students.

A Second Chance to Make a First Impression

In June 1953, Gerald Prosterman, a childhood friend of mine, was about to begin his senior year at UT dental school. He was home for a break between quarters, and we arranged to meet at the Jewish Community Center, just minutes away from the U.C. college campus. He told me they were starting a Jewish dental fraternity at UT under the guidance of Dr. Ben Dent, a well-known Jewish dentist in Memphis. Gerald told me that Dr. Dent was a friend of Dean Ginn and that he would talk to him about me.

Shirley came to Chattanooga for the Fourth of July weekend. We had a great time enjoying the holiday with family and friends on the lake. We quietly concealed our disappointment that I had not heard yet from Dr. Ginn. The summer quarter at the dental school would soon be starting.

Shirley wrote me on Sunday night, July 5, as soon as she returned to Atlanta. She thanked me for a wonderful time. "I hope you get the phone call on Tuesday from Dr. Ginn."

The call from Dr. Ginn's office came on Monday morning, July 6. "The dean would like to see you tomorrow in his office for an interview. Can you be here tomorrow for a 1 p.m. appointment?"

I hung up and called my dad at the coal yard. His excitement was dampened by the reality that his physical condition wouldn't allow him to accompany me on the long drive to Memphis on such short notice. I was on my own since my mother wouldn't be able to leave my dad alone. I would have to develop a plan. Before I could gather my thoughts, I heard back from my dad.

In just a few minutes, my dad had convinced his friend Dr. David Karr to cancel his next-day office schedule and accompany me to Memphis for my meeting at the dental school with the dean. Fourteen months had passed since my rejection from Emory. I didn't have to be reminded how lucky I was to be getting a second chance.

We met Dr. Karr early the morning of Tuesday, July 7, at Lovell Field, Chattanooga's municipal airport. The original terminal building had been expanded in 1950, and the airport featured a new runway. I had never traveled by air, and I felt lucky to have a senior flying companion.

We made one stop in Nashville, the state capital. Over half the passengers deplaned and were replaced by westward-bound passengers. We were now on Central Standard Time, which meant that we were picking up an hour. An hour and a half later, we landed at our destination. It didn't take me long to learn just how different the culture was in western Tennessee. People weren't joking when they bragged that Memphis was the largest city in Mississippi.

Having no luggage, we moved quickly through the plane and down the steps to the tarmac. We entered the doors leading to the terminal, and followed the small crowd through the causeway.

Dr. Karr was cheerful and optimistic during the taxi drive from the Memphis airport to the dental school. It had been quite some time since he had been in Memphis, and he eagerly pointed out familiar landmarks, including John Gaston Hospital, the Memphis city hospital.

Although the dental, medical, pharmacy, and nursing schools were located not too distant from the busy downtown district, there was a quiet atmosphere surrounding the campus.

The UT College of Dentistry was founded in 1878, making it the oldest dental college in the South and the third oldest public college of dentistry in the United States. It was located at 875 Union Avenue.

We arrived with time to spare for my one o'clock afternoon appointment with Dean James T. Ginn. He was seated comfortably behind his uncluttered desk awaiting my arrival and stood to greet Dr. Karr and me. Dr. Karr excused himself after a brief introduction. After months of guarded expectation, the moment had finally arrived.

Dean Ginn maintained a pleasant smile during our meeting. This put me at ease. Before coming to Tennessee, he had spent years teaching at Loyola in New Orleans. While there, he had acquired the local dialect. His "th's" were pronounced as "d." I found out later that the students referred to him as "Der Dean of der dental school." His questions were of a general nature, sparing me the discomfort of discussing details of my experience at Emory dental school. I did mention that I had only seen Dean Buhler once, at my class orientation, and added that I had never been called to his office or anyone's office for a warning. I thought I saw the smile on Dr. Ginn's face widen. What was that about?

Dr. Ginn was young, only 44 years old, but presided over our conversation with the wisdom of a seasoned judge. In effect, that's what he was: an arbiter, the person who had ultimate authority in deciding my future.

The imaginary scale of justice sitting on Dr. Ginn's desk contained, on one side, my record at Emory dental school. However, my original application to UT dental school (I had been accepted to both Emory and UT in 1951), my high school and college transcripts, the positive results of the dental aptitude test I had recently taken in Nashville, and a number of letters of recommendation mitigated my concerns.

At the time, I was unaware that Dr. Ginn's final decision was likely influenced by additional circumstantial evidence. Years later, while browsing the *Journal of the American Dental Association*, I discovered that Dr. Ginn was one of seven founding members of the Southern Regional Conference of Dental Schools, which had its initial meeting in March 1953, just four months before my meeting with him. Among those at the first meeting were Joseph Volker of Alabama, James Ginn of Tennessee, and John Buhler of Emory. Having just met his imperious colleague from Emory for the first time, the impression of Dr. Buhler was fresh on Dr. Ginn's mind.

At that very moment, Dr. Ginn's smile broadened. With his soft Louisiana Cajun accent, he said the magic words, "Son, we are going to let you come to school here. I think *dat* you're going to do real fine."

That was it. I was in!

Dr. Karr was waiting for me in the dean's reception room. From the smile on my face, he knew the outcome of the interview. Dr. Ginn's secretary graciously called for a taxi, and we danced through the lobby on our way out the building.

I could hardly wait to share my happiness. Before takeoff, I called my parents and Shirley with the exciting news. When Dr. Karr and I returned to my house that night, several cars were parked outside, and we could see lights on all over the house.

My uncle Ted Brickman had purchased a bottle of champagne, and a small crowd of family and friends were awaiting our arrival to pop the cork. My sister Rita, normally the model of composure, was giddy after her second drink.

My mother and I excused ourselves, and we climbed the stairs to my room where she had already begun packing my bags. She was so happy for me, but she already knew how difficult it would be for her to take care of my dad. I would later describe the scene in a letter to Shirley. "You're still my little boy," my mother said with tears in her eyes. "Give me a big hug–like you would give Shirley." I left the next day, Wednesday, July 8, on the morning train to Memphis.

I wrote Shirley on Thursday morning from Memphis. The return address on the envelope disclosed my address: 874 Union Avenue, Memphis, Tennessee. There were no zip codes in 1953.

Dearest Shirley,
Sweetheart, would you have ever thought that it would
happen? Oh, golly, I didn't believe it when he called me
and told me to come right down. I've gotten everything
straightened out except my room. I'm sleeping on a cot in
a friend's room now. There are two boys who flunked and
who are asking for readmission, and if either one doesn't
get re-admitted, I get his room. If not, I'll find a room
somewhere. It's really beautiful here and huge. They have
dentistry, medicine, hygiene, pharmacy and nursing all
together. It's in a real nice section with a park, and tennis
courts, a pool, bowling alley, etc. In an hour I've got to go
to my first class - - - anatomy.

I continued the letter that evening.

There are 37 in the class including one girl and seven boys
who are repeating the quarter. We cleaned our cadavers and
got our bone boxes. I think I've got a room in the dorm
across from the school. Both of those boys were denied re-
admission. I'll find out tomorrow.

Shirley's return letter was overflowing with happiness. She told me
how proud she was of me, and that she always knew a door would open
for me. She said there were rumors circulating that Art Burns and Allen
Shaw had also been flunked out of Emory dental school and were already
in the Army. I felt so sorry for them. Two wasted years. Suddenly, I was
reminded how fortunate I was to have gotten out of that miserable place
after only one year, and now I was getting a second chance.

I am often asked if, upon hearing about Art and Allen, it finally
occurred to me that there might have been a religious element involved
in our dismissal from Emory. Years later, I asked Art and Allen that same
question. We shared the same response. Even if we had suspected it, we

didn't dare hide behind a reason that no one would believe. Even if it were true, we had to avoid seeing ourselves as victims. We had to put it behind us and move forward to something positive.

What we did know was that at Emory dental school we had felt isolated and intimidated. We didn't feel like we belonged. When you're overwhelmed, you become terrified. When you're terrified, you're dominated by what others are thinking. Even when you're in the shower, you're thinking, *what are the others thinking?* You begin to doubt yourself. Doubt paralyzes. You no longer have any spirit. You have lost.

CHAPTER 7

A Phoenix Rises

The fear that once paralyzed me vanished the moment I received the rejection letter from Dean Buhler. It seemed so strange and ironic that the person who exercised the terror hold over me was the same person who enabled my release from that terrible burden. Without that fear, I was then left to struggle with the twin yokes of anger and embarrassment.

I soon realized that anger went hand in hand with fear. Thank God family and friends surrounded me. It would be unfair and counterproductive to direct any residual anger and hostility toward them. My anger gradually disappeared.

However, the embarrassment was beyond my control. The rumor mill was porous and unfiltered, and it didn't take long for the news of my failure to reach far beyond Atlanta and Chattanooga. Even though my fraternity friends sent a steady stream of encouraging letters, and even though my family was totally supportive, I couldn't shake off the dirty feeling of shame. Sixty years later, my fellow classmates confided in me and said, "We never told anyone, but the shame and embarrassment never left."

Dental School, Round Two

The moment Dean Ginn accepted me, I resolved not to share my past experience at Emory with anyone in Memphis. I vowed to never look back over my shoulder again. In modern parlance, I rebranded myself.

I was stepping into a new world. Actually, more than just a new world. For me, it was גַּן עֵדֶן ·(a Hebrew/Yiddish phrase pronounced in English, Gan Aden), translated as the biblical Garden of Eden. Memphis was going to be my Paradise on earth.

It was late Tuesday night in Chattanooga when the celebration party ended. My parents would be taking me to the train station early in the morning, so we agreed to save that time for our final goodbyes. Instead, my parents, my sister, and I took a few last minutes to sit down and reflect on the miracle that had suddenly changed our lives. I told them how much I appreciated everything they had done to set the stage for my success. My parents always taught me that "God helps those who help themselves." They carefully avoided mentioning that this was a reenactment of a previous episode in my life. Appreciative of their sensitivity, I acknowledged that I was grateful for this second chance.

Chattanooga was already a bustling railroad community long before Glenn Miller made the world-famous "Chattanooga Choo Choo" an American icon. In 1906, the Southern Railway Company purchased a prominent downtown property and cleared ground for construction of its new station completed in 1909. Many of the railroad's most prominent trains stopped at Terminal Station including the *Birmingham Special* (Washington-Birmingham), *Pelican* (New York-New Orleans), *Ponce de Leon* (Cincinnati-Jacksonville), and the *Tennessean* (Washington-Memphis). The latter ran two trains daily, with a regular stop in Chattanooga. Three years later, Elvis Presley and his bride Priscilla would travel eastward from Memphis on the same train.

The train pulled out of Terminal Station promptly and, after reaching the city outskirts, reached its maximum allowable speed. My mind was moving at an even faster pace. Suddenly, the porter interrupted my thoughts: "Please adjust your watches one hour backward"- we were entering the Central Time Zone. It wasn't as if we were crossing the border into a foreign country, but it was a forceful reminder that I would soon be settling into a new address and a life-changing adventure.

I stepped off the train six hours later, gathered my baggage, and joined the crowd walking along the concrete sidewalk to the main building. We entered single file into the large downtown reception area. As I moved across the room toward the outside street exit, my eyes were drawn to a newsstand situated just inside the departure doors. The bold headlines of the *Memphis Commercial Appeal* caught my attention: "**Reds Say They Are Ready to Negotiate Final Details of a Korean Armistice**." Good news was coming in clusters. It was worth the five cents I paid for the privilege of reading the details of the article in the cab on my way to my dorm.

I stepped outside to grab a taxi. The heat and humidity coming off the nearby Mississippi River were crushing. As I stepped from the curb to the street, I could actually feel the asphalt pavement buckle beneath my shoes. I asked myself, "What's going on? Wasn't I here just yesterday? It must be at least ten degrees higher today."

A large flashing thermometer on an elevated marquee outside the train station provided the answer. The three o'clock afternoon temperature was 96 degrees. As we pulled away from the curb, the cab driver informed me that it was a record high for Memphis. I had no idea I would receive such a warm reception to Paradise.

I had memorized my new address. "874 Union Avenue," I told the driver. With undisguised pride, I added, "It's the dorm right across the street from the dental school." Those were my last words on the 20-minute ride to the campus, as the driver immediately took over the conversation. He must have been an employee of the Memphis Chamber of Commerce.

"Memphis is the largest city in Tennessee. We've got 400,000 people livin' here—some say half a million. The university is one of our largest employers. There's lots of construction goin' on. You'll see—all over. You like baseball? The Memphis Chicks play at Russwood Park. It's on Madison Avenue, just two blocks away from your dormitory. After the seventh inning, they'll let you in free.

"You ever heard of Holiday Inn motels? They started here in Memphis just last year, and they've already opened up three more on the roads leading into town. Word is that they'll soon be buildin' them all over the country. Mr. Wallace Johnson, one of the founders, is a local builder. He can build anything. He's a hero around here."

He was right. Holiday Inn had tripled its number of motels by the time I graduated. Branded as "The Nation's Innkeeper," it opened its 1000th motel in San Antonio, Texas, in 1968.

Fourteen years later, in 1967, I was practicing oral surgery in Decatur, Georgia. Hospital beds were scarce in the entire Atlanta area, and West Paces Ferry Hospital in northwest Atlanta was one of the private hospitals being built to meet the need. I attended its opening. The builder, Wallace E. Johnson of Memphis, participated in the ceremonies. I remembered my cabbie's complimentary remarks about Wallace Johnson: "Mr. Johnson can build anything."

After the ceremonies, I approached the venerable Mr. Johnson and shared my cabbie story with him. I told him that several doctors and businessmen in nearby Decatur were in discussions about the need for a second hospital in our community. With twinkling eyes and a ready smile, the jack-of-all-trades entrepreneur drew a business card from his pocket and placed it in my hand. "Call me." We did, and he was hired to build our hospital. In the summer of 1973, on the eve of the opening of Decatur Hospital, the 72-year-old Wallace Johnson was the featured speaker at the pre-event ceremonies in the luxurious penthouse Sky Room of the Decatur Savings and Loan Bank in downtown Decatur.

******

It was after four o'clock in the afternoon when we pulled into the narrow alley adjacent to the three-story dormitory to which I had been temporarily assigned. The dean's office had called the building superintendent, a Mr. Hearn, and told him that I was a last-minute addition to the first-quarter dental school class and needed a room.

I was told that the status of room #309 was in question pending a final decision on two students who had been flunked out of school. Aware that I was from Chattanooga, Mr. Hearn asked Oscar B. Hecklin, a first-year medical student from Cleveland, Tennessee, if he would agree for a cot to be set up temporarily in his second-floor room. O.B. had been my Sunday school pal at B'nai Zion Synagogue in Chattanooga for years, and he welcomed the opportunity to help out his old buddy. When I knocked on his door, O.B. was headed out to join his medical school classmates, who would be viewing an emergency autopsy. "Set down your bags and come with me," he ordered. "It'll just take a few hours. Then we can go out for supper and celebrate."

O.B. had always been the largest boy in our Sunday school crowd. It was his lifelong dream to become a doctor, and he advertised his obsession by wearing a light green scrub suit (extra-large) wherever he went. I obediently followed him on foot to the University Hospital two blocks down the street, where I changed clothes. None of his classmates questioned my presence. We took our seats in the autopsy room just before they wheeled in a white female who died earlier that day of stomach cancer. This proved to be more excitement in one day than I had over the course of my entire stay at Emory dental school.

Next to becoming a doctor, eating was O.B.'s favorite pastime. His food didn't have to be fancy—just plentiful. We lost no time hitching a ride over to nearby Pappy's and Jimmy's restaurant at 2100 Madison, a noisy and cluttered restaurant that could accommodate as many as 400 diners—and most nights it did. I knew that this would be my last extravagance for a long time, and I savored the experience.

Outside the restaurant, the oppressive heat had eased off a bit, but there was no additional relief when we returned to the dorm. Those days, a Fedders window air conditioner cost $400. You also had to pay for converting the wiring to a 220-volt outlet. There was only one in the entire building, and it didn't belong to O.B.

We showered and got ready for bed. O.B.'s pajamas looked familiar. He had changed to a different color scrub suit, still extra-large but now light blue. I stretched out on the narrow cot, barely a foot off the floor. After setting my alarm, I began thinking about the following day, which would be my first day at UT dental school. Although I had vowed to discard all memories of my former dental school, I couldn't avoid contrasting my past and present situations. I suppose it was a subconscious way to boost my morale. Positive images scrolled up, reminding me of how fortunate I was.

Back at Emory I would have to wake up before daybreak to drive my way through the morning traffic to arrive on time for my first class. Here I would only have to walk across the street. In downtown Atlanta, my classmates and I were isolated from the rest of the Emory community. Here we were totally integrated with the medical and nursing students, and I could already sense the camaraderie. The university provided convenient and inexpensive student dormitories. In Atlanta, you were on your own. At Emory, you weren't allowed to do any lab work outside the school. I guess they didn't trust us. At UT, there was a lab in the basement of the dormitory. We were on the honor system. My tuition was $700 per year at Emory. My annual in-state tuition at UT was $375.

At Emory dental school, Jews were not invited to join non-Jewish fraternities. In fact, my three Jewish classmates and I were so isolated that we were totally unaware of any other Jewish students in the school. At UT, not surprisingly, Jewish students were also not invited to join non-Jewish fraternities. But at UT there was an Alpha Omega fraternity chapter, and the Jewish students told me they enjoyed a friendly relationship with the administration. I also learned that there were a few veteran Jewish faculty members.

Another huge plus: Tennessee was the lone holdover from the WWII years that saw medical and dental schools adopt an accelerated three-year program. At Tennessee we would be on a quarter system, thirty-six months with no interruption. I would finish in three years instead of four. God willing, I would be graduating in June 1956, just one year later than I would have graduated at Emory. Amazing.

While all the above was comforting, reality wouldn't allow me to fall asleep. I couldn't dismiss the fact that Memphis was 340 miles from Chattanooga, and 460 miles from Atlanta, and Shirley was always in my thoughts. But reality prevailed—I had been failed once before, and nothing was going to prevent me from succeeding this time.

My classes began at 1 p.m. the next afternoon—Gross Anatomy in Room 304 in the Anatomy Building, where they taught us basic sciences. No introductions, no orientation. Just take a seat, take notes, and listen. The professor announced that each of us would get a bone box and a microscope for histology. Then he told us that four students would share a cadaver, which we would clean up that afternoon. The protocol was the same as Emory's. No jokes or smart remarks around the table. The cadaver we were dissecting had once been a live person just like us and deserved our respect.

I didn't see my name on the class list. Not a surprise, but it was time for me to become an official member of the class. I quietly, and with as little detail as possible, reported in to the professor. With full authority, he inserted my name into the list and assigned me to cadaver #1. I slipped into the alphabetical order. There would be five of us at our table instead of four. One of my classmates was female, and in her thirties, a Latvian transfer student named Lydia Baumanis. With her quiet demeanor and pronounced Baltic accent, she added continental class to our group.

I learned to adapt to the six-day schedule. The accelerated system required a concentrated curriculum and varied noticeably from the one I had at Emory. It was top-heavy with sciences and was a perfect segue from my courses at The University of Chattanooga. There was just one dental subject, a one-hour Introduction to Dental Anatomy, our only class at the dental school.

On Sunday night, July 12, I penned a two-page letter to Shirley, who had just graduated from Grady High School and was working at the Atlanta Jewish Community Center day camp. "I finally got a room here in the dormitory. There's a small living room and a bedroom. I'm rooming with a third quarter dental student from a small town in western

Tennessee. His name is Harold Russell, and he's a nice guy. He's a pretty hard worker, and I'm going to work hard, too."

I told Shirley that I was very lucky with my cadaver partners. Two of them had comparative anatomy in college (as I did), and they were all inquisitive. "Friday, we completed our dissection quicker than any of the other groups. Saturday, in histology class, it felt great to know what I was doing. Half of the guys didn't even know how to look through a microscope. There's one other Jewish boy in my class who went to college at The University of Alabama. I told him that you were probably going there this fall. He said his girlfriend who lived in Birmingham might also go there this fall." A connection that would lead to a close lifetime friendship.

On Sunday afternoon, July 19, I wrote home about a gross anatomy exam coming up on the following Thursday. I found it noteworthy to mention that my anatomy professor was Jewish, the first Jewish professor I had ever had, even including college.

"I made a 98 on the Anatomy quiz, the highest in the class," I wrote in my July 26 letter to Shirley. I also wrote, "...my friend O.B. and I spent Saturday night in the emergency room of John Gaston Hospital. O.B.'s physical bearing and his oversized scrub suit allowed him (and me by extension) to 'set up our tent' in one of the treatment rooms, and treat emergency patients. We went in at 11:00 p.m. and walked out at 5:00 a.m. We were busy the whole night giving tetanus shots and sewing up minor lacerations." What a tremendous boost to my morale.

On August 10, I wrote Shirley about my first major chemistry exam, which was given the previous Wednesday. There were 2 E's, 8 G's, 15 S's, 5 P's, and 9 X's. I made a G. The following week I wrote that I got back my second gross anatomy exam, and I made a 95 and a 91 on the practical. "The Chemistry grades aren't back, but the rumor is that ten guys failed. My class meets with the dean for a progress report tomorrow. I don't ever remember receiving grades at Emory. And my class certainly never met with Dean Buhler."

On August 26, I wrote Shirley that the dean only called in nine students. "I'm glad I wasn't one of the nine. I really feel sorry for them. The only consolation is that if you have to repeat a quarter, it's only three months instead of a year. I hear that it's not too unusual for a student having to repeat two quarters, just so they are not consecutive. That's still less than a full year." And it wasn't considered something that would cause you to hang your head in shame.

During my first eight quarters, I continued to live in Room 309 of the student dorm. My first roommate got married. My second roommate, from Corinth, Mississippi, moved to private housing, and my third roommate was a first-year med student from Birmingham. They were all perfect Southern gentlemen.

My letters home continued to be upbeat, especially with regards to my grades. My parents were pleased to know that I had become close friends with my classmate, Stanley Rubenstein, and was studying with him almost every weeknight at his Grandma Sokol's house, where he was now living. Stanley grew up in Milan, Tennessee, where his parents owned and operated The Toggery, a specialty-clothing store. His three sisters were very grown up and sophisticated, but Stanley was as country as it gets. His father died suddenly, and his mother was running the business. It would have been natural for Stanley to remain in Milan, with no connection to a Jewish community.

Stanley's older sister, Margie, was married and living in Birmingham. She was determined to get her brother out of Milan, and as soon as he graduated high school, she invited him to spend the summer with her and her husband Ralph in Birmingham. That's where he met and fell in love with Micky Friedman, a smart and popular high school girl who was three years younger than him. Micky, the youngest of the three Friedman children, had also lost her father.

Now Margie had to convince Stanley to leave Birmingham and go to college at The University of Alabama at Tuscaloosa, 60 miles away. Two years passed quickly, and Stanley was accepted to dental school at The University of Tennessee in Memphis. He and Micky wanted to get married. She would work in Memphis and help pay for expenses. Both families intervened and convinced Micky to go to college at The University of Alabama for at least one year.

In August 1953, Stanley told Micky that his classmate's girlfriend, Shirley Berkowitz, was enrolling at Alabama. She reacted excitedly. "I know Shirley from Young Judea youth conventions. I had a date to a dance with an Atlanta boy the night Shirley was crowned JAC sweetheart."

Stanley and I drove down in his car to Tuscaloosa the first Friday in September to see our girlfriends. It was strictly against sorority rush rules for the girls to go off campus or participate in non-sorority activities. Hoping just to catch a glimpse of them, we drove by the SDT sorority house, cruised by the campus post office, and finally succeeded in sneaking a few hours with them at a nearby lake. We were back in Memphis late Sunday evening. A few days later, Shirley wrote that she and Micky accepted bids to SDT sorority.

On Saturday, September 19, I broke the Yom Kippur fast at Baron Hirsch Synagogue, located about three and a half miles north of the dental school in the Vollintine Evergreen area of Memphis. In the 1950s, Baron Hirsch was the largest Orthodox congregation in North America, with a membership of over a thousand households. Yom Kippur is supposed to be a time for repentance, but I spent at least half the day praying for success on my final exams taking place the following week.

During the breaks in the service, it was customary for young and old members to mingle on the street outside the synagogue. I recognized several of the girls who were home from college, and quite a few were from Alabama. I asked Rochelle Goldstein and Diane Leach, Alabama SDT sisters of Shirley, to send my regards to her. A few years later, Rochelle married Ed Wiener, a UT dental graduate, and Diane married Larry Wruble, a med student from Miami who lived in my dorm. We all remain active members of our respective Orthodox congregations.

We had our final histology practical the following Monday. On Tuesday we had the chemistry final. Friday, the histology final, and Saturday, gross anatomy, after which I took the plane home to

Chattanooga for a short two days with my parents. When I returned, I received my first-quarter final grades—E in gross anatomy, G in chemistry, and S in histology. Over the next quarter I knew I would have more anatomy and chemistry plus physiology. The biggest challenge would be dental anatomy, the "killer" course taught by the notorious Dr. Virgil Bolton, the "Red Man," so called because when someone angered him, a frequent occurrence, his face flushed, and as we would find out later, his blood pressure skyrocketed.

On Tuesday, October 13, I received the results of Bolton's first pop test—97. I was ecstatic. He had already okayed the first three teeth I carved, the central and lateral incisors and the cuspid.

Two weeks later, I had the first and second bicuspids under my belt. By November 12, I got the first and second molars checked. I had a 90 average in dental anatomy. Every time I got a tooth checked by Dr. Bolton, the hardest teacher in the school, I thought about those jerks at Emory. Strangely, I didn't see it as revenge. I just continued to question their ulterior motives. It would take many years for the complete picture to unfold.

At my mother's suggestion, I dropped by Dean Ginn's office to tell him how much I appreciated what he had done for me. He told me that at a recent faculty meeting, he asked Dr. Bolton how I was doing. "Dr. Bolton told me, 'He's got it.'" We were both smiling this time.

As the end of the second quarter neared, I was making consistently high grades in all my courses. The hard work was paying off. I made hotel reservations for the December weekend in Birmingham when Stanley and Micky were getting married. I encouraged Shirley to try to make it to the wedding. I was secretly (maybe not so secretly) hoping that she and I could do the same thing a year later. At the same time, I depended on my parents for financial support and could not muster the courage to ask them to support two people. I was unfairly expecting Shirley to more or less hang in the air for an unstated period of time. That we were able to surmount this emotional and psychological barrier is a testimony to her unfailing love and support.

My afterschool schedule was predictable. I didn't feel like a prisoner as I did at Emory, but I maintained a highly disciplined and regimented lifestyle. It was impossible during the summer heatwave to study in my room, even in the evenings. So, I ate an early supper at the nearby Nightingale restaurant and then headed to the air-conditioned student center, where I would find a quiet corner to pore over my books. Alternately, I would sleep from six to eleven o'clock in the evening and then walk over to the nearby all-night drugstore, where I would have a midnight chicken salad sandwich and a strawberry soda at the counter, and then spend the next three hours memorizing the names of the facial muscles, their nerves, and their blood vessels. I often wrote Shirley at 3 a.m. before catching a few hours of sleep before morning classes.

The newlyweds, Stanley and Micky, were living in nearby university apartments. Micky would have her girlfriends over to play cards, and Stanley would drive over to study with me at the student center. On weekends they would drive to see Stanley's mother in Milan or to see Micky's mother in Birmingham. I didn't mind going alone to the baseball park to watch the minor league Memphis Chicks take on Chattanooga, Birmingham, Nashville, Knoxville, Mobile, New Orleans, or Little Rock. Occasionally, I would catch a bus downtown to see a movie. Once in a while some of us guys would drive over to West Memphis, Arkansas, to view a movie that had been censored in Memphis. Those few hours of diversion were always followed by study, study, study.

1954 began on a positive note. Stanley and I advanced to the third quarter. Our friend Jack Bern from McMinnville, Tennessee, joined us. Two years later, the three of us would graduate in the same class. We have remained life-long friends.

My Emory fraternity brother Ted Wolff from Miami, who had been a faithful correspondent during my "blue" period," was now a freshman med student at Emory. Ted was my guest in early March 1954 when he visited his girlfriend Elly Blumenthal, who was a second-year dental hygiene student in Memphis. Ted had recently seen Art Burns and Allen Shaw, who were both flunked out after two years at Emory. They were both in the Army and hoping to avoid service in Korea. Ted brought news that our fraternity brother Phil Nathan and several more of our boys were having a rough time at Emory dental school. Just a few months later Shirley confirmed that Phil had failed his sophomore year and was not given an opportunity to repeat. I located Phil in California 58 years later. He was a hugely successful business consultant, as well as a proud and loving husband, father, and grandfather. He told me that he had vowed never to look back. Yet, when he heard from me that Emory was going to offer a public apology, he felt moved to write the vice president of Emory University about how devastated he was at the time of his failure, and how he bore the pain of rejection.

The third quarter was known by all to be a major hurdle, but I took it in stride. I continued to maintain a high grade-point average during the fourth and fifth quarters. I was first in my class by the end of the sixth quarter.

I finished my sixth quarter on December 15 and got a ride home to Chattanooga with my friend Bruce Backer. We arrived late that evening. My parents and I had plenty to talk about, but we agreed to cut our conversation short, as they had to get up early the following morning to go to work at the coal yard.

The winter months were the busiest time of a coal dealer's year, and I insisted on going with them to help out. After a long and productive day, we returned home, cleaned up, and ate a late supper. Then my parents and I, and my sister, who was home from college, sat down and discussed my wedding plans.

Sitting in front of the living room fireplace, we talked about how my parents had first met Shirley when she visited me in Chattanooga for Thanksgiving 1952, six months after I had been dismissed from Emory dental school, eight months before I was accepted to UT, and 10 months before she went to college. From the moment my parents met Shirley, they loved her. They would have preferred that we wait until I graduated dental school to get married. But they understood how much we cared for each other and felt that we had matured sufficiently to assume the responsibilities of marriage.

By the fall of 1954, our parents had agreed to allow Shirley and me to get engaged during the Christmas break. Now we were making plans to drive to Atlanta, where Shirley and I would announce our engagement. Shirley would remain in Atlanta and work until a few weeks before our wedding in June 1955.

Shirley's parents invited family and close friends to an engagement party in Atlanta at the Progressive Club on December 26. Shirley and I were so happy that our parents had become such close friends. We vowed to model our lives after them.

The day after the party, Shirley and I had another tearful separation, but this time we knew that our hopes and dreams would soon be realized. My parents and I drove back to Chattanooga, and after a brief stay, I returned to Memphis to begin my seventh quarter on January 6, 1955.

I ran into Dean Ginn on the clinic floor soon after I returned to school. The dean told me that the Conference of Southern Dental School Deans had just met in Memphis. Dean John Buhler and Associate Dean L. Berry Brown represented Emory there. Dr. Ginn told me that Doctor Buhler and Dr. Brown had both asked him how I was doing in school. He told me that it gave him great pleasure to inform them that I had completed the past quarter first in my class. Soon after, one of the senior students, Ruben Robinson, told me that he had recently attended an Alpha Omega event in Atlanta, and Dr. Marvin Goldstein asked him how I was doing. Dr. Goldstein told Ruben that he had written letters to the dean when I first applied to the school. I was constantly reminded of how many people had intervened on my behalf, and I was so grateful.

No one could ever become complacent or overconfident in dental school, but I had reached the point where I looked forward to life after dental school. Senior students were advising us to look into joining an Army or Navy reserve unit with the hope that we could have a timely transition from school into one of the branches of the military.

There were several advantages to serving two years as a dental officer before starting private practice. You would gain two additional years of practical working experience before opening a practice, you would earn a decent income, and you could set aside some of your salary in a savings account. Equally important, you would avoid being drafted after going to the expense of setting up a practice. Everyone said it was the thing to do.

Two of our instructors were active members of the Naval reserve unit situated at nearby Millington Naval Station. I lost no time requesting application forms. After completing the forms, I received notice to report for a physical examination at the naval station. Everything seemed to go well, and I was told to expect to hear from them within a reasonable period of time. I informed my parents of my decision, which they questioned. That made me uncertain, but I felt that I had to be proactive rather than take a passive stance. I made several follow-up calls to the naval station and was assured that I would soon hear from them.

The first two quarters in the clinic were exciting. I was treating real live patients and enjoyed my work immensely. Though Shirley had loved her time at the University of Alabama, she insisted on postponing her studies so that we would not have to rely completely on our parents for support. She completed a speedwriting course and was lucky to get a job with Dr. Harold Levin, a prominent Atlanta dermatologist. We supplemented our numerous letters with lengthy evening phone calls. Shirley and many of her girlfriends were planning their June weddings, and she shared every intricate detail with me. My last letter from Memphis to Miss Shirley Berkowitz was postmarked June 6, 1955. I told her that I had placed a $75 down payment on a furnished apartment at 1165 Poplar Avenue #8, which would be ready for occupancy when we returned to Memphis after our honeymoon. The rent was $65 a month.

Our wedding picture

Our June 26 wedding was held at 7 p.m. at the Progressive Club in midtown Atlanta. Shirley was 19 years old and I was 22. We first met almost five years before, and it was truly love at first sight. We flew to Miami early in the morning and stayed at the oceanfront Nautilus Hotel on Miami Beach, a popular honeymoon destination. Several of my fraternity brothers who lived nearby dropped by to see us. They had played a vital role in our long-distance romance and were happy to share in our happiness. The Miami scene was vibrant, and we gave some thought to settling there one day. But that was just a fleeting thought.

Back in Atlanta after a glorious honeymoon, we shared our pictures with Shirley's parents and her sisters, Marilyn and Helen. Shirley's dad surprised us with a used 1950 DeSoto, and we loaded it down with all our new belongings. We stopped overnight in Chattanooga to spend a few precious moments with my family, and then we headed back to Memphis to begin my last four quarters in dental school.

Shirley was pleased with our apartment. It was convenient to the dental school and situated on a busy bus line. Within a week,

Shirley found employment with Charles T. Wheat, a manufacturers' representative with offices near the historic Main Street/Beale area in downtown Memphis. When added to our parents' financial support, her $50-a-week salary made it possible for us to make ends meet. The apartment wasn't too much larger than my former dormitory room, but as far as we were concerned, it was heaven.

The next four quarters quickly moved by. With hard work and relentless encouragement from Shirley, my parents, and my friends, I graduated on Monday, June 11,1956. Only half of my original classmates graduated with me. We began our first quarter in July 1953 with 39 students. On the way to graduation in 1956, we lost 15 of our original classmates. Nine members of our graduating class of 28 joined us somewhere along the way. It was a bittersweet moment.

My U. of Tennessee dental class graduation picture (June 1956)

They announced the Dean's Honorary Society members at the graduation ceremonies. I finished fourth in my class, only four-tenths of a percentage point below the top student. My wife sat between my parents, and they held hands throughout the ceremonies. As I walked across the stage to receive my diploma, I said a silent *Shehecheyanu*, thanking God for allowing me to reach this long-awaited day.

I have never forgotten The University of Tennessee and its dental school for giving me a second chance. I served as president of the Tennessee Dental Alumni Society from 1992-1994 and was recently inducted into the Tennessee Society for philanthropic achievement. Shirley and I established the James T. Ginn merit scholarship for deserving students to honor the memory of my benefactor, Dean Ginn.

My parents left the day after my graduation and returned to Chattanooga. Before they left, I reminded my father that a month before graduation, I finally heard from the Navy. They regretted to inform me that an incompletely-healed cyst had disqualified me for a Navy commission. "Try the Army," they advised me. "They're not as strict as the Navy." I asked my dad to start working his connections to get me an Army or Air Force commission. I figured that if he could get me into dental school, he could get me into the service. Shirley was three months pregnant, and we were resigned to moving in with my parents in Chattanooga, where I would look for part-time work with a local dentist. Shirley would have the baby in Chattanooga, and I would continue to pursue getting a commission.

Love at First Sight

Following graduation, Shirley and I stayed in Memphis so I could take the Tennessee State Board examination, which was conveniently scheduled the day after the June 1956 graduation ceremonies.

The Tennessee State Board examination was given in Memphis biannually, June and December. My newly acquired diploma merely permitted me to take the board exam. Passing the State Board was the legal requirement to practice dentistry in Tennessee. It was also a prerequisite to being accepted to the dental corps of each branch of the armed forces.

Most but not all the dentists taking the Tennessee Board were recent graduates, and most were graduates of UT. Those of us UT graduates who had scored a B or higher on our senior clinic practical enjoyed a huge advantage. We were exempted from the clinical portion of the test, which comprised the major part of the examination. But there were still some laboratory requirements, and everyone had to take the jurisprudence part of the exam.

After arriving at the dental school where the exams were being given, I confidently took the elevator to the familiar third-floor clinic area.

I didn't allow myself to become overconfident. I knew I had to pass the Board to practice in Tennessee. I was also going to take the Alabama State Board exam the following week and the Florida State Board two weeks later, and I figured that passing this test would not only look good on my resumé, but would also provide me with valuable practical experience.

As happy as we were to have completed this chapter of our new life together, Shirley and I needed a few days to say goodbye to our friends and pack our belongings.

We had lived at 1165 Poplar Avenue in a furnished one-bedroom apartment, so moving furniture was not an issue. We had clothes, books, a few cooking utensils, a wedding album, and a bulging duffel bag of June 1952 to June 1955 love letters from me to Shirley and from Shirley to me. They were the glue that kept us together when we were apart for three years.

Sixty-two years later, those more than 600 letters, still in mint condition, provided incredible details of our developing relationship.

******

By the summer of 2017, I reached the point in my storytelling that I realized the need for details of what happened between 1952 and 1955.

After all, it was so long ago. Time had passed by. Lots had happened. How could I bring back memories into sharp focus? A thought came to mind, but I was afraid to pursue it because I didn't want to be disappointed. But it was my only real chance.

I casually inquired of Shirley, "Did you happen to save any of the letters I wrote you?" knowing that she never throws away anything but hoping for just a few. She calmly replied, "Between 1956 and 1961, we made seven moves, starting in Memphis and ending in Atlanta. There's an old duffel bag full of all the letters you wrote to me in the back of the closet next to our bedroom. That may be where some of your letters are."

Five minutes later I heard her cry out, "Oh my God, look what we have! Letters from you to me *and* letters from me to you. Three cent stamps on all of them. Handwritten. From June 1952 when you left Emory to June 1955 when we got married." She was so excited.

I walked the few steps from the adjacent study. There they were on the floor where she had emptied the duffel bag. Hundreds of letters all over the floor. The letters from me to her were numbered in chronological order.

"I don't even remember your giving me the letters I wrote to you," she said. "I didn't even think you had saved them. You even kept the letters your parents sent you. And the ones your friends sent you, and the ones my parents and sisters sent you. They are all here with the ones I sent you."

We carefully gathered the letters and placed them chronologically in seven file boxes.

Then Romeo and Juliet started reading the long letters aloud to each other, sometimes reading nonstop for three hours, only stopping when our voices became hoarse and our mouths dry. They provided long-forgotten facts and distant memories. We recalled the author Kent Nerburn's stressing the importance of bridging time gaps: "Care less for your harvest than for how it is shared and your life will have meaning and your heart will have peace."[51]

Shirley, a 15-year-old, described our first date in Atlanta and the ensuing drama of young love. She continued writing to me with trust, encouragement, and increasing love when I had to leave Emory and return to Chattanooga. She never doubted me. Her lengthy letters from college revealed our mutual desire to get married. After our engagement, she shared the bliss of a soon-to-be bride.

The letters in my handwriting were equally amorous but revealed my despair as I described my exile in Chattanooga after the Emory disaster and the frustration of being apart from Shirley, detailed my miraculous rescue by an understanding dean, and chronicled the next two years in Memphis where, alone, I began my rehabilitation. My love for Shirley was the spark that fueled my desire to succeed.

From the day I arrived in Memphis, the stars above guided me. I had risen from the ashes. My spirits were lifted by the kindness of everyone around me. I, somehow, intuitively knew the importance of observing and documenting my everyday activities. The day would come when I would discover a broader landscape.

CHAPTER 8

Smooth Sailing

Priming for the Real World

They offered the Tennessee State Board exam at the UT dental school. It began early on the morning of June 12. Being on familiar territory, I was able to complete the written exam and the lab requirements in a day and a half. I arranged for the results to be sent to my Chattanooga address. We were advised that we would have to wait two weeks for the results, but I felt reasonably confident that I would pass.

Shirley and I had a few personal goodbyes to say. A few months before, when we first suspected Shirley was pregnant, we asked friends to recommend a gynecologist. Dr. Rivers was everyone's favorite. He was a young UT graduate and had taken his residency at one of the affiliated hospitals. We told him up front that we would only be in Memphis a few more months and wouldn't be around for him to deliver our baby. Nevertheless, he was kind and spent lots of time with Shirley and refused to charge us for his services. I told him that although I was a student and had limited income, I would still like to pay him something for his services. Furthermore, I told him that we would be moving far away from Memphis, and I would never be able to reciprocate his kindness.

Dr. Rivers reached out and grasped my hand. "Not too long ago, I was a student just like you. People took care of me, and when I told them exactly what you just told me, they said, 'The time will come when you can help someone else.'" He paused and continued, "You will be paying me by helping someone else." I always remembered this powerful lesson.

We also wanted to spend a few more hours with our dear friends Stanley and Micky Rubenstein before they left for Birmingham. We didn't know when we would see them again, and we wanted to thank them for their many kindnesses. How many times had we told our parents, "Look at Stanley and Micky. They're married, and she's working to help get Stanley through school, and they are doing just fine." They served as a role model for us. We promised to keep in touch, and we did.

While my first choice was to find a job in Chattanooga while I was waiting to get in the service, there were no immediate offers. During my last quarter of school, I had heard that one of the large steel mills in Birmingham had an opening in its dental clinic. I was told that I could apply for the job, but I would have to pass the Alabama State Board exam, which was going to be given the third week of June. They offered to find me patients for the practical part of the exam. They casually mentioned that the steelworkers' union was threatening a strike but felt that it would be quickly resolved. Thus, my job was contingent on the outcome of these negotiations.

I drove to Birmingham the week after the Tennessee exams. I did really well on the Alabama exam. I already had one test under my belt, and I sailed through the three days without any surprises or complications. We were told that we wouldn't hear the results for two to three weeks. I returned to Memphis confident that I had passed and hopeful for a job offering. The following morning, Shirley and I turned in our apartment keys and headed due east to Chattanooga.

I had no sooner arrived in Chattanooga than I read in the local paper that negotiations between US Steel and the steelworkers' union had reached an impasse. On July 10, 1956, 650,000 workers went on strike nationwide. The company sent a telegram the following day, withdrawing the job offer. It was small consolation when I heard from the Alabama Board that I had passed its exam. Never one to make snap decisions, I kept the license active for the next ten years.

Shirley was not surprised, but noticeably disappointed, when I told her I didn't intend to take the Georgia Board exams. My reluctance to return to Atlanta was understandable, given my previous experience at Emory. The truth was that, in my mind, I worried I wouldn't get a fair shake from the Georgia examiners. I wasn't going to give them a second chance to flunk me.

Instead I decided that I would take the Florida Boards, scheduled a week after the Alabama examination. I would drive down alone, having as my sole companion in the back seat of my car the bulky dental paraphernalia required by the Florida Board.

It took less than an hour to reach the Georgia state line from my house in north Chattanooga, but I knew this was the shortest part of a long trip ahead. Georgia is the largest state in landmass east of the Mississippi, and it took me 10 hours to reach the Florida state line. The summer sun was still bright when I arrived 30 minutes later in the business area of Jacksonville. I had made reservations at the Seminole Hotel, whose 10-story presence dominated the downtown landscape and quickly came into view.

I was all keyed up during my drive down to Jacksonville. Despite my unquestioned success at Tennessee, I still harbored memories of my year at Emory. In my mind, passing the prestigious Florida Board would erase anyone's doubt of my abilities. Those thoughts faded from my mind as I parked my car and entered the hotel. I had safely reached my destination and was finally able to relax, settle down in my room, and get a good night's sleep.

The Florida Board was arguably the most challenging dental exam in the country. Everyone, especially Northerners, wanted to move to Florida. Florida wasn't interested in an ingress of old retired dentists who would practice part-time, so they made their test practically impossible to pass. There were endless lawsuits challenging the legality of the Florida Board exam, but they proved unsuccessful. The failure rate continued to exceed the numbers who passed. Word had it that very few Northern students were successful. I was fresh off two successful board exams, and with nothing to lose, I decided to take the challenge. If I passed, I could only dream of where in Florida I would practice.

The logistics were as formidable as the exam itself. Florida did not yet have a dental school and wouldn't until 1972, so a temporary testing area was set up each year in the mezzanine of the Seminole Hotel, a legendary landmark in downtown Jacksonville.

There were 320 applicants from all over the South and the Eastern Seaboard. They arrived two days before the exam to check in the neighboring hotels, register for the exam, and look for patients. The Florida applicants had already found their patients, but the majority of the applicants had to find theirs in the next two days.

A local dental supply house advertised in the local and regional newspapers for prospective patients, who were attracted by the opportunity for free dental work. I joined the line of board applicants, eager to meet our prospective patients. The line stretched for two blocks along the sidewalk leading to the dental supply house.

The dental supply dealer provided X-ray machines, which were necessary to determine the presence and extent of the patients' dental cavities. There was a fierce competition for patients. It was often necessary to locate more than one patient to find the type of dental disease you were looking for. In that case, after finding your first patient, you would have to go to the end of the line and, an hour or two later, identify a second patient. After suitable patients were identified, financial deals were made to ensure the patient would show up for the exam. No patient, no license.

The elevators to the hotel mezzanine were overcrowded on the day of the exam. When the elevator doors opened, the sight was surreal. Mazes of electrical cords were strewn across the entire periphery of the staging area. Wooden bridge chairs for the patients were set up five feet apart all along the wide expanse of the open mezzanine. A gooseneck lamp with a 50-watt bulb provided the illumination. Each candidate brought his own jackrabbit engine, slow-speed hand-piece, and dental instruments. There were no plumbing facilities. When necessary, the patient would empty into a paper cup. It was a zoo. Yet the hotel engineers must have known what they were doing. There wasn't a single circuit break the entire day.

To give the appearance of anonymity, each applicant was assigned a number to wear on his dental jacket. That same number would be affixed to the lab work you completed and handed in to the monitor at the end of the day. Six very officious-looking board examiners roamed the aisles and approached whenever a candidate raised his hand asking for permission to start a procedure.

Now was the time to assert my Southern credentials. "Suh, I would appreciate you givin' me a startin' check for a Class 2 D-O restoration on the upper left second premolar."

"Where did you go to dental school?" he replied.

"I just graduated from The University of Tennessee, suh."

He looked at me approvingly. "Okay, show me what you can do."

The written exams were very tough, especially the oral pathology section. But I was prepared, and I wasn't under the same pressure as the Florida boys, who desperately needed to pass so they would be able to practice in their hometowns. If they were unsuccessful, they would have to wait another year to have a second chance. After three failures, you were ineligible to reapply.

The exam lasted three full days. Very few applicants went home with a positive view of their outcome. Most were accustomed to taking an exam in a dental school environment and were not prepared to deal with the primitive accommodations.

On the other hand, I was upbeat. My two patients showed up, and I was able to complete all the operative procedures. The written exams were long and challenging, but I finished them with time to spare. It was late afternoon, and I wouldn't be leaving until the following morning.

I can't say that it slipped my mind because I know full well that it didn't. My friend Art Burns came from Jacksonville, and I wondered what had become of him. Shirley had written me from Atlanta in June 1953 that she heard Art and Allen Shaw had been flunked out of dental school after their second year. At the same time, I also heard from friends that they had joined the Army. What happened after that, I had no idea.

I reached for the phone. I wanted to call Art's home and find out where he was and what he was doing. But I demurred. I was afraid it might be hurtful if he learned that I had already graduated dental school. The Emory experience was still messing with my mind and didn't seem to want to let go.

Some 50 years later I discovered that while I was in Jacksonville, Art was in town for the summer break between his first and second years of dental school. And Allen Shaw was in Miami, recently discharged from the Army and preparing to be readmitted to Emory to repeat his sophomore year.

The next morning, I gathered my belongings and headed north out of Jacksonville. I was in Georgia in less than an hour, and two hours later I was in Savannah. Atlanta was my next stop. This time I decided to spend the night with Shirley's parents in Atlanta. They were eager to hear about my post-graduation experiences, and how Shirley was getting along in Chattanooga. I reassured them that she was being taken care of by a young OB/GYN physician, Dr. Sam Binder from Philadelphia.

Sam met and married my cousin Claire Siskin after graduation from medical school, and they had recently settled in Chattanooga after three years in the military. In just a few months, our baby would be his first private practice delivery. Shirley's little sister, Marilyn, now 16 years old, sat spellbound with the realization that she would soon be an aunt. Shirley's older sister, Helen, a PhD candidate, was home for a short visit and promised to return from New York when our baby arrived.

During my brief stopover in Atlanta, I made no effort to see or hear what was going on at the Emory dental school. If I had, I would have been troubled and deeply disturbed to know that the fates of Jewish students Dick Arnold, Bucky Bloom, Stanley Krugman, Shep Masarek, Jerry Summers, Gerald Wernick, Jay Paulen, and Coleman Socoloff were in peril. Or that Larry Fall, David Hoffspiegel, Melvin Mitchell, Phil Nathan, and Sheldon Waldman were already flunked from the dental school. I might have learned that the first whistleblower, Arnold Hoffman, my former AEPi fraternity advisor, had just written to the American Dental Association, calling to their attention his concern that Emory dental school was engaged in antisemitic behavior. I might have become aware of the embattled efforts of ADL's Art Levin and Dr. Marvin Goldstein, who were desperately urging the Atlanta Jewish community leaders to confront Emory authorities about the situation at the dental school. Because of my reluctance to open old wounds, I wouldn't know any of this until 50 years later. It was only then that I came to suspect that I was not alone—that my Emory experience was part of a sinister conspiracy.

I returned to Chattanooga the following morning, prepared to answer all the questions about my recent experience in Florida. I played it down because even if I passed, it would be years before we would seriously consider where to settle. For now, we had to concentrate on getting into the dental corps of one of the armed services. By the end of June, I received letters from Tennessee and Alabama informing me that I had passed their board exams. On August 14, I received my dental license from Florida.

One day in late June, my dentist, Dr. Ewing B. Connell, called me with news that there was an opening in the dental clinic at Baroness Erlanger hospital. One of the oral surgery residents had been suddenly relieved of his duties, and they were in desperate need of someone to treat indigent patients four days a week in the outpatient clinic. The remaining oral surgery resident, Robert Strahley, was delighted to see me, as he was currently the only resident left to treat the in-house trauma patients and the ambulatory surgery patients. I thought back to my first weekend in Memphis working with my friend O.B. Hecklin in the emergency room. It was like receiving a battlefield commission. I was being given a responsibility over my grade, but I welcomed the opportunity. Moreover, I was going to be paid for the on-the-job training. Strahley even offered to let me assist him on Fridays in the operating room. I had never considered specializing in oral surgery, but this would be a taste of things to come.

Family and friends asked if I would be interested in taking care of their dental problems. I told them I was trying to get into the service and couldn't promise them how long I would be around. I could only offer them evening appointments. This suited them fine, as they were happy not to lose time from work. A friend of mine, Dr. Arthur Saloshin, offered to let me use his office at night. Shirley, now in her fourth month, acted as my receptionist, chair-side assistant, and bill collector.

My father went back to his contacts, this time to move along my effort to enlist in the Army or Air Force. By August, Garrison Siskin, my mother's cousin, was confident that he could work through Tennessee Senator Estes Kefauver's office to get my commission.

After leading a much-publicized investigation into organized crime in the early 1950s, Kefauver twice sought his party's nomination for president. In 1956, he was selected by the Democratic National Convention to be the running mate of presidential nominee Adlai Stevenson. He was eager to get as much support as possible and did what he could to help his constituents.

Cousin Garrison called my dad and told him that he wanted me in his office at Siskin Steel that afternoon when he called the senator's office. I was seated across from him as he personally dialed the senator's private line. He turned on the speaker while the senator's secretary summoned her boss to the phone. Despite being in Congress for 17 years, the senator retained his pronounced eastern Tennessee accent. Having appeared on television so often during the past five years, he seemed to project himself right into my cousin's office.

My cousin didn't beat around the bush. "Senator, I have my cousin in my office, and we need to get him into the service right away. He's eager to serve his country. He's a Tennessee native. Grew up here in Chattanooga, and just graduated dental school at UT in Memphis. He's already got his license." He swiveled in his chair and winked at me.

The senator responded quickly but with a slow drawl, "It might take me a few months to get him in the Army." My cousin didn't hesitate, "He wants the Air Force, and he wants to be stationed in Spain. He tells me that we have a big Air Force base in Spain, and that's where he wants to be."

"Look, Gary," he replied, "I'll get him in the Air Force, but that's as far as I can go. He'll have to go wherever they assign him. Send me his resumé so we can move things forward. By the way, we're going to be in Chattanooga in a few weeks. I need you to help me out."

My wife received my orders in the mail one day in early October while I was working in the hospital clinic. She called me with excitement in her voice. "You're to report on November 24th for basic training at Gunter Air Force in Montgomery, Alabama. After that, we're going to be stationed at Dobbins Air Force Base. Can you believe that? Dobbins is in Marietta, just outside Atlanta."

I called Shirley before I left work and told her I would be home in a half-hour. She was outside the house waiting for me with the orders in her hand. "I've already called my mother and told her that we're going to be stationed in Georgia. Momma and Daddy were so excited, and so am I."

She handed me the orders, and I slowly turned the pages. The military jargon made it difficult to decipher the document. "Where does it say Dobbins?" I asked.

She had read the orders several times and knew exactly where to find it. "There," she said, pointing to the exact spot. "D.O.B., Dobbins."

I hesitated, knowing that Shirley's eyes would soon be full of tears. I didn't want it to sound like I was making fun of her. "Sweetie," I said as tenderly as possible, "D.O.B. stands for Date of Birth. See, it's followed by 12-23-32, my birth date."

Shirley wasn't offended. She handled it better than I expected. "Then where will we be going?"

"It says Stony Brook Air Force Station, AMC, Chicopee Falls, Massachusetts. I'll have to check a map to see where it's located."

After searching through an atlas of the United States, I was still left wondering exactly where we were going to be stationed for the next two years. I made inquiries the following day, and the best I could do was find that there was a very large Strategic Air Command (SAC) Headquarters at Westover Air Force Base, also located in Chicopee Falls, Massachusetts.

I called my cousin Garrison Siskin to bring him up to speed, and to thank him for making all this possible. I told him that I was unable to find anyone who knew anything about Stony Brook Air Force Station. Without waiting for me to ask his advice, he told me that he would contact Senator Kefauver's office. "I'll thank him for helping us, and at the same time I'll ask him to get the information we need."

Two days later I received the elusive information, along with instructions. After completing my three weeks of basic training in Montgomery, I was to report to duty in Massachusetts on December 23, 1956. I was to arrive at Westover Air Force Base no later than ten o'clock in the evening. I would show my orders to the guard at the gate and be directed to the base commander's office. After confirming my credentials, they would give me specific instructions on how to proceed on to Stony Brook.

The summer in Chattanooga passed quickly. Shirley bonded with my parents, my sister, and especially my mother's parents. They couldn't believe that my wife could speak Yiddish fluently, and this became their special connection. Shirley's everyday companion and confidant was Evelyn, the maid who had been with my family since I was six weeks old.

Shirley was due with our child on November 13. My "due date" was November 24, the date I was to arrive in Montgomery to begin my basic training. That seemed to be a comfortable margin, but as the day approached, the doctor suggested that the baby might arrive a little later than we expected.

By mutual agreement, I worked my last day at the hospital on Friday, November 16. Shirley felt her initial labor pains at about ten o'clock the morning of Tuesday the 20th. She still reminds me that first Evelyn made lunch for me, and only then did I take Shirley to the hospital. Lori, our beautiful six-pound-six-ounce daughter, was born six hours later. I was fortunate to spend my last three days in Chattanooga celebrating with Shirley the birth of our first child.

Before leaving for Alabama, our DeSoto suddenly broke down and had to be towed to a repair shop. The estimated cost of fixing our used car was not justified when considering that I would soon be driving a thousand miles to Massachusetts. Shirley's dad, who had given us the DeSoto, agreed that we should trade it in for a new car. My dad and I found a relatively new '55 Chevrolet, which would serve us well for the next 10 years.

The four-hour drive to Montgomery in the new car was smooth and uneventful. Before reporting in to Gunter Field, I first visited the PX at nearby Maxwell Field where I purchased winter uniforms and insignia. I then drove across town to Gunter Air Force Base where I would receive my three-week officers' basic training.

I had attended military school in high school and was familiar with starched uniforms and military discipline. I was even able to disassemble and reassemble a rifle, but, as dental officers, we were not issued a weapon. We did receive training on setting up a field hospital with portable dental units. It vividly reminded me of the primitive set-up on the mezzanine of the Seminole Hotel in Jacksonville.

The first letter I received was from my daughter Lori. Of course, it was in Shirley's handwriting. Postmarked November 29, 1956, it was sent to 1st Lt. Stanley P. Brickman AO3074673, 3882 School Group BOC 56P, Box 48, Gunter Air Force Base, Alabama.

Dear Daddy,
I love you and I miss you and I wish you were here. I ask Mommie about you every time I see her, and she gives me your kiss on the nose. I look forward to that kiss every four hours. We have lots of visitors, and Mommie tells me I am the talk of Erlanger hospital. Please hurry home to

us. Here's a kiss from us both. We love you dearly. Lori (Mommie, too)

I completed my three-week tour at Gunter and returned to Chattanooga to pick up Lori and Shirley. We expressed our deep gratitude to my parents before departing the next day for Atlanta. It was time for Shirley's parents and sisters to surround her and Lori with their love and attention. They would be staying in Atlanta until I could secure permanent housing on or near the base in Massachusetts. Following up on last-minute advice, I had my car undercoated to prevent rust and erosion from the harsh New England weather, I bought chains for the tires, and of course a scraper for the car windows.

The following three days passed far too quickly. I left Atlanta on Friday and arrived in Chicopee Falls, Massachusetts, two days later. It was the oldest-looking town I had ever seen. Forty-five minutes later, in uniform, I drove up to Westover Air Force Base and was saluted by the airman at the gate. I presented my orders, and he gave me instructions for the three-mile ride to Stony Brook Air Force Station. The scenery changed after the first mile passed. There were no buildings or vegetation on either side of the flat narrow two-lane road. The last hundred yards, a prominent road sign ordered vehicles to decelerate to 10 miles per hour. It was eight o'clock in the evening when I faced an armed air policeman who emerged from the guardhouse, leaving his companion inside.

I had my credentials bearing my photo in order, but my unmarked vehicle with a Tennessee license plate received a rigid check. One of the guards affixed a temporary pass to the window of my car. Now satisfied, the airman pointed to the BOQ where I was to be lodged for the next two months. Snow began to fall as I entered the miniature base, which was formally designated a station. I parked my car and walked into the one-story building just inside the gate where I was told I would find the OD, Officer of the Day. The captain, one of the skeleton crew on duty during the holidays, gave me the keys to my room. He told me he would see me at the mess hall at breakfast the next morning.

When I awoke, I could see from my dormitory window that my car was almost completely covered with snow. Once outside, I was able to process Stony Brook station with only a few glances. The entire complex measured maybe a hundred yards in width. The administrative complex was comprised of two rows of one- and two-story buildings facing each other across a 30-yard courtyard.

I walked over to the mess hall and celebrated my 24th birthday, sharing breakfast with a few of the unfortunates who had picked the short straws and were not able to go home for the holidays. This would be my working domain for the next two years.

I met Shirley and Lori at the Springfield/Hartford airport on February 4, 1957. Their arrival was delayed almost a month because of the scarcity of on-base housing. The Cold War with the Soviet Union had resulted in the massive deployment of personnel to Westover Air Force Base, and career officers were rightfully given housing priority. I was finally able to find a nice apartment 30 minutes from the base in nearby Springfield, and our young family settled in for two useful and blissful years, a thousand miles away from our families and friends.

Stony Brook Air Force Station was in fact a secret base whose role was to arm the hundreds of B-52s and B-47s flying out of Westover, one of the largest Strategic Air Command bases in the world. I was the lone dentist, and my colleague Dr. Steven Bauer was the only physician. I was also the designated morgue officer, trained to identify and classify victims of a potential attack by the Soviets. I had learned a few months before in Alabama that I had been thoroughly vetted and given top-secret clearance before receiving my assignment.

Fortunately, our country's massive buildup of nuclear weapons and willingness to go to the brink caused the Soviets to back down, and war was averted. I was able to devote most of my attention to providing dental treatment to my small but special community. Shirley thrived in her long-desired role as loving wife and mother. She also met many new neighbors and service wives, some of whom would become lifelong friends.

I received citations for exemplary work and my captain's bars after my first year of duty. Near the end of my second year, I respectfully declined offers to become a career officer.

Shirley supported my decision to specialize in oral surgery, which would require four additional moves and another three years of hospital-based training. We departed the Air Force in November 1958 with a new family member, Lori's five-month-old little sister, Teresa, who already had her own personality.

CHAPTER 9

A Happy Wife Is a Happy Life

I spent my final year of residency in New Orleans at the renowned Ochsner Clinic. I was flattered when Dr. James Quinn, head of the oral surgery department, urged me to remain as a junior member of the staff. But I knew that Shirley yearned to go home to Atlanta. She knew that to practice in Georgia, I would have to take the same Georgia Board exams that I had steadfastly avoided five years before. She also knew that the exam tested applicants on their knowledge of general dentistry, not oral surgery. For sure, I would be at a disadvantage.

I had not practiced general dentistry for three years. I had not waxed up dentures or cast a gold crown in five years. Nevertheless, I had to demonstrate to Shirley my willingness to make the effort to pass the Georgia State Board exam, which was being given at the dreaded Emory dental school May 29-31, 1961.

There was a glimmer of hope. My AEPi fraternity friend Dr. Bob Triff, now practicing dentistry in Atlanta, surprised me with a phone call on April 13. Without even identifying himself, he said, "The king is dead," followed by the news that Dean Buhler had resigned the previous day. Bob told me the *Atlanta Constitution* reported that the dean would leave Emory at the end of the current school year. It sounded like good news to me. I then told Bob that I had decided to take the Georgia Board exams, and he offered to find a patient for me at the Ben Massell Dental Clinic, a clinic for needy individuals sponsored by the Atlanta Jewish Family Services.

Shirley and our little girls would need our car in New Orleans, so I took the train to Chattanooga to see my parents, and then boarded a bus to Atlanta. Bob had already found two board patients for me, and I met them at the Ben Massell Dental Clinic just to be sure they would show up for the exam on Monday the 29th. I also made several stops around town, hoping to get a feel for the need for another oral surgeon. I didn't even have a license yet, so I had to be cautious about whom I approached. I got conflicting views, but nothing totally negative.

I wrote Shirley from Atlanta on May 29, 1961, the night before the exams. "A hundred and twenty-one people are taking the exams, seventy from Emory. So you can see that quite a few outsiders are here." After a few comments about the beautiful weather in Atlanta, I added, "One thing I have heard—Buhler is really out, and the local Jewish dentists are angry with a Jewish faculty member who, I am told, sided with Dean Buhler against the Jewish dental students. They are calling him a 'quisling,' a collaborator against his own people."

I returned to New Orleans after the exam, and only then did I tell Shirley how spooked I was when I walked into the dental school the first day of the exam. "Once inside the front door of the school, I felt a strong urge to take the steps down to view the basement lab where I had spent most of my freshman year, but I just couldn't do it. Too many bad memories. When I asked someone where the exams were being given, I was told to take the elevator to the clinic on the third floor. I was ten years late, but I had finally made it to the Emory dental school clinic."

I told Shirley that I fully expected to be recognized by some of my former Emory faculty instructors. A glance around the room convinced me that the state board examiners were a totally different crowd, and I breathed a sigh of relief. My self-esteem was at risk, so I urged myself to do the very best I could. Still, I wasn't wild about practicing in Atlanta, and my Florida license was burning a hole in my pocket. If I passed, fine. If not, I had other attractive options.

The examiners made the results of the Georgia Board available to the public two weeks later, and I could now boast four licenses. I was a

28-year-old oral surgeon with a wife, two children, and one on the way. It was time to get serious.

We left New Orleans in mid-June. Shirley was six months pregnant, and still comfortable enough to take a leisurely automobile trip through Florida to evaluate prospective practice sites. Her sister Marilyn flew down from Atlanta and happily agreed to share a back seat with her two nieces.

We moved eastward along the highway leading out of New Orleans, through the coastal cities of Mississippi and on to Mobile, Alabama, where we enjoyed lunch with my uncle and aunt, Lewis and Ida Brickman. When we reached Pensacola, Florida, one hour later, Shirley began her self-imposed assignment to grade each city on its relative merits. The first ballot was announced. In her opinion, Pensacola was out of the question. Simply too far from Atlanta.

We motored on to Panama City, where we decided to eat supper. After a ride around the city and a review of the business section of the local phone book, another decision was made. Too touristy, and only one small synagogue. We checked into a motel and, after a fitful sleep, resumed our adventure the following morning.

We decided not to consider any inland cities, so we hugged the coast and arrived in Tampa six hours later. The Tampa/St. Petersburg area appeared to be a viable choice. I checked us into a busy motel and suggested that the four ladies enjoy an afternoon swim in the motel pool. I set out to see three oral surgeons my former chief, Dr. Quinn, had recommended to me. They were very cordial but showed no interest in taking on a young associate. By the time I returned to the motel, another decision had been taken. Too industrial—not what they had in mind.

It was only an hour's drive to the Bradenton/Sarasota area, which was beautiful. We stopped at a service station to gas up and use the restrooms. When the ladies came back to the car, they were visibly agitated. There were huge roaches all over the place. The attendant told them they would get used to them. The vote was unanimous—NO.

Ft. Myers was our next stop, where people were reportedly flocking into the area, and where I knew there wasn't an oral surgeon. It was a short two-hour drive. Connie Mack, whose father was the legendary owner of the major league Philadelphia Athletics, had built a huge development for retirees at nearby Cape Coral. Trailer parks dotted the area. Small fishing boats were docked in tiny slips as far as the eye could see. "Get us out of here!" they screamed in unison.

I called ahead to my friend Ed Zwig, a fraternity brother who graduated dental school in 1956 and was practicing in Coral Gables, a suburb of Miami, only two and a half hours from our current location. Ed offered to make reservations for us at a motel and invited us to come over to his office when we arrived. Ed was familiar with my story but had not seen Shirley and me since 1953, just before I was accepted to UT dental school.

Ed came to Emory in 1950 and joined AEPi fraternity. Ed and fraternity brother Bucky Bloom, who came to Emory in 1951, later became brothers-in-law when they married identical twin sisters Jane and Joan Margolies.

Bucky was one year behind Ed at Emory dental school. It was a terrible shock to everyone when Bucky flunked out of Emory in 1955 after his second year. Ed escaped the hatchet and was one of the few Jewish boys who graduated Emory dental school in four years.

Ed proudly told me that Bucky rebounded and graduated from the University of Miami medical school in 1960. He said that Bucky was currently doing a rotating internship at Cook County Hospital in Chicago and had been offered a residency in general surgery. Ed seemed uneasy talking about any of the other boys who had been in the dental school, so I didn't push the issue.

Ed did not encourage me to practice in Miami. "I'm leaving. I'm saving money to take a periodontal residency in New York. I plan to sell this practice as soon as possible." That's all Shirley needed to hear. We left Miami the next morning and took the causeway to Miami Beach.

We checked out Miami Beach from one end to the other. The corned beef and pastrami were fabulous, but the location just didn't seem right for us. We proceeded to Ft. Lauderdale, West Palm Beach, and Daytona Beach. The decision? Too hot, too many mosquitoes, too congested.

I checked the map. Tallahassee, the state capital, was four hours to the northwest, situated just 15 miles south of the Georgia state line. It wasn't on our itinerary, but my research notes reminded me that it offered several attractive advantages. Besides being the capital of the state, it had two large universities and, best of all, did not have an oral surgeon. We reached the city limits shortly after noon. All my occupants were tired, thirsty, hot, and fidgety. But it was my last chance.

I stopped at a service station and received directions to the main hospital. I called the administrator's office and told his secretary the nature of my call. "An oral surgeon? We really need one," she said, confirming my findings. "My boss will be returning in a few minutes from his regular Rotary meeting. Come on over and meet him."

I invited my four passengers to come with me into the hospital, but they insisted on staying in the car. I sensed that they had already made up their minds and didn't want to be confused by the facts. I rolled down the window on the driver's side, knowing full well that it wouldn't offer them very much relief. I knew I was pushing the limits of their patience, but I had a hunch I would get a favorable reception.

I returned to the car 15 minutes later with a big smile on my face. I leaned over and spoke to Shirley through the open car window. "Honey, they really want me. They have to send all their facial trauma patients all the way to Thomasville, Georgia. I think this is a great opportunity."

Shirley looked up at me with a half-smile and softly but firmly replied, "I agree. It does sound like a great opportunity. And if you don't mind commuting to Atlanta on week-ends to see me and the kids, this is the place for you to be."

I didn't bother to go back into the hospital to thank the administrator for his offer. I opened the car door, inserted the keys into the ignition, and headed north to Atlanta.

Planting the Seeds of History

I was raised to understand that two countervailing factors control your life experiences. I continue to believe, more than ever, in divine intervention, in Hebrew, *hashgacha pratit*. And equally do I affirm the concept of *hishtadlut*, the Hebrew term for using one's free will to exert one's best effort.

The story that will unfold in the pages to come never would have surfaced if we hadn't come back to Atlanta. Part of that was ordained, *hashgacha pratit*, and part derived from a combination of love, faith, strength, resiliency, and determination—*hishtadlut*.

So, on the twin wings of destiny and hard work, we finally ended up in Atlanta in the late summer of 1961. We arrived later in the evening than we had planned. We stopped at the all-night pharmacy on Ponce de Leon Avenue to make a phone call to Shirley's parents, who were still awake and expecting our call. Ten minutes later, five tired vagabonds crawled out of our car and climbed the steps of the Berkowitz home in northeast Atlanta.

Lori was almost five, and Teresa had just turned three, and Shirley's parents embraced them. They had already prepared our beds and quickly bid us goodnight, as they had to get up early in the morning to go to work at their grocery store in southwest Atlanta, eight miles away. Mother's parting words were, "You'll stay here to have the baby. In a few weeks when you get your strength back, you can look for a place to live. You're welcome to stay as long as you like." We would live at 1350 Pasadena Avenue for the next 12 months.

Jeffrey was born at 1 p.m. on September 15 at the Georgia Baptist hospital. Dr. Abe Velkoff (who died recently at the age of 102) opened the door of the reception room and announced the arrival of our new son. We named him after my dad's father, Joseph Herschel Brickman.

Atlanta was still a relatively small city in 1961. The official population was 487,455. The metro population was 1,312,474. The first MARTA station wouldn't open until June 30, 1979. There were nine oral surgeons in the seven-county Atlanta area, including those in full-time teaching. There were fewer than 20 in the entire state, including the military.

Actually, there were only four oral surgery offices in the Atlanta area, as several of the men had associates. It didn't take much time or effort for me to set up appointments with all of them. Having a family of almost five and without a dollar in my pocket, I hoped I would find someone who wanted and needed an associate. They were all as cordial as possible but offers were not forthcoming. In less than two days, out of necessity, I would find a different kind of partner—the C&S Bank.

C&S originated in Savannah but had multiple offices in the Atlanta area. I visited the nearby branch at the corner of Clairmont and North Decatur Roads and met the chief financial officer, Merriell Autrey, to explain the nature of my visit. He knew practically every dentist and physician in DeKalb County and was involved in the building of the 200-bed DeKalb General Hospital, which had opened its doors only three months before.

There were practically no banking restrictions at the time. Bank officers could use their discretion, and helping a dentist to open a new office was good business. Mr. Autrey assured me that he would be pleased to help me with my banking needs.

The only problem was that there were no medical offices available in DeKalb County or in nearby Decatur, the county seat of DeKalb County and the working address of many of the prominent dentists and physicians of the area. Decatur Federal Savings and Loan was building an eight-story state-of-the-art building two blocks from Decatur Square, but it wouldn't be ready for occupancy until February 1962. Mr. Autrey advised me to use the intervening time to go out and meet all the medical and dental community and tell them that come February they wouldn't have to refer their patients all the way to downtown Atlanta anymore. He knew I was impatient to get started, but he told me the extra time would give me the advantage of designing efficient office plans and hiring the proper personnel. Six months would fly by, he said.

I was amazed at the positive reception I was accorded. No one even bothered to ask me where I was from, where I had gone to dental school, or where I had trained. They all told me the same story. When they found it necessary to refer a patient to an oral surgeon, their patient would have to travel to downtown Atlanta for treatment and often be required to make several post-operative visits. One dentist jokingly offered to sell me his set of extraction forceps. "I hate doing surgery," he said.

I quickly noticed from the diplomas hanging on their office walls that most of the dentists were Emory graduates. I wondered if and when my past situation would come up, but I knew that I would have to get that out of my mind. If I were given an opportunity to prove myself, I hoped that would become a non-issue. I soon noticed that at least a half-dozen Decatur dentists had been in my original freshman class at Emory dental school 10 years before. There were also three former instructors practicing in the area. I decided not to bring up the past, and it never surfaced as an issue.

Seneca, a first-century Roman philosopher, allegedly said, "Luck is what happens when preparation meets opportunity." Action is the vital part missing from this quote. Without action, luck can evaporate. Your ship can leave the port, leaving you at the dock. I signed the loan documents and committed to a five-year lease of office space, Suite 715 in the new Decatur Federal Bank building in downtown Decatur.

Mr. Autrey was right. The time passed quickly. I opened my office on February 6, 1962. The telephone number, 378-2331, soon needed an extension. That first day, Dr. Bill Avery called and asked if he could refer an emergency patient. When the patient arrived at my seventh-floor office, she was noticeably disturbed. She said it was the first time she had ever been on an elevator. She paid seven dollars for the extraction of her decayed upper left first molar.

I had the great fortune to have wonderful professional neighbors in the Decatur Federal Building. Drs. Herschel Hatcher and Charlie Davis occupied the adjacent suite of offices. They were active in the Northern District Dental Society and the Hinman Dental Society and sponsored me for membership. Dr. Robert Fine, a dermatologist, also in my building, sponsored me for membership in the DeKalb Medical Society, and I became its first and only dental member. Dr. Richard Smoot, chief of surgery at DeKalb General Hospital, who also had offices on the seventh floor of our building, sponsored me for membership on the staff at DeKalb General Hospital and supervised my first surgical procedure. He was supposed to monitor me for a year, but after my first surgery he told me that henceforth I would be on my own. "I'm a general surgeon," he said. "I don't know anything about oral surgery. Just don't mess up."

I entered my specialty of oral and maxillofacial surgery at the very time that innovations in general anesthesia and advanced surgical procedures were being introduced. Under the auspices of the American Society of Oral and Maxillofacial Surgeons, I was the youngest of a small contingent chosen to travel to Zurich, Switzerland in 1964 to learn orthognathic surgical procedures with the world-renowned Professor Hugo Obwegeser. The experience gained allowed me to return home with the knowledge and skill to perform advanced maxillofacial procedures. However, there were negative aspects of that trip to Europe that strongly influenced my thinking. How they impacted my future will be revealed in a subsequent chapter.

I had the great fortune of coming to the Atlanta area at a time of business and professional prosperity, well before the intrusion of the government into medicine. I enjoyed the additional benefit of Shirley managing the business side of the practice. She was there at the opening of the office, and with only a three-year break in the mid-1960s, she continued as office manager until 2002.

I recognized the importance of becoming an active member of my professional societies and was a willing participant in their scientific and educational programs. I was a regular volunteer at the Ben Massell Dental Clinic and received a citation for 50 years of service in 2012.

I joined the Atlanta Alpha Omega Alumni chapter as soon as I returned to town. I served as president of the chapter in 1963-64 and 1971-72. In 1972, as AO president, along with Dr. Marvin Goldstein, past international president of Alpha Omega, I presented the Alpha Omega National Achievement Award to Dr. George Moulton, who followed Dr. John Buhler as dean of Emory dental school. In Dean Moulton's declining years, I was honored when his wife, Dr. Pat Moulton, asked me to treat the Dean's dental problems.

Not until I began my Emory dental school research, did I uncover unknown details of Alpha Omega's role in the denouement of Dean Buhler and the eventual exposure of the antisemitism at the dental school. There were hints along the way, but the crucial role frater Dr. Marvin Goldstein played cannot be exaggerated. That is why I take special pride in having received, along with Dr. Alan Lease, the Marvin C. Goldstein Medal of Achievement from the Atlanta Chapter of Alpha Omega International Dental Fraternity, awarded in 2002. In 2012, I received the Presidential Award from the Alpha Omega International Dental Fraternity.

While in dental school at UT, I became a student member of the American Dental Association, and 73 years later I maintain my membership in the ADA and attend local, state, and national meetings. In 1965, I joined the Southeastern Society of Oral Surgeons and the American Society of Oral and Maxillofacial Surgeons (ASOMS) and have been an active member in both groups. When the ASOMS held its annual meeting in Atlanta in 1973, Shirley and I were chosen as chairmen of local arrangements.

In 1965, just three years after setting up practice, I was one of the three founders of the Georgia Society of Oral Surgeons. Soon afterwards, Dr. James Harpole, chairman of the Department of Oral Surgery at Emory dental school, asked me to join his staff as a clinical instructor. Insignificant as that may sound, it might qualify as the champion turnaround of all time. Kicked out as a student in 1952. Appointed to faculty in 1967.

Our three children became very attached to Shirley's parents. We all knew that we would have to move eventually, but we never thought that we would stay at 1350 Pasadena for an entire year. With the help of our realtor, Janis Fields, we found a one-owner three-bedroom house in the Merry Hills subdivision off LaVista Road, less than 10 minutes away from our temporary location. We are blessed. Sixty-three years of marriage, three children, six grandchildren, and 55 years in the same home.

Shirley worked part-time in my office from the very beginning. When Jeffrey reached school age, Shirley was able to work additional hours. She had experience, and it relieved me of my administrative duties and allowed me to concentrate exclusively on surgery. She took pride in seeing Dr. Ed Green, Dr. Charles Rosenberg, and Dr. Harvey Silverman become partners. She remained a vital part of our office staff for 40 years.

When we first returned to Atlanta, Shirley joined Hadassah and the Synagogue Sisterhood and became an active member. She also joined the auxiliary of the dental society. When we moved to Reindeer Drive, she participated in neighborhood activities. She became an active participant in the Atlanta Jewish Welfare Federation and remains an active member today.

She enjoyed working in the PTA and library at Kittredge Elementary School. When the kids reached high school age, Shirley merely transferred her attention and PTA support to Briarcliff High School, conveniently situated next door to Kittredge.

Although my practice and my family required much of my time, I found the time to become active in the community. We lived less than 10 minutes from the Emory campus, and I decided to drop by the AEPi fraternity house early one evening. I was invited to become their advisor, and I continued in that role on a regular basis for the next 20 years. Many of "my boys" became active members in their communities, and we remain in touch. That was therapy for me.

I look back on that first return to the Emory campus as a beginning point in my emotional readjustment. When asked where I had attended school, I learned to casually respond that I had gone to college at Emory and dental school at Tennessee. That served as a Band-Aid, but the underlying wound was still there. I remembered being told by Emory that I was a failure back in 1952. But I had later seen that I was not the only one. My three classmates suffered the same fate. By 1953, all four of us would be gone. And I had later learned that Bucky Bloom had been cut loose. I had also heard about Phil Nathan, but I didn't know the details. It was a nagging pain, not enough to paralyze me and not enough to cause me to lose sleep. But it was always there.

The fraternity connection led to my becoming the official liaison between the Atlanta Jewish Federation and Hillel, the Jewish campus organization. I was a frequent visitor to the campus and the "go to" person when joint events were planned. When Elie Wiesel and other dignitaries visited the campus in 1972, Shirley and I were there to welcome the Atlanta Jewish community to the university.

In 1974, Emory established its first chair of Judaic Studies and installed Dr. David Blumenthal as the first holder of the chair. Shirley and I were invited by the Jewish Federation, as members of the Jewish community who had made a financial commitment to the chair, to participate in the celebration. Some probably thought I was attending as a proud and loyal Emory alumnus, but in fact, as far as Emory was concerned, I was a friend with an unknown background. That suited them fine, and it was a situation I was likewise comfortable with.

As Chairman of the Board of Decatur Professional Investors, I led a group seeking to bring another hospital to DeKalb County. In 1973, I cut the ribbon at the opening of Decatur Hospital, a 120-bed hospital in downtown Decatur.

I was inducted into the American College of Dentists in 1977 and named Honorable Fellow of the Georgia Dental Association the same year. I was chairman of the United Way Dental Division in 1969 and 1988.

B'nai B'rith jointly honored Shirley and me in 1989 with the Community Service Award. We were co-honored by the State of Israel Bonds in 1993 and were honored by Yeshiva High School of Atlanta in 1995. In addition, I received the DeKalb Medical Society Julius McCurdy Award in 1992. This award was established in 1977 to recognize outstanding community service by a DeKalb County physician. This was the only time the award was bestowed on a dentist.

I was appointed by Governor Zell Miller to the Georgia Board of Dental Examiners and served a seven-year term from 1994-2001. This blue-panel board of 10 sits judgment on dentists and hygienists who have been charged with violations of the state dental practice act. We met monthly for the seven years I served. I never failed, at the beginning of each of those meetings, to reflect on a decision I made before applying to take the Georgia State Board exam in 1961. In submitting my transcript to the Board as part of my application, I omitted the nine months I spent at the Emory dental school. I always had a transient moment of deep concern that, after 30-plus years of dental practice, I might be called before this very Board and charged with fraud and deception. I hope it won't be held against me one day in the heavenly tribunal.

My principal efforts outside my practice focused on Federation activities and programs. Shirley and I traveled to Eastern Europe in 1983 and 1987 to bring comfort to Jews trapped behind the Iron Curtain. We made 25 trips to Israel, the first of which was in 1967 just after the Six-Day War and the liberation of Jerusalem.

In 1990, I was elected president of the Atlanta Jewish Federation for a two-year term. At the 1992 meeting of the General Assembly of Jewish Federations of North America, in my capacity as chairman of the Atlanta delegation, I congratulated Professor Deborah Lipstadt on her recent appointment to Emory University's faculty and invited her to be a member of the Atlanta Jewish community. In January 1993, Professor Lipstadt moved to Atlanta as associate professor of religion at Emory. Deborah's first Shabbat meal in Atlanta was in our home.

Lipstadt's signature book, *Denying the Holocaust*, appeared in June 1993 and garnered simultaneous front-page favorable reviews in the Sunday *New York Times* and *Washington Post*. That fall Emory promoted Lipstadt to Dorot Professor of Modern Jewish and Holocaust Studies.

During all this time, Shirley and I never had even a private discussion about the Emory phase of our lives. Our three children knew that their parents had met on the ball field at Emory during my undergraduate days. But they had no reason to suspect there was a dark side to my Emory experience. After our son Jeff graduated in 1986 from the University of Florida law school, we openly encouraged him to enroll in Emory University School of Law in 1988 to earn his Master of Litigation degree.

My parents and my in-laws, following my graduation from Tennessee, never uttered a word about my days at Emory. My three oral surgery partners, one of whom graduated Emory in the 1960s after the Buhler years, never knew that I had attended Emory. At an AEPi reunion, where several of us met for the first time since our Emory days, there was absolutely no mention of our common experience at the Emory dental school. My wife, with amazing insight and sensitivity, labeled us a "Fraternity of Silence." No one ever suspected our deep underlying resentment.

CHAPTER 10

The Real World

Having three willing partners allowed me time outside the office. I met Dr. Sid Winter, who was the chief of dental services at the United States Federal Penitentiary in Atlanta. He oversaw a large operation and needed an oral surgery consultant. After being cleared for the position, I served 20 years as oral surgery consultant at the penitentiary. I became aware of certain inmates who were in the witness protection program. When indicated, I performed orthognathic surgery on those who had distinguishing facial irregularities. Following recovery, these patients were transferred to an undisclosed location where they would embark on a new life.

The penitentiary operating room was part of the hospital infirmary, supervised by a full-time US Public Health physician. It was located on the fourth floor of the prison, and its doors were situated just across the hall from the nursing station. On the opposite side of the room, large curtain-less windows overlooked Boulevard Avenue and the visitors' parking lot, which was located outside the prison walls. This was where I always parked my blue 1973 Buick Riviera.

The anesthetists, like me, were not prison employees, but instead were outside professionals who attended when needed. The operating room nurses, on the other hand, were prisoners. There were usually two nurse/inmates in the operating room for major procedures. It was established protocol that the inmates didn't fraternize with the civilian consultants. Just enough conversation to get the job done.

I was surprised one day to see that we had been assigned three nurses. The two familiar nurses were setting up the room in preparation for the arrival of my patient. The new inmate was gazing out the windows. The view from those windows was the closest connection a prisoner could have with the outside world. With his back to all of us, he spoke in a slow, deep, monotone voice. His anger was obviously directed to my car and by extension to me, and everyone heard his menacing message: "I hate Buick Rivieras." He had his desired audience.

I should have allowed the regular nurses to handle the situation, but I automatically responded, "Why do you hate Buick Rivieras?" Still facing the windows, he continued, "Me and my buddy robbed a bank in east Arkansas and made a clean getaway. We weren't two blocks from the bank when the drive shaft of his Riviera fell out, leaving us dead in the water. I hate those damn Buick Rivieras."

One of the nurses slipped out quietly and summoned the guards. We never saw that prisoner again.

With Love, from Israel

While appreciative of the surgical skills I acquired at the 1964 maxillofacial mini-residency in Switzerland, the trip was marred by an open hostility to the United States and Israel our group encountered in casual after-work conversations with the locals. It was clear to me that the "neutral" Swiss, who sat out WWII, considered Americans and Israelis aggressors, and continued to harbor anti-American and anti-Jewish resentment. Stung by that anti-American and anti-Jewish attitude, I resolved, when I returned home, to become more involved in Atlanta Jewish Federation programs, particularly as they related to US/Israel activities.

The Six-Day War began between Israel and her Arab neighbors Egypt, Jordan, and Syria on June 5, 1967, and ended on June 10. During that brief time, Jewish communities around the world followed the news from moment to moment. Israel emerged victorious, having thoroughly vanquished her enemies. All of a sudden, the world loved Israel.

A month later, I received a call from Birmingham from my dental school classmate Stanley Rubenstein. Did I want to go to Israel? One of the Birmingham community leaders was part of a national mission planning to leave in two weeks. There were two remaining openings, and Stanley's friend was chosen to fill the spots. My passport was still valid, and with Shirley's blessings, I packed my bag.

The Birmingham group made a short stop in Atlanta, and I met my mission companions. We landed at Kennedy International Airport a few hours later. Following our written instructions, we proceeded to the terminal where we joined the national mission group preparing to depart to Medinat Yisrael, the biblically prophesied State of Israel.

I wasn't prepared for the scene behind the double doors of the meeting room. The room was packed with oversized men, many years my senior, who were smoking Coronas and kibitzing while awaiting their departure. The smoke was overwhelming. No one seemed to notice us enter the room.

The noise suddenly abated as a well-dressed middle-aged man moved to the podium. Herbert Friedman was an American Reform rabbi and US Army chaplain who during the American occupation of Germany served as the chief military aide to the advisor on Jewish affairs to the commander of US forces. He also played a key role in supporting the efforts of the Bricha organization to move thousands of Jewish survivors from Eastern Europe into the American zones of occupation to facilitate their immigration to Palestine.

It was the best speech I had ever heard up to that point. A brief review of the recent war served as a backdrop for the rabbi's charge to the group. "You are the first to embark on the 'Prime Minister's Mission.' You will be the first American Jewish group to officially visit the liberated Western Wall of Jerusalem. You will see the Jewish flag waving over Sharm El Sheikh at the southern tip of the Sinai Peninsula. You will stand on the Golan Heights where our brave men defeated the Syrians and sent them fleeing back across their southern border. When you return, it will fall on you to energize your communities, and raise record sums of money on behalf of Israel." His message was so powerful I believed our plane would be able to take off without any fuel. We were still excited when we landed in Israel the following day.

We were quickly waved through customs at the austere Lod airport outside Tel Aviv and led to waiting buses. During the ride, we remained glued to the windows of the bus, mesmerized by the local scenery. For miles and miles, the narrow highway to Jerusalem was bordered on both sides by the broken frames of tanks and relics from the recent war.

We pulled up to the historic King David Hotel in Jerusalem an hour and a half later. We were told to check into our assigned rooms where our baggage had already been placed, freshen up, and return quickly to the lobby. We would be addressed by a member of the Israeli government. We were about to hear an even better speech than the one we had heard less than a day before. Our speaker was Abba Eban, the distinguished Israeli foreign minister who was fluent in 10 languages. In his Oxford English, he held us spellbound. An hour later we were driven to a nearby Air Force base and transported south by military aircraft to the Gulf of Eilat. While being briefed by a top Navy officer, we heard gunfire in the distance. The officer told us there were still some minor skirmishes taking place.

My friend Stanley and I soon learned that we were about to spend a week in Israel in the company of the elite of American Jewish leaders. We were the lucky ones, as we took the two remaining slots. They told us not to be intimidated when they announced their gifts at the conclusion of the mission. We were advised to keep our eyes and ears open and let it serve as a lesson for the future. I would visit Israel 24 more times during the course of my life, but never again at that level. It was an unforgettable teaching moment.

That experience increased my interest in all Jewish communal activities. Shirley and I became more active in B'nai B'rith, ORT, JNF, Israel Bonds, the Jewish Community Center, the Atlanta Jewish Federation, and later the Georgia/Israel Law Enforcement Exchange.

I became more involved in our synagogue and gradually returned to biblical study, which I enjoyed so much as a youngster in Hebrew school.

In 1983, Shirley and I were part of a Federation group that visited Communist Poland to reach out to survivors of the Holocaust and visit the former death camps of Auschwitz and Treblinka. We were fortunate to take a side trip to the small town of Lask where Shirley's father was born and raised, and from which he escaped in 1919 to come to America. Shirley's mother was also born in Poland. After the death of her mother, she was raised by a great aunt and uncle in Zamocz. She then emigrated from Poland to New York in 1921, sponsored by another relative.

In 1987, Shirley and I were part of a group of five who were selected by the Federation to travel to the Soviet Union for two weeks to bring aid and comfort to refuseniks, Soviet Jews who had been dismissed from their jobs because they wished to emigrate to Israel or the United States. Our children were proud of our efforts and were fortunate to have grandparents to take care of them in our absence.

I gradually moved into the leadership ranks at the Federation and served as president from 1990-1992. I was still actively practicing oral surgery, but my younger partners graciously relieved me of my nighttime call rotation. During all this time, we were blessed to see our three children graduate college and begin to raise families of their own.

I celebrated my 70th birthday in December 2002, at the end of my 40th year of practice. I was spending an increasing amount of time volunteering in community activities and gradually reduced my time working in my office and in the hospital.

Long Time Coming

I voluntarily retired in the spring of 2005 after 43 years of private practice. I always considered every accomplishment I achieved, every reward I received, and every blessing I was granted a "mulligan." It's a golf term denoting a second chance to perform an action, usually after the first chance went wrong through bad luck or a blunder.

I was ready to close the books on a long chapter in my life and enjoy the dividends I had accrued—namely my trophy wife, my three outstanding children, my six wonderful grandchildren, and a host of family and friends.

I continued to treat needy patients at the Ben Massell Dental Clinic, which provided my State Board patients in 1961. The extra time with Shirley and the family was long overdue. I also had more time to work on behalf of Yeshiva Atlanta High School where two of my grandchildren were attending.

But life would prove to be unpredictable, and my experience at Emory would not leave me. There were questions to be answered, and whether intentional or not, I would be the one answering them.

And So, It Begins

It wasn't long after I retired that life presented me the opportunity to launch a new career— investigative journalism. It was only about a year after I left my practice that Shirley and I attended the exhibit at Emory. The stark simplicity of the section on antisemitism at the dental school was seared in my memory. There were three panels, and two of them were directly related: Dean Buhler's resignation (he could have remained if he wished to), and Emory President S. Walter Martin's insistence that there was no antisemitism at Emory. I had some vague memory of hearing about that when I returned to Atlanta in 1961. Those two items were certainly important and deserved my further attention.

But I decided to concentrate on the third panel, the one about which I had no previous knowledge. The panel included a bar graph showing that 65% of the Emory Jewish dental students were flunked out or made to repeat one or more years between 1948 and 1958, Dr. Buhler's tenure as dean. A footnote credited the ADL's book *Some of My Best Friends* for having provided the information illustrated on the panel.

I was eager to read *Some of My Best Friends*. I asked around but was unable to find a copy of the book in Atlanta, not even in the ADL Atlanta office. Fortunately, Amazon had a used copy. Farrar, Straus and Cudahy originally published it in March 1962. The original price was $4.50, and I acquired my initial copy for about the same amount plus shipping. I decided to purchase additional copies as they became available.

The book was co-edited by Benjamin R. Epstein, national director of the Anti-Defamation League of B'nai B'rith from 1947 to 1978, and Arnold Forster, general counsel of the ADL from 1946 until 2003. Their 274-page book told the story of how, during the 20th century, discrimination operated in the fields of education, employment, housing, and many aspects of American life. Even today, its 16 chapters and copious footnotes offer a useful historical guide to the problems Jews faced in the first half of 20th-century America.

Chapter 11 was titled "The Graduate School" and featured the Emory dental school in Atlanta as the prime example of antisemitism in professional schools in the United States. The book was dedicated to "the men and women of the Anti-Defamation League of B'nai B'rith whose united effort made this book possible." I called the national ADL office, and they claimed to have no papers or records relating to the anonymous field workers who provided the critical documents. They also had no files on their former executives who authored the book.

I turned to the local ADL office, seeking information on its staff during its early days. The Atlanta ADL had recently moved to its new Peachtree Road address. The receptionist referred me to one of the young associates who was, not surprisingly, totally unfamiliar with the dental school story. She made a quick search but was not able to come up with a dental school file. She promised to undertake a more thorough search and eventually call me back. She called me the following day to share the unfortunate news that practically all their old files had been lost in the recent move to the new office.

The information and statistics presented in Chapter 11 of the ADL book were shocking. The drama leading to the ultimate resignation of the dean was compelling and left little doubt that the decade of rumors about the dental school was based on factual evidence. Dr. S. Walter

Martin, the Emory president, and Boisfeuillet Jones, the vice president for medical services, were clearly portrayed as unfeeling officials who denied the accusations in spite of the overwhelming facts. There was no criticism of Emory University medical school or Emory undergraduate school. Likewise, they didn't target the dental school faculty.

Chapter 11 continued, "Two weeks after the dean's resignation, President Martin sent a letter to a leading member of the committee: 'You brought to our attention a matter that involved principles which are important to all of us. I am sure that our discussions have served to remind all of us that, despite our constant vigilance, there is always the possibility that someone may err, even without conscious or deliberate intent." It continued, "We hope from it that we may have achieved some closer relationship and understanding with the Jewish community."

The authors concluded, "Here the matter rests. But all concerned—students, faculty, administration, community—are convinced that the long period of foul air at Emory University Dental School caused by religious discrimination has been finally cleared—for good."

After reading the chapter numerous times, I thought I understood why the authors chose the Emory dental school story, out of all others, as their example. It was an epic struggle in which the antisemites were identified by the ADL, and good overcame evil. The ADL, virtually alone, was able to do all the heavy lifting and then exited the scene, allowing the adversaries to bury the hatchet. Seemingly a win-win public relations success story. While it made for an impressive overall read, I was left unsatisfied. There were too many unanswered questions. Peace without retribution. Damage without repair.

The dean had come and gone, leaving behind a trail of tears and broken lives. His dismissal seemed to me a hollow victory. The anonymity of the scarred Jewish students blunted the impact of the outcome. The authors cited devastating percentages but offered no vital details. A half-century had already passed, and the facts remained buried in the sand. I felt a deep responsibility to identify my fellow dental students.

I found that very few people in the community were aware of the story. Two of my close friends (who had barely survived the dental school bloodbath) were still practicing in Atlanta. The wife of one forbade him to discuss it. The wife of the second was unaware of that part of his life, and he also refused to help me. A few native Atlantans remembered the controversy but were unwilling to cooperate or even talk with me.

As I mentioned in Chapter 1, I began making regular visits to the Emory campus after viewing the September 2006 exhibit. The parking deck was just a few blocks from the Woodruff Library. As I walked past the Goizueta Business School and turned the corner on Asbury Circle, I encountered the large bronze statue of Mr. Woodruff standing on a marble pedestal, hat in hand, welcoming students and visitors to the second-floor entrance of his namesake library. A double set of doors led to the security desk. Students with ID cards were being electronically ushered through the checkpoint. A separate entrance accommodated visitors.

The visitors' checklist required several answers. I identified as an Emory alumnus C'53, and stated that I wished to go to MARBL, the Manuscript, Archives, and Rare Book Library. I didn't yet have a topic for my research, so I left that category unanswered. Unsatisfied, the student/employee called over a uniformed security personnel, who checked my briefcase, asked me to empty my pockets, and finally allowed me to enter through the mechanical turnstile. I was directed down the entire length of the library to the elevators, which would take me to my destination on the 10th floor. This was the same floor of the museum I had visited in September to view the exhibit curated by Dr. Eric Goldstein. Unfortunately, the exhibit had been taken down on January 6, just a few days before my present visit.

MARBL was located on the top floor of the Woodruff Library. As I exited the elevator, I faced a bare wall that until recently had supported artifacts of the Jewish exhibit. Turning left, I followed the narrow walkway to the check-in desk. It had been years since I had done any research at an Emory library. During my undergraduate days, we used the old Candler Library, which is still located on the Emory quadrangle. What an amazing change had transpired.

Before signing in, I was led to a metal locker in which I was asked to check my briefcase and its contents. I was restricted to my camera and my laptop computer. There was another sign-in sheet. I knew I had to finally declare the purpose of my visit. I slowly wrote in my best handwriting, "Emory dental school." The librarian informed me that they (Emory library) never held the papers or records of the dental or medical schools. She added, "The medical school still retains its own papers, and nobody knows what happened to the dental school records after the school closed in 1988."

I asked to see the Emory annual yearbooks and was delighted to find that they were openly stacked in wooden bookcases lining the front wall of the main reading room, directly across from where I was now standing.

I was directed to one of the many wooden desks in the main reading room. They gave me a large cradle to support the open books I would be viewing. White gloves were issued to avoid soiling the pages with greasy fingerprints. No pens were permitted. The clerk at the front desk issued a lead pencil. I combed the *Campus* yearbooks, with special focus on the dental and medical schools. I was able to determine with accuracy the matriculation of the Jewish students, how many graduated, and at what rate. I became intimately involved with each of them, although I had never personally known many of them. I decided to photograph every page, which I transferred to my computer when I returned home each day. Many of the images that at the time appeared meaningless turned out later to disclose valuable and revealing evidence. I spent many days and many hours accumulating evidence.

Not surprisingly, the Woodruff Library preserved all the personal papers of former Emory president Goodrich C. White. Dr. White was president from 1942-1957 and chancellor from 1957-1979. The papers (1905-1979) consisted largely of personal and professional information. A substantial number of White's letters concerned the Emory dental

school and provided a valuable insight into White's involvement in the evolution of events at the dental school.

The letters provided details of Emory's purchase of the Atlanta-Southern Dental College in 1944. President White maintained an increasing friendship with Dean Ralph R. Byrnes and relied on Byrnes to keep the troubled dental school running in the pre- and post-WWII years. Intramural infighting at the dental school was disruptive, and no viable candidate for the deanship emerged from the faculty. White convinced the aging Byrnes to remain as dean until together they could identify and hire his successor. An extended correspondence between Dr. White and Dr. John Buhler, who was hired in 1948, revealed a developing personal relationship. Buhler's sycophantic letters, many handwritten, are over the top. They began from the time White hired him in 1948. White seems to have enjoyed the praise. While in all correspondence with others he was very proper and discreet, White tolerated Buhler's bigoted racial and religious comments.

The letters make it clear that Buhler was very disappointed when White's presidency ended in 1957, though his long letters and reports to the new president, S. Walter Martin, were also flowery and flattering.

Buhler often played the religious card. His 1959 annual report to Dr. Martin ended by stating that the "most important attribute necessary for admission to study in the profession of dentistry is a high level of moral and ethical standards and an acute sensitivity to God and His purpose as revealed through Jesus Christ."

President Martin did not encourage Buhler's hyperbolic remarks as did his predecessor, Dr. White. Buhler continued to exchange letters with (now Chancellor) Goodrich White in which Buhler's distrust of Martin's support was noticeable.

By this point, I had finally acquired a basic understanding of the administration's involvement in the dental school story. Although I had not yet found Dean Buhler's papers, I had learned much about him and his personality from his correspondence with President White and later with President Martin. That part of the equation was becoming clear. I decided that I needed to take a library break to refocus on the enigmatic bar graph that appeared on the third panel of the Emory exhibition. It was obvious from the panel that the ADL had been Emory's protagonist, but personal and historical details were conspicuously absent. My outreach to the local and national ADL offices had been fruitless.

CHAPTER 11

Hurry Up and Wait

A Much-Needed Break

I reached the point where I had accumulated large numbers of poorly organized files on my laptop. I made the change to an Apple computer and transferred all my personal and research records to the new format. I needed the break both to upgrade my computer skills and to boost my morale, which, depending on my daily progress, was swinging up and down like a yo-yo.

I signed up for the popular one-to-one computer learning sessions at a local Apple store, where I spent three days a week for several months organizing my digital files. The instructors, who were trained to be impersonal in a highly professional manner, were soon paying attention to my source material. They were all young and totally unfamiliar with the concept of quotas that excluded certain groups from college. They had only heard of minority preferences, which were quotas enacted to increase the numbers of minorities. Soon they asked if I had uncovered any additional information. They taught me how to do digital recordings, with the goal of producing CDs and PowerPoint presentations. This encouraged me to get back in the research mode.

In late November 2008, out of the blue, I received a phone call from Arthur Burns of Jacksonville, Florida, one of the four Jewish boys in my first-year dental school class. Art had recently retired from his orthodontic practice. We had not seen or talked to each other since we were both kicked out of Emory dental school 56 years earlier.

"How are you doing?" he asked. "I have thought of you and all the rest of the guys every day of my life. It has been a constant burden." I knew what he meant. Just like me, he hadn't shared his experience with anyone else. At that moment, I decided to find out as much as I could about what had happened to him during and following the Buhler years.

Art and I came to Emory as freshmen in 1949. We joined different Jewish fraternities, but we were friendly competitors. After two years, we were both admitted to Emory University School of Dentistry, along with two more of our fraternity brothers. What we didn't know (at that time nobody knew anything) was that one of our college fraternity brothers had just been flunked out of the dental school after his second year, with no option to repeat. We were also unaware that another Jewish boy from Savannah had to repeat his sophomore year. A Jewish boy from Atlanta was starting his second year and was to find out nine months later that he would also have to repeat. And another of our fraternity brothers was to find out nine months later that he would also have to repeat his second year.

Just as bad, there were no Jewish students in the junior or senior classes. Including us four freshmen, a total of seven Jewish students were in the entire school. There was no fraternity house, nor a lab for us to work in. In short, we were alone and, as we would soon find out, isolated and vulnerable. Within two years, all four of the boys in our class would be gone. Other naive, innocent young men would be entering the school over the next few years. For the most part, they had no clue what they would face.

As I reconnected with Art, I told him about the exhibit at Emory and about my preliminary research at the Emory library. He was very excited, and challenged me to continue my investigation. But he hesitated when I invited him to collaborate with me. The "burden" he referred to, the long emotional struggle he had endured after being kicked out of school, prevented his active participation. Decades later, the wounds were still fresh.

I learned from Art that Dean Buhler told him that he was the worst in our class, number 72 out of 72. In stark contrast, and eight years later (1959) at Temple University School of Dentistry, he won the Alpha Omega award for having the highest scholastic average in his class of 131 and won the "Faculty Award for the highest proficiency in dentistry," a reflection of his "manual skills." He took two additional years in orthodontics and returned to Jacksonville to practice his specialty. Despite his remarkable turnaround, he was permanently scarred. "I'm really not doing so well," he said to me. "You will have to do the heavy lifting—I'll help as much as I can."

It would take him seven months to put together a packet containing highlights of his life after Emory. But it was worth the wait.

Meanwhile, I accelerated my efforts to bring clarity to a long-suppressed story. There were so many disparate pieces to the puzzle— a veritable scavenger hunt. Days stretched to months, and months to years.

February 26, 2009 was a sad and dreary day in Atlanta. Shirley and I attended the funeral of Dr. Morris Benveniste. Morris was Shirley's former brother-in-law and our longtime friend. The soft winter rain had begun at daybreak but appeared to be letting up. Mindful of the uncertainty of Atlanta traffic, we started out early from our home in northeast Atlanta and arrived at Greenwood Cemetery a full 45 minutes before the 11 a.m. graveside service. I spotted my former college classmate, Miles Alexander, who was Morris's Emory fraternity brother. Miles asked me for an update on my research, and I told him about my numerous phone calls with Art Burns, who was also one of Miles' fraternity brothers. As Morris's family arrived, friends gathered under the tent at the gravesite. Miles urged me to continue my work and insisted that I keep him apprised on my progress. "It's time something was done," he said. Miles, a Harvard law graduate, never wasted words. His support was genuine. It was the best anyone could hope for.

The support from Miles encouraged me to return to the Emory library and intensify my search for new information. I discovered *Emory University, 1915-1965; A semicentennial history* by Thomas English, published in 1966, just a few years after the ADL charges. Professor English carefully avoided discussion of the Emory dental school. On page 175, he wrote, "Some unpleasantness developed in 1961 when it was charged that a disproportionately large number of Jewish students in the dental school had been failed in their work. President Martin made a personal investigation after which he stated his belief that there had been 'no willful or intentional discrimination.'" Dean Buhler's resignation coming at this time, it was rumored that his leaving was a direct result of the unfavorable publicity that the school had received. This charge also Dr. Martin dismissed as 'pure coincidence.'"[52] That was the full treatment of the matter in the official Emory historical account. They whitewashed it. It seemed that nobody wanted me to discover what really happened. I would have to find information elsewhere.

The Federation

While still at Emory, I chose to veer slightly off my current path. I checked out the papers of Dr. Judson Ward, dean of the faculties and vice president of the university. Dr. Ward had a reputation for careful modulation. He was the steadying force during the change of administrations in 1957 and 1962. I discovered that Dr. Ward kept "two sets of books." One folder contained dry administrative protocols. The other contained trivia and even gossip. I was attracted to the latter. There were personal letters concerning the Emory dental school between Dean Ward and prominent leaders of the Jewish community, including Rabbi Harry Epstein, Rabbi Jacob Rothschild, and William B. Schwartz, Jr., chairman of the Jewish Community Relations Committee. I realized that I should seek additional information, if it existed, at the Jewish community archives. The archives were housed downtown at the Jewish Federation building at 1440 Spring Street NW. One end of the mystery was slowly unraveling. I needed to tug at the other end.

On Thursday morning, June 25, 2009, I made a preliminary visit to the Cuba Family Archives in the Breman Museum in midtown Atlanta. Sandra Berman, the archivist, was a long-time friend. She invited me into her compact office and offered me the lone chair across the desk from her. She knew that I was a past president of the Federation and probably figured that I was in the building for a board meeting. She was surprised to learn that I had begun a research project and wanted access to the archives inventory. I told her the nature of my research, the former Emory dental school, and asked if she could point me in the right direction. It was my turn to be surprised. Sandy told me without hesitation that most of the information I sought was restricted. I sat up straight in my chair, incredulous. But she had a ready explanation. "There are three issues," she explained. "One is the sensitivity of the matter. Many of the people whose names you will run across are still living and might not appear to you in a favorable light. The second is a legal matter. Our attorneys are still working on legal documents governing how we make our papers available. Finally, we are still uncertain as to who will be eligible to see the material in our archives"

I remained silent. Sandy looked down at her appointment book. "Can you come back next Tuesday at one o'clock? I'll pull the Dr. Marvin Goldstein papers. It will be eyes only– no copies will be permitted. You may take notes, but you will have to sign a form promising not to speak or write about the information without our prior approval. Okay?"

I nodded my head and thanked Sandy for trusting me. I could hardly wait to see the Goldstein files. I returned to the Cuba Family Archives to view the Goldstein papers on June 30, 2009, at approximately 1 p.m.

This would be the first time I ever viewed a volume of documents collected by or representing the thoughts of someone I had actually known. Marvin Goldstein had supported me ever since I returned to Atlanta in 1961. At some point I learned that he played an important role in my acceptance to The University of Tennessee dental school after having been flunked out of Emory. A role model in so many ways, he was a leader in the dental community and the general community. He was active in the Jewish community, serving as president of his synagogue and the Jewish Federation. He had served as international president of Alpha Omega, the Jewish dental fraternity. He was politically active in local, state, and national politics. The walls of Marvin's orthodontic office were lined with plaques and trophies citing his numerous awards. He never sat by the sidelines. He was a fighter and an advocate for the underdog until his death from pulmonary fibrosis in 1997.

Although Marvin never brought up the subject, it was rumored that he and his older brother Dr. Irving Goldstein were early opponents of Dean John Buhler. In 1948, they had received word from their dental colleagues at Temple University that Buhler was leaving Philadelphia and coming to Atlanta as dean of the Emory dental school. Their friends had warned them that Buhler was an antisemite. It didn't take long after Buhler's arrival for the Goldsteins to be convinced that it was a well-founded warning. That's why I was extremely hopeful that there would be useful information about the dental school matter in the Goldstein archives.

When I arrived at the Breman, the Goldstein folders were neatly arranged on a portable bookshelf that had been transferred from a temperature-regulated room into the open research area. Library rules were in force. Whispering—no talking. The usual white gloves and pencils.

The files were organized into categories: Soviet Jewry, Synagogue, Federation, Red Cross, Hire the Handicapped, United Way, Politics, Hotels and Real Estate, Dental, Miscellaneous, etc. Sandy Berman pointed out that there were several dental folders and told me I would be allowed to look at them one folder at a time. It appeared that the dental folders were a repository for complaints on dental school-related matters. Apparently, everyone knew that Marvin was the "go to" man, for he received correspondence from a variety of sources.

By chance, my first selection was a series of typed letters from a desperate dental student to Dr. Goldstein describing in detail the terms of the student's dismissal from the dental school. I had to hold back tears when I read of the horrible verbal abuse the student received from Dean Buhler when he was asked to justify his dismissal. A letter followed this from the student's father pleading with the dean for a second chance for his son. "You have not treated him well. I will pray for you on Yom Kippur."

The student described Buhler's tirades, directed back to him. "It's people like you who make it hard for the rest of the Jewish students. Look how nice we have been to Shaw and Krugman to let them stay in school and repeat the year." There was an original 1956 letter to the American Dental Association from Arnold Hoffman, Emory business school graduate and AEPi undergrad fraternity advisor. Hoffman demanded that the ADA investigate the Emory dental school. "Something wrong is happening there to the Jewish students. If you don't do something about it, I will not allow my nephew to go to Emory. I will send him elsewhere." There was no reply from the ADA headquarters in Chicago.

There was a copy of an application form that Dean Buhler was planning to send out to 1961 applicants. It asked for the religion of the applicant and offered three choices: "Caucasian, Jew, Other." There was a copy of a memo from Eugene Howard, a local Jewish dentist to a Jewish dental colleague, Gerald Reed. Howard told Gerald Reed that the lone Jewish dentist on the Emory faculty, Marvin Sugarman, was trying to undermine Reed's Christian associate, Allan F. Shaw. Sugarman was sabotaging Shaw's application for part-time Emory faculty status by insinuating that Shaw was hiding his Judaism. I would need to find out why Sugarman was undermining Allan F. Shaw.

Several internal memos indicated that the Jewish Community Council members were well aware of the continuing complaints of discrimination at the Emory dental school but were resistant to speaking up. Marvin Goldstein took the matter to his national dental fraternity, Alpha Omega. At the December 1960 AO meeting in Washington, DC, Marvin authored a resolution praising the ADL and especially their Southeast director, Arthur Levin, for "their exceptional efforts and help to Alpha Omega." Marvin was able to bring pressure to bear from the outside when local community leaders were dragging their feet. A copy of that resolution was in the Goldstein files.

There were *Atlanta Journal* newspaper reports of the dental school episode, including President S. Walter Martin's cynical rejection of the ADL's charge of discrimination at the dental school. There was a typed copy of a list of dental students who had been flunked out or had to repeat. There was a notation that a few had gotten in other schools and graduated with honors. I was stunned to see my name on that list along with my Chattanooga home phone number, 62258, handwritten in blue ink along the margins.

I couldn't write fast enough. I was finally on the inside of the storm with all kinds of new information and new names swirling around me. Until now, the public was privy only to Emory's interpretation of the dental school story. That narrative had held sway for more than 60 years. I was now certain that there were other players in the drama. The curtain had to be drawn, and these newly announced players—Arnold Hoffman, Eugene Howard, Gerald Reed, Allan F. Shaw, Marvin Sugarman, William Schwartz Jr., and others—needed to be brought on stage, introduced, and allowed to tell their stories. Having now seen the Goldstein papers, I concluded that there were at least two other individuals (Arthur Levin and John Buhler) and two other groups (ADL and the Atlanta Jewish Community Council) whose stories were equally critical to unmasking the truth.

In my opinion, Arthur J. Levin, the ADL's Southeast director, must have been the principal figure in developing the case against Dean Buhler—ultimately leading to his resignation. The ADL book *Some of My Best Friends* didn't give any of their field workers credit by name in the Authors' Acknowledgement section. But you didn't have to be a Sherlock Holmes to figure out that Marvin Goldstein, in his Alpha Omega resolution, was identifying Levin as the driving force in the investigation. I needed to find Art Levin.

The second individual, Dean John Buhler, was deceased. Yet it was inconceivable to me that a person with his oversized ego would depart this world without leaving a recorded legacy. I absolutely needed to find his papers.

I was still unconvinced that there were no ADL files. I was willing to concede that the Atlanta office didn't put a premium on maintaining 60-year-old records. But the elusive ADL files had to be somewhere in New York. Their side of the story was critical.

Finally, the Jewish Community Council papers. Why wouldn't they be at the Breman? It was near closing time, but Sandy Berman was still around. I walked over to her office and asked if the Council papers were in-house. She told me I could return to see those files, but that most of the minutes were either misplaced or lost. She commented that Ed Kahn, the Federation's first professionally trained executive, preferred to keep most of the Council's proceedings in his head. She told me that when I returned to review the Council minutes, the same rules would apply. She was still playing by the rules, but so far, she was giving me everything I wanted, and even more. I was grateful for the opportunity.

I returned the following week, prepared to spend the entire day. In fact, the information in the CRC file was much less expansive than what I found in the Goldstein file. There were lists of regular members and invited guests who attended the meetings, and some reference to the topics discussed, but in general the minutes were a huge disappointment. I hand-copied all the names, as I recognized many whom I knew to still be alive.

Suddenly, beginning in the fall minutes of 1960, a new name appeared. Fred I. Baker was the new assistant director, and his signature at the end of the minutes indicated that he was also serving as the recording secretary. The conversation came alive as Baker finally provided a window into the committee's proceedings. Familiar names emerged as the principal players in the drama. As the opposite sides aligned, Baker's narrative provided the reader with a sense of the struggle taking place.

From my perspective, Baker's arrival at the Federation was perfectly timed. By the fall of 1960, when Baker arrived, the minutes indicated that the ADL's Art Levin was now confident he had sufficient evidence to take to the university. He was looking for partners but was willing to go it alone if necessary. At the last minute, Kahn and the Federation leaders reluctantly agreed to accompany Levin to the Emory president's office. Baker's minutes were professional, but it seemed clear to me that he had a favorite side. He seemed eager to report the outcome of the high-level meetings and the ensuing turn of events.

Baker's minutes carried us into the spring of 1961, by which time Dean Buhler "chose" to resign. After this time, I had to rely on newspaper reports of the dental school episode. I needed some live testimony.

I was spending much time on the phone unsuccessfully talking with the ADL New York office. Fortunately, Deborah Lauter, formerly with the ADL in Atlanta, and now a national vice president, stepped in and introduced me to the ADL archivist Aryeh Tuchman, who immediately mailed me all the Art Levin documents that were in the New York office. I was beyond emotional when I heard from Aryeh a month later that he had also discovered previously unknown 1959-1960 ADL documents in an off-site storage space in Brooklyn. They included valuable correspondence between Art Levin and his superiors. Tuchman warned me, "The documents are in poor condition. They will require careful restoration." He was right. The documents were in terrible condition—but what a treasure trove. The new documents preserved most of Levin's correspondence. Those records were in sync with Fred Baker's minutes.

Deborah Lauter, along with Atlantan Dale Schwartz, also helped me find 93-year-old Arthur Levin in Coral Gables, Florida. After having exposed Dean Buhler, Levin was told by the Atlanta CRC to stand down and allow bygones to be bygones. He was not allowed to hold Emory accountable. Unsupported by his board and his superiors in New York, he left Atlanta and the ADL for a new career. He was now living alone in retirement in Florida. Email exchanges and subsequent audio and video interviews with Levin would leave no doubt that Art Levin was the principal hero of this story.

But what of Fred Baker? He departed Atlanta in the late spring of 1961 and left no visible trail. His last minutes were dated April 20, 1961. In 2013, no one in Atlanta seemed to remember Fred Baker. I googled and surfed until I found a possible clue that suggested he might have moved to Dallas. After running down all my leads, I finally dialed the Baker residence in Dallas. Fred had passed away six years previously, but his wife Edith, known by her friends as Didi, received my call with amazement. I followed the call with more calls and letters, and finally a trip to Dallas.

Reaching Out

The process had been slow and often frustrating, but my patience and persistence finally started to pay off. Suddenly, I had so many promising options that I actually had to prioritize my schedule, taking into account the age and health of my respondents and their geographic locations. From my research at the Woodruff Library, I had a list of all the Jewish students who were at the dental school during Dean Buhler's tenure. I couldn't afford to delay finding them. I needed to find out what they had made of their lives. With the help of the Emory Alumni office, I developed a mailing list and sent the following letter:

July 6, 2009
Dear Friends,
I have begun writing a biographical memo which will serve as a record of who was the young person (SPB) who was one of the statistics in the Emory University School of Dentistry episode. Before I complete the memo, I thought it would be appropriate to state why I think it is an important thing to identify the victims and survivors of the tragedy. Ultimately, I would like each person to write a memo. I think it will be a useful and long overdue archival record. I urge your involvement.

Early on, when I began asking questions, I was asked, "Why do you want to know what went on during the Buhler era at the Dental school? What do you intend to do with the information? It's over... why not leave it alone?"

My reaction was defensive. It seemed that I was being asked to believe that because an injustice had been rectified, it was not in anyone's interest to delve into the past and its uncomfortable details.

Instinctively, I retreated into my own domain. I realized that I would have to proceed in a less direct fashion. I could not be confrontational. I had to be sensitive to the fact that long suppressed feelings and emotions were involved.

Also, I had to reach deep down to re-examine my motivation. I think what had always bothered me more than anything else was that one moment I was part of a society, and the next moment I was in total exile. No one called. No one offered support. It was as if I had disappeared from existence.

Much later, when I was able to access newspaper articles and other private documents, certain facts became clear. Those who originally pursued the case only had anecdotal evidence and were painfully aware of their lack of scientific data. The Dental School and Emory University fought hard to deny that discrimination had existed and made it very uncomfortable for their accusers. When the ADL entered the fray and accumulated hard data, they were welcomed by some in the Jewish community but were viewed at a distance by others because the University characterized them as unwanted trouble-making intruders. The records reveal that the pressure increased as Buhler panicked and contributed to his own downfall. His resignation appeared on the front page of the Atlanta Journal accompanied by a statement by Emory that this in no way indicated that there was any institutional antisemitism involved. Certain editorials actually placed the blame on the Jews. "Why didn't they work as hard as the other students instead of just whining about discrimination?" Though there was heated debate in the Jewish community, especially in Alpha Omega, the Jewish dental fraternity, it was agreed that there would be no continued criticism of the University. The issue was over. Buhler was gone, and, after all, that was the desired goal. Soon thereafter, Jewish financial support for the new dental school was manifest, with Dr. Irving Goldstein being selected by Emory to chair the campaign.

Having been involved in Jewish politics over the past forty years and being an avid student of Jewish history, I recognize and applaud the wisdom of quickly reconciling differences and turning the page to a new chapter. It was a turning point for the Jewish community, particularly with reference to Emory and the Dental school.

However, one glaring fact remained. Over a period of twelve years, as documented in the ADL report, there were an inordinate number of Jewish victims at the Emory Dental school. It never occurred to Emory University that it was on their watch that such a travesty occurred. They had no conscience in this matter. But forget Emory University. A Jewish army never leaves its wounded on the battlefield. With the battle over, why didn't the organized Jewish community immediately reach out? Although it has been over fifty years, it's still not too late.

I always realized that it was not just my experience, but I had no idea of the scope involved. I no longer consider it a purely personal matter. Rather, it belongs in the public domain. It is such a fundamental principle. Truth needs to be exposed and examined. And part of the truth is to seek out the victims and offer some degree of comfort and recognition to them. I have come to learn that there are many lessons to learn from the survivors. At the very least, we can gain satisfaction from their accomplishments. We

can also learn about some of the heroes who helped them get back on their feet.
The telling of the story has fallen to me. But it is not just my story. I encourage everyone to contribute to this effort.

Sincerely,
S. Perry Brickman
1731 Reindeer Drive
Atlanta, Ga. 30329
simchaper@aol.com

There was an overwhelming response. Not only did I hear from the students, but also from a wide range of individuals who had heard about my project. I quickly learned not to underestimate seemingly dull and uninteresting clues, and to pay attention to patterns that ordinarily could have been taken for granted. On the other hand, there were plenty of "wow moments." I realized an investigator finds patterns hidden in the chaos.

I found the unexpected in Ithaca, New York, in the person of Elizabeth Reed, widow of Dr. Gerald Reed. Elizabeth, with her daughter Janice Nigro at her side, told me how her husband and Art Levin had first met. While I waited, Elizabeth asked her daughter to retrieve her deceased father's personal files, which had not been opened since his sudden death in 1976. They revealed vital information about Gerald's unlikely collaboration with ADL's Art Levin. Elizabeth's own testimony, even more amazing and incredible, will be recounted in a subsequent chapter.

I met face-to-face with the story's 93-year-old hero, Art Levin, in his Coral Gables, Florida, apartment overlooking Biscayne Bay. Soon afterwards, I interviewed Levin's 95-year-old former adversary, Dr. Marvin Sugarman, seven months before his death in Atlanta on November 8, 2010. Sugarman wanted to explain his side of the story.

My interviews with these two key players are also recounted in detail in later chapters.

Dr. Leon Feldman welcomed me, in his deep traditional Charleston accent, to his lovely South Carolina home. There, he told me about an unpleasant encounter he had with Dean Buhler. "I was president of the South Carolina Dental Association in 1966 and would be presiding at the annual meeting. I told Dr. Buhler that I would allow him, as the new South Carolina dean, to speak at the annual meeting, even though I knew he was antisemitic. He replied that if he had been dean when I was a student, I never would have graduated."

On August 17, 2010, a full two years after our initial phone call, my former classmate, Art Burns, readied himself for an interview in the study of his home in Jacksonville. I turned on the switch of my video camera and recorded 29 single-spaced pages of his inspiring story. In 1953, Dr. Buhler told Burns that he was the worst in his class at Emory. "Do something you're better suited for," he told him. Six years later, Burns graduated first in his class in every category at Temple University dental school.

I interviewed Eugene (Bucky) Bloom in his home in Savannah, Georgia. Bucky and his wife Joan had retired after 40 years in Miami, where he was a prominent gastroenterologist. Bucky excelled in his undergraduate studies at Emory. During his two years at Emory dental school, he was a popular member of the student council. "At the end of my second year, I got the infamous letter that said, 'Dentistry is not a profession for you. Go seek some other profession.' Essentially, they told me, 'Hey, you're canned. If you don't resign, we're going to flunk you out. You're not coming back.' So, I wrote them a letter of resignation, obviously. And then sat around on my couch for about a week deciding I better do something with my life. And then I decided, 'You know? You made A's and B's in all of your basic sciences. You love that. Why don't you go to medical school and become a physician?' But to do it—I had only had two years of undergraduate school and I needed certain subjects, so I enrolled in the University of Florida right away that summer, started taking some of my required courses, and by December of that year I had already been accepted to the University of Miami medical school.

"I knew some individuals who had been fraternity brothers of mine who had been in dental school who didn't make it through their sophomore year—either their freshman year or their sophomore year—they were gone. And so, you know, you had a little trepidation about this, but one can rationalize anything and it's just like a cigarette smoker. The cancer of the lung is going to happen to somebody else. It's not going to happen to me. But from the beginning, the experience in dental school was not a pleasant one. You were always walking on eggshells. And there were clues. So many of the Jewish boys ahead of me were being flunked out.

"The instructors were worthless. They were absolutely worthless. You know, my dog could have done as good a job. They didn't teach. They just didn't know how to teach. They sat at their desks reading their *Mad* comic books and didn't do anything to come down and say, 'This is how it's done.' Medical school was entirely different. They were there to help you get through. They were there to educate you. And I did very well. Heck, I was in Alpha Omega Alpha. It's the Phi Beta Kappa of medical school. I graduated high in my class. Following that, I interned in Chicago with Cook County Hospital. And interestingly enough—of course I didn't get through dental school because I didn't have good hands, but nonetheless, I was [laughs] offered a surgical residency at Cook County Hospital because apparently my rotation through surgery showed my hands were pretty good in operating on the human body.

"I don't want an individual apology. Listen, my life has been quite successful, okay? But they owe the Jewish community and the Jewish kids who've suffered that indignation a global apology: 'Hey, we were wrong. We turned our backs. We didn't look at what was going on. We should have been more proactive at the time. We apologize for what scars we might have left on you.' And believe me, it's left a scar on me. I'll be the first to admit it. It's left a scar on you. You wouldn't be here today if it hadn't left a scar on you. They told me I was a 'failure.' Now I really wasn't a failure. They were failures, but I was the brunt of their failure and somehow or another, that gets ingrained into you and it's troubling, and globally, all of the students at Emory dental school deserve an apology because they didn't get the education they paid for."

I continued to seek out evidence and information elucidating all sides of the story. Top items on my bucket list were to:

1. Obtain as many live interviews as possible;
2. Confirm the accuracy of Art Levin's data that he employed in developing his 10-year statistical analysis of the dental school;
3. Undertake a comprehensive investigation of Dr. Buhler that would explain his animus for Jews;
4. Explain the Jewish community's unwillingness to cooperate with the ADL and in some cases actually combatting it;
5. Revisit the role of the Council on Dental Education (CODE) and its Executive Secretary Harlan H. Horner, author of the infamous Horner report;
6. Determine the American Dental Association's role (through CODE) in enforcing the implementation of Emory's dental school quota that began in 1944, four years in advance of Dean Buhler's arrival;
7. Produce a documentary presenting my findings.

CHAPTER 12

A Tale of Two Men

D r. Eric Goldstein, the professor who curated the Emory Jewish History exhibit, provided me with my second major break. In addition to his role as a full-time professor of history, Eric (no relation to Marvin and Ron Goldstein) was the chair of the Emory Tam Institute for Jewish Studies. On January 29, 2010, I met with Eric at his Tam Institute office to review my progress. I bemoaned not having found Dean Buhler's papers.

Eric calmly powered up his desktop computer. "Didn't you tell me once that Dr. Buhler had surfaced in Charleston as dean of the new South Carolina dental school? Let's see what they have in their library." He was undeterred when his initial search was unsuccessful. He scrolled further down the page. "It says here there is a medical school library. It's called the Waring Library. Let's try that."

Bingo! There they were: 1.85 cubic feet of papers dating from 1923-1972, and only 310 miles away in Charleston, South Carolina. We called the library and were told that the papers could be viewed during regular hours. There were no restrictions. I absolutely would need to add a trip to Charleston to my calendar.

On April 19, 2010, Brooke Fox, librarian at the Medical University of South Carolina, wheeled the Dr. John E. Buhler files to my study desk at the Waring Historical Library. Ms. Fox told me that her records indicated I was the first outsider to see these long-sought documents. I spent two days photographing Dean Buhler's memorabilia. In contrast to the ADL files, they were in pristine condition.

When I returned to Atlanta from Charleston, I assembled on my desk, side by side, the Jewish Community Relations files, the rescued ADL correspondence, copies of the newly acquired Buhler papers, and the revelatory documents from the Woodruff Library. I was able to compile a near-seamless account of internecine feuds, inter-agency warfare, and institutional conspiracy. At the core of the intricate web lay a theme of discrimination at the Emory dental school. And much more.

The story goes that once Dean John Buhler arrived in Atlanta, he penned his lengthy missives and schemed his devious plots from his dental school office at 106 Forrest Avenue NE (now Ralph McGill Boulevard), six miles away from the main Emory University campus.

Edward Kahn, executive director of the Atlanta Jewish Welfare Federation, and Arthur Levin, Southeast director of the Anti-Defamation League, operated from their completely separate offices at the 41 Exchange Place building in downtown Atlanta. Geographically, Levin and Kahn were located less than a mile away from Buhler, a mere five-minute car ride. But in every other way they were worlds apart.

Arthur J. Levin, Executive Director of Southeast Region of ADL

Arthur J. Levin was born in Brooklyn, New York, in 1917. His parents were immigrants from Russia and Poland. Levin graduated from the City College of New York (CCNY) in 1937, after which he attended the University of Iowa, where he studied parasitology. He was almost finished with his PhD dissertation when WWII intervened. After the war was over, he moved with his family to Atlanta for a job with the Communicable Disease Center (the "CDC," now known as the Center for Disease Control). In his spare time, Levin became active in the civil rights movement, which led in 1953 to an offer with the Anti-Defamation League in Atlanta as regional director. In 1954, he advanced to the position of director of the ADL's Southeastern region. He served in that capacity from 1954-1962.

The Anti-Defamation League of B'nai B'rith was organized in 1913 as a direct result of the infamous Leo Frank case. Frank, a 29-year-old Jewish factory superintendent, was wrongly accused of murdering a 13-year-old female employee. The trial took place in Atlanta and ended with Frank's conviction. His appeal was rejected by the US Supreme Court, but in June 1915, on his last day of office, Georgia Governor John M. Slaton commuted Frank's sentence to life.

Slaton's decision enraged much of the Georgian populace, leading to riots throughout Atlanta, as well as a march to the governor's mansion by some of his more virulent opponents. The governor declared martial law and called out the National Guard. When Slaton's term as governor ended a few days later, police escorted him to the railroad station, where he and his wife boarded a train and left the state, not to return for a decade.[53] In this antisemitic climate, Jews were threatened and physically attacked, and many fled Georgia to neighboring Jewish communities in Alabama and Tennessee.

Two years later, on October 16, 1915, in the dark of the night, Frank was dragged from his jail cell in Milledgeville, Georgia, transported 170 miles to Marietta, Georgia, and lynched the following morning in front of a large crowd who had gathered to watch. They were shouting "Hang the Jew."

The activities of the ADL centered on combatting antisemitism and other forms of discrimination and bigotry. The organization, in its formative years, often found itself in conflict with the established Jewish communities, who were accustomed to handling community relations in their own way. This was particularly true in Southern towns with small Jewish populations. They resented outsiders telling them how to get along with their non-Jewish neighbors and how to manage race relations.

Art Levin was definitely an outsider, and the ADL was new on the Atlanta scene. He was a liberal New York Jew who was actively involved in the civil rights movement. However, he and his family became active members in the Atlanta Jewish community, where they developed many friendships. Levin attracted several influential Jewish leaders to his Southeastern board and was soon known for his successful opposition to and exposure of the KKK and other radical hate groups. Nevertheless, the members of the Jewish Community Relations Council (CRC) considered the ADL a threat to their autonomy. They guarded their authority and resented the ADL "meddling" in their affairs. Additionally, the ADL and other groups such as the American Jewish Committee, National Council of Jewish Women, and others were introducing outside agendas and competing financially with the established Jewish Federation.

From the time Levin was named Southeast regional director of the Anti-Defamation League on March 12, 1954, his calendar was full, combatting hate speech on radio, marginalizing KKK marches, fighting segregation issues in the schools, and standing down rallies by the American Nazi Party. Levin operated openly. Ben Rabinowitz, president of the local B'nai B'rith chapter, praised Levin as "the bravest man I ever met."

Levin's focus was narrowed when numerous former Emory dental students approached him about extreme cases of antisemitism at the local dental school. They told Levin they had complained to members of the Atlanta Community Relations Council but were told by those CRC members that they were simply trying to blame others for their own inadequacies.

Levin's basic education was in the sciences, and he was trained to be objective. The complaints were subjective, but he was open to checking out the facts. Being an outsider, he knew his limitations in collecting local data. He found a kindred soul in Dr. Marvin Goldstein, who was willing to spend hours helping Levin accumulate data on the Jewish students. Their statistics were shocking. Between 1948 and 1958, 65% of the Emory Jewish dental students had been either flunked out or made to repeat one or more years. Efforts to convince the community leaders that something sinister was going on were futile. Levin finally got their attention when he threatened to go alone to the Emory administration to present the data. On the one hand, the CRC didn't want to participate, but on the other hand, they didn't want Levin and the ADL to represent the community. Dr. Goldstein told Levin that he would enlist outside help from his national dental fraternity, Alpha Omega.

John E. Buhler was born in Marion, Indiana, on June 28, 1908. His grandparents were Swiss/German immigrants. Buhler spent his childhood in Arizona but returned to his native state to attend Indiana University. He entered dental school at Indiana in 1931 and graduated in 1935.

While in school, Buhler was befriended by his fraternity faculty advisor, Dr. Gerald Timmons, who had taught at the school since 1925. Buhler graduated from dental school in 1935 and spent the next six years teaching at Indiana. He was on course for an academic career.

Buhler's mentor, Dr. Timmons, was appointed interim dean of Indiana in 1938. When the permanent position eluded him, he left in early 1940 for Chicago to become Secretary of the American Dental Association (ADA). Buhler remained at Indiana, maintaining a steady correspondence with Dr. Timmons. In his letters, Buhler frequently described the shaky political climate at the dental school. Timmons responded by advising Buhler to stay clear of the in-fighting.

Meanwhile, Harlan H. Horner PhD, a retired demographer with a 35-year career in the New York State Commission of Education, joined the ADA staff in July 1940 to become the first Executive Secretary of the Council on Dental Education (CODE). His job was to conduct a national survey of the 39 US dental schools, and he sought Dr. Timmons' advice on how best to accumulate useful data. Timmons was helpful but was unwilling to share confidential information about the dental curriculum of his alma mater, Indiana. Instead, in a July 12, 1940 letter, he introduced Horner to his former protégé Dr. John Buhler, who was still on the Indiana dental school faculty. Thus, began the Horner, Buhler, Timmons connection. This trio would ultimately shape the destiny of the Emory University School of Dentistry.

In 1942, Gerald Timmons was offered the deanship at Temple University dental school. He knew that the school was struggling but recognized its potential. He eagerly accepted the challenge of turning the school around. He had been very helpful to Dr. Horner at the ADA headquarters in Chicago and felt secure that Horner and his CODE committee would assist him in the curricular and administrative changes he would have to make in Philadelphia.

After his arrival at Temple, Dean Timmons received a frantic letter from John Buhler—he no longer held his position at the Indiana dental school.

When Dr. Timmons received his protege Buhler's desperate plea for a job, he graciously came to his rescue. After joining Dr. Timmons in Philadelphia in 1942, Buhler was groomed to learn administrative skills, especially how to comply with the increasing demands of the accreditation process being formulated at ADA headquarters in Chicago. Guided by Dean Timmons, Buhler soon became secretary/treasurer of the American Association of Dental Schools, where he developed a close connection with the members of CODE. Only recently on the ropes, Buhler's star was suddenly rising.

The Horner committee made survey visits to all operating dental schools in 1942-1943. Only two-thirds of the schools received a "full approval" status. Fourteen schools, including Temple, Atlanta-Southern (Emory), New York University (NYU), and Georgetown were given "provisional approval," with the warning that they would lose accreditation if they weren't able to correct their deficiencies. This would result in the ineligibility of their graduates to practice anywhere in the US.

Timmons knew that Temple had many deficiencies and at best would only be granted provisional approval status by the Horner committee. He and his administrative assistant Buhler, with close ties to the committee, learned what it would take to turn things around. What were they told, and how did they succeed in accomplishing this task?

I found the answer at the Samuel Paley Library at Temple University. A 1948 state-of-the-school letter from Dean Gerald Timmons to Temple President Robert L. Johnson stated that the dental school had been, in 1943, rated **next to last**, of the dental schools examined. In his report to the president, Timmons said that the Horner report described the horrible shape of Temple dental school's physical plant. Under Timmons' leadership, money was raised, and a new state-of-the-art school was built. That, he said, was his first most important accomplishment.

What Timmons considered his second most important achievement concerned a change in the student body. He was careful not to mention that the Horner committee mandated the change. But, as we will see, there can be no other explanation. Timmons illustrated, in charts, the number of students of the "Jewish faith" beginning in the 1942 freshman class (71.05%) and posted the figures for the next six years. Timmons noted that in 1942-43, 71.05% of the freshman class was Jewish. By contrast, he boasted that in the recently selected 1948-1949 class, Jewish representation had dropped to 28.46%.

1942–43

	JEWISH		CATHOLIC		PROTESTANT		TOTAL	
	No.	%	No.	%	No.	%	No.	%
Freshman	81	71.05	23	20.18	10	8.78	114	100.0
Sophomore	69	59.48	27	23.28	20	17.24	116	100.0
Junior	58	54.21	25	23.36	24	22.43	107	100.0
Senior	54	58.61	18	19.57	20	21.74	92	100.0
TOTAL	262	61.07	93	21.68	74	17.25	429	100.0

Religious makeup at Temple University dental school (1942-1943)

1948–49

	JEWISH		CATHOLIC		PROTESTANT		TOTAL	
	No.	%	No.	%	No.	%	No.	%
Freshman	37	28.46	42	32.31	51	39.23	130	100.0
Sophomore	43	33.33	30	23.26	56	43.41	129	100.0
Junior	53	44.91	31	26.28	34	28.81	118	100.0
Senior	43	53.75	23	28.75	14	17.50	80	100.0
TOTAL	176	38.51	126	27.57	155	33.92	457	100.0

Religious makeup at Temple University dental school (1948-1949)

Timmons went on to explain to President Johnson the purpose behind the actions he took following the Horner visitation. He explained that this was not a quota, and it wasn't about Jewish students. He simply had decided to discontinue accepting applications from New York State students. Henceforth, Temple would only accept applicants from Pennsylvania and nearby states without dental schools. This would be a temporary action but would be maintained until there was no longer any "provincialism." Of course, the action resulted in a dramatic decline in Jewish students, but it wasn't, according to Timmons, because they were Jewish per se. It was just because there was a disproportionate number of Jewish applicants from New York. Timmons proudly reported to President Johnson that their school, now in compliance, was fully approved and accredited. This occurred at the same time the Atlanta-Southern Dental School (precursor to Emory) was also given provisional approval. What do we know about that? We know that the ubiquitous

Horner and his committee also visited Atlanta in 1943. Atlanta-Southern Dental College (ASDC) was the last surviving proprietary school in the United States and was in the crosshairs of the Horner committee. It was given provisional approval, but only after it agreed to sell its assets to Emory University. The exact rank of ASDC with respect to the other 38 schools was previously unknown, as all records were lost when the Emory dental school closed its doors in 1988. But we have a January 30, 1964 letter from Buhler to President Goodrich C. White reminding him that in 1943, Emory, then Atlanta-Southern Dental College, was ranked last in the country by the Council on Dental Education.

The transaction was reported in the July 1944 *Journal of the American Dental Association.* The editor, Dr. L. Pierce Anthony, wrote: "It is indeed with much pleasure that we announce the merger of the Atlanta-Southern Dental School and Emory University and the incorporation of the dental school into the Emory University educational system.

"The affiliation of the Atlanta-Southern with Emory has been under advisement for some time (1943); until the desirability of such an association became so apparent that the directing bodies of the two institutions delegated President White of Emory and Dean Byrnes of the Atlanta-Southern as a conference committee to determine the consummation of the association. The merger here announced is due in part to the efforts of the Council and particularly those of the Executive Secretary, Dr. Horner."

Like Temple, Emory was told that it must build a new school as soon as possible. Although there are no available documents suggesting the need to adjust their "racial" profile, the record speaks for itself. The ADL, in its book *Some of My Best Friends*, states that prior to the merger in 1944, Jews came to Atlanta-Southern Dental College from 10 to 12 states, and non-Jews from 28 states. After 1944 and for the next 18 years, no Jews from New York, New Jersey, or any Northern state were accepted to Emory. In fact, between 1944 and 1962, Emory accepted

Jews from only three states, Georgia, Florida, and South Carolina, while non-Jews continued to be accepted from 23 states.

On September 1, 1944, Emory University School of Dentistry inaugurated its first class. Dean Byrnes agreed to remain as head of the school until a replacement could be found. None of his faculty was interested in the position, and the troubled school was unable to attract a viable candidate from the outside.

Then, in late 1947, John Buhler's career was once again advanced to a higher level. Dr. James R. Cameron, a native of Australia, was the crown jewel of the Temple faculty. He founded the oral surgery department at the prestigious Pennsylvania Hospital and had been on the Temple dental school staff since 1933. When Dr. Timmons asked Dr. Cameron in 1942 to allow the recently arrived Dr. Buhler to teach part-time in the extraction clinic, Cameron likely agreed with reluctance. Buhler was not a fully-trained oral surgeon, having only served a one-year internship.

James Cameron was a legend at Temple. My former classmate Art Burns, who graduated with highest honors from Temple in 1959, shared with me a senior faculty member's remembrance of the Cameron/Buhler episode. Professor Louis Herman, Cameron's longtime friend and associate, confided to Burns that Buhler was annoying Cameron with his pretentious behavior in the clinic and his unfounded claims of surgical superiority. According to Dr. Herman, Cameron barged into Dean Timmons' office one afternoon in late 1947 and announced in his distinct Aussie accent, "It's him or me," with an emphasis on "me." Timmons had been hearing rumors and needed no explanation. Buhler, with all his flaws, was his pet. But Cameron was untouchable. Buhler would have to go, and there was a perfect solution.

Timmons called Atlanta and recommended Dr. Buhler to his Emory colleague Dean Ralph Byrnes, who was intrigued with his suggestion. Dean Byrnes was reminded that Buhler had several useful assets. He had assisted Timmons in moving Temple into a modern dental school facility. He had recently been appointed secretary of the American Association of Dental Schools. He was also thoroughly familiar with the Council on

Dental Education requirements and, under Timmons' supervision, had just completed Temple's successful application for full approval status.

Four years had passed since Emory had acquired Atlanta-Southern Dental College. A candidate was finally identified and hired. That person was Dr. John E. Buhler. Buhler was totally aware of the Emory situation when he arrived in 1948 to assume the deanship. He knew that President Goodrich C. White had instituted fundamental changes in the school's admission process. There were only six Jewish students in the entire school. The Jewish quota had already been established. Unfortunately, the worst was yet to come.

Buhler began to pick a fight with his imagined Jewish adversaries almost as soon as he arrived in 1948, long before Art Levin arrived on the scene in 1954 to take over the leadership of the Southeastern office of the Anti-Defamation League.

The March 1952 issue of the *Journal of the South Carolina Dental Association* featured excerpts from a letter written by Dr. John E. Buhler to Dr. J.W. Douglass Jr., president of the South Carolina Dental Association. Douglass was a 1928 graduate of the Atlanta-Southern Dental College. His private letters to Buhler, discovered in the Buhler collection, revealed undisguised rabid antisemitic sentiments. Buhler was adept at identifying those who shared his views. He was skilled in consolidating his followers while marginalizing his opponents.

Buhler wrote: "It is sometimes unbelievable how much trouble we can seemingly get into in trying to do the right thing—in trying to avoid the pressure brought on us. Some of the loudest critics depend so heavily upon the hope that we will not be so inconsiderate as to stand up and publicly tell the whole story about some applicant in whom the critic has an interest. There are just a few persons who are really critical of Emory's admission procedure, but they usually follow pretty much the same general tactic of rumor mongering or gossiping and will only criticize and falsify when they are pretty sure there is no one present who can actually show the facts of the case."

In a February 23, 1961 letter to Emory President S. Walter Martin, Buhler wrote, "… two Jewish dentists, as principal offenders, prostituting their own dental fraternity and manipulating by deception at least one other Hebrew organization, have seen fit—seemingly without conscience—through race baiting tactics to malign the faculty and the Dean of the School of Dentistry by charging racial discrimination." "… The atrociously damaging and maliciously false charges of alleged discriminatory practices against Jewish applicants and students which have been made…have caused us to become aware that we can no longer be indifferent to race and religion. We must become able to provide factually accurate data with which to refute the lies and innuendoes … and expose them to the light of truth."

Buhler, at the conclusion of his letter, wrote, "… it appears to us that many fine, honorable and well-meaning members of Atlanta's—and of the nation's—Jewish faith are being innocently sucked into a quagmire of consternation and defamation as unwitting pawns in helping to achieve goals of personal ambition of less than a handful of Atlanta's Jewish community. We are confident that this confusion could have been easily aborted beginning as far back as 1949, had I, as Dean, been willing to have prostituted the standards of the School of Dentistry, to have brought upon myself the very righteous and deserving condemnation which would have issued, had I been willing to have encured [sic] the disgust and disintegration of the Faculty, by the simple expedient of recommending appointment to the Faculty two members of the Jewish Community who requested that they be appointed." "… These observations enjoy the support and endorsement of many of Atlanta's Jewish Community who have personal knowledge of the circumstances, and these observations also enjoy the support and endorsement of the faculty of the School of Dentistry."

Buhler received support from the upper ranks of his faculty. Dr. James Garland, associate professor of prosthetics and director of clinics, in an interoffice memo wrote: "In looking over Thursday night's Atlanta Journal, I found this TV column to be of particular interest since the writer is discussing pressure groups (minorities) and their activities. In view of our present problem with another of these pressure minorities, I thought you would find this of interest since it points up how they operate and indicates there is *no end* to this sort of thing and no solution."

The truth is that Emory officials at the highest level had been hearing for years that something was not right at the dental school. They were comfortable isolating it from their minds and their consciences because in their minds there was no hard evidence against them. Additionally, they were certain that they had a good standing in the Jewish community. Moreover, they felt sure that they could rely on the local Atlanta Jewish community's reluctance to confront them, quite content that their reputation was unassailable.

Enter the ADL Southeast Regional Director Arthur J. Levin. During the 1950s, Levin and his staff were dealing with Klan activities, hate speech in the newspapers and radio, and the infamous October 12, 1958 Temple bombing in Atlanta. Despite being consumed by the above events, Levin did not discount disturbing reports his office was receiving on possible antisemitic discrimination at Emory's dental school.

The reports actually began as early as 1954 and came from students who had been flunked out of Emory University School of Dentistry. On his own, Levin accumulated affidavits from these students and others. He also received invaluable data and support from Dr. Marvin Goldstein, a fearless Jewish advocate. Goldstein told Levin that, over the past five years, he and others had made informal presentations to the President and the Chairman of the Board of Emory without any results. This was in addition to conversations with Vice President Boisfeuillet Jones in 1955, 1956, and again in 1960. Goldstein told Levin that he and several other dentists also had discussed the problem with Dean Buhler directly over at least the past five years. The point is that Emory's knowledge of the situation began as early as 1955, and not 1960.

Levin's superiors in New York told him that under normal circumstances the evidence he had accumulated would be sufficient to prove his case. But they seemed certain that Emory would take the case to court, in which case Levin would need additional statistics, particularly pertaining to the non-Jewish Emory dental students, so that a valid analysis could be made. It was a disappointing set-back for Levin, but his fortunes were soon reversed. The next day, Levin received a letter from an ADL field worker in New York City. Levin's colleague, Sol Rabkin, had received a disturbing call from his dentist, Marvin K. Rubin, a part-time faculty member at NYU. Dr. Rubin told Rabkin that a recent NYU dental graduate, Dr. Gerald Reed (originally Rubenstein), was having legal and professional problems with his local Atlanta, Georgia dental society and with Dean John Buhler of the Emory dental school. These problems at their core were fueled by Reed's religion and additionally by his involvement in local civil rights activities. Reed was nervous about taking on the Emory dental school and Dr. Buhler by himself. Rabkin asked Art Levin to reach out to Dr. Reed. The die was cast. Reed and Levin, with similar interests and goals, became a team.

Levin had already determined that during Buhler's tenure, 65% of Jewish students were flunked out or had to repeat one or more years. I have live-recorded testimony that Dr. Gerald Reed obtained the corresponding data on the non-Jewish rate of attrition so critical to Levin's report. Reed located and delivered to Levin solid indisputable evidence that "only" 15% of non-Jews were flunked out or had to repeat during Buhler's tenure. This additional information enabled Levin to take his case to the Emory authorities. A week following Buhler's April 12, 1961 resignation, Levin wrote Reed stating that he (Levin) couldn't have made his case without him. Levin kept a copy of the letter and showed it to me following a 2010 interview at his home in Coral Gables, Florida.

Much to my dismay, I learned that Gerald Reed died suddenly in the Atlanta Jewish Community Center gym of a cardiac arrest on December 30, 1976. I was able to contact several of Reed's dental and medical friends and associates. I interviewed his former dental technician who, upon graduation from dental school, had become his dental partner. I interviewed the widow of a dental student whom Reed had helped when he was flunked out of dental school in the mid-1950s. I learned that the threats Reed described in the letter to Rabkin were not overstated. It was common knowledge among his close friends whom I interviewed that Reed had been threatened by Dean Buhler and had worked with the ADL to overthrow Buhler and his henchmen at the dental school. According to his friends, after Buhler's departure in 1961, Reed changed his focus to politics and other business interests.

I was told that Reed's widow had moved to Ithaca, New York, soon after his death. Reed's friends told me that Elizabeth Reed might be able to provide the clues I was seeking about how her husband procured the vital information. I flew into Ithaca on May 12, 2010, and interviewed Elizabeth Reed and her oldest daughter, Janice Nigro, on May 13, 2010. Elizabeth was an amazing font of information. She described her courtship with Gerald, their dental school days, and the reason they had left New York for Atlanta. She confirmed her husband's problems with the Emory dental school and his friendship with Art Levin but, initially, could not remember details of their collaboration.

During the interview, Reed's daughter, Janice Nigro, sat quietly as her mother described her dad. Tears came to her eyes as I described her dad as a hero. I was surprised when Janice suddenly left the room. She was gone for what seemed like a long time and finally reappeared with a large set of files. They were Gerald's business and personal files, which neither mother or daughter had ever examined. Janice opened the file, and suddenly, much of the ADL/Emory story unraveled. There were lists of Jewish dental students who had been flunked by Dean Buhler. I saw many familiar names, including my own name, my Tennessee address and phone number, and my grades at The University of Tennessee. There were legal papers describing how Reed had successfully defended himself from actions taken by Dr. Buhler and others. And there was the original letter from Art Levin stating that he would not have been able to accomplish what he did without Reed's help.

I asked Elizabeth what indeed had her husband done that was so important? It took some time for her to reconstruct the story. It required recalling some personal information, which she had not thought about for a long time. I told her to take her time. I encouraged her not to be selective; I wanted to hear all she could remember.

Elizabeth and Gerald met the summer of 1943 at Rockaway Beach in Queens, New York. Gerald was 18 years old, employed as a lifeguard for the summer. Elizabeth was 16 and worked as a mother's helper/babysitter for a family that was spending the summer at the beach. Elizabeth and Gerald quickly became engaged. They were married in September 1945.

Elizabeth and Gerald Reed

Gerald was classified "1A limited" by the Army. The "limited" was due to his faulty eyesight. Nevertheless, he was called to duty at age 18, right after the marriage, and was sent to Louisiana for basic training. He was a private. He didn't serve very long, as the war was soon over. He got a job in a dental laboratory and also enrolled in Long Island University. He was accepted to NYU dental school in 1949 and graduated in 1953. After dental school, he enlisted in the Army as a dentist with the rank of lieutenant. He served from 1953-1955. At some point in this time period, he changed his family name from Rubenstein to Reed, thinking it would shield his children from antisemitism.

Elizabeth's family was violently opposed to her marriage to a Jew. She found it difficult to live in New York, where she would have to be in contact with her parents. Gerald's married sister was living in Atlanta and encouraged her brother and sister-in-law to come South where they could live in peace. Elizabeth, Gerald, and their children moved to Atlanta in 1955, where he began his dental practice as Dr. Gerald Reed.

Elizabeth remembered her husband's early involvement in the civil rights movement in the 1950s. He welcomed black patients in his office, a very unpopular activity at that time. Word filtered back that the dental establishment viewed him as a trouble-making outsider.

He got off to a quick start in his practice and soon opened a dental laboratory adjacent to his dental office. He hired a dental student to work in his lab at night. He was soon able to attract more lab work from other dentists by charging them less than the commercial labs. This also caused controversy in the dental trade community.

Elizabeth's testimony complemented the written evidence in Reed's files, which on closer scrutiny revealed even more cases of Reed's assistance in uncovering antisemitic activity in the dental school. I recalled the letter to Dr. Reed in the Goldstein file at the Breman Museum, regarding an Emory faculty member who allegedly had sabotaged the application by Reed's partner Alan F. Shaw to join the faculty. Reed felt that Emory and the local dentists were after him because they knew that he was Jewish and were now insinuating that his partner Alan F. Shaw was Jewish.

I interrupted Elizabeth and told her I could see that Gerald was fighting his own battles with Emory even before he met Art Levin.

But what did she think was her husband's unique role that earned him that special letter of appreciation from Art Levin? Until this time, she was unaware of the letter, so she had never had reason to consider its importance, nor the reason that Levin had written it. I had interrupted her train of thought, and she needed a moment to readjust.

She recalled that her husband had written someone in New York, seeking advice regarding the concerted effort of certain local dentists to take away his dental license. "He was always self-assured," she said, "but the matter had accelerated, and he was obviously concerned that he was a lone person against a unified enemy. He normally didn't share details of his business matters, but he did share some of his concerns with me. After all, he had considered my feelings in making the move to Atlanta, and now we were facing even larger problems. I'm not sure whether he told me that he was going to meet someone who could possibly help him. But I do remember that after his meeting with Art Levin, he was rejuvenated. Art Levin had told Gerry that he was also having problems with Emory and was faced with having to find statistics that were next to impossible to get from the dental school. Gerry had found a friend in Art Levin, and he was obsessed with finding a way to help him. He was a member of the American Dental Association and wrote them asking for statistical information. Whenever we went out socially, he told friends about his new mission."

Elizabeth seemed somewhat hesitant to continue, but the gravity of the story carried her on. "I have already told you that my family practically disowned me for marrying Gerry. This caused me to have bad feelings about my religion, and I decided that I would no longer belong to a Christian church. Gerry's family wasn't too excited either, but they accepted me. Gerry still considered himself Jewish, even though he was not that religious. He had joined the Jewish War Veterans, and later was commander of his post. Out of consideration for me, he agreed to attend a meeting of the local Unitarian Congregation. I had learned that the membership was comprised of people who were formerly Jewish or Christian, but who had opted out in favor of a non-denominational community."

Elizabeth told me that she and her husband walked into the vestibule of the Unitarian congregation at the same time that another young couple entered. The couple had moved from Macon, Georgia, and were also leaving behind their church affiliation.

"They were both liberals and wanted intellectual freedom. I can't remember their names, but I do remember that he said that he was a schoolteacher and had taken a position in the Atlanta school system. At that point, my husband took over the conversation.

"He told the new couple about his problems with the dean of the Emory dental school. 'The people over there,' he said, 'are racist and antisemitic. The Anti-Defamation League, the ADL, is trying to develop a legal case against them, and I'm trying my best to help them develop their case. The problem is that they need the grades of all dental students between 1948 and 1958. The information is located at the registrar's office at Emory, and the university is unwilling to let the ADL examine their records. The ADL case relies on having those documents.'

"My husband suddenly stopped talking. It wasn't so much the fact that he was dominating the conversation. That was his style, especially if he had a platform to express his views. It was that he noticed that the young lady from Macon was frowning and appeared to be in deep thought.

"My husband modulated the tone of his voice. 'Did I say something to offend you?'

"'No,' she answered. 'I'm just thinking. Give me a moment.'

"Then she spoke up. 'I think I can help you. I'm the assistant to the Registrar at Emory.' "She told us that she also had a colleague who worked in the secretarial pool at the dental school."

Elizabeth told me that she never asked her husband about any of the details concerning how the transaction was carried out. Her husband never discussed it, and it was never mentioned in future social encounters with the mild-mannered couple from Macon.

The rest of the interview was anti-climactic. The next morning, Elizabeth's daughter Janice took me to a copy center and duplicated every one of the documents in her father's files. I returned to Atlanta, eager to receive a follow-up phone call with any further details about the couple from the Unitarian Congregation.

There were several false alarms. Finally, Elizabeth located a man she had worked with in Planned Parenthood. He had also belonged to the Unitarian Congregation. He remembered that the Macon couple's last name was Hall. He didn't know if they still lived in Atlanta, or if they were even still alive.

I decided that, if necessary, I would call every Hall in the phone book. I finally reached Eugene Hall, and he quietly acknowledged that he was the person I was seeking. His wife Dolores was no longer living, but she was definitely the one who willingly responded to Dr. Reed's plea for help. Yes, he would be glad for me to interview him, and he would proudly corroborate the story Elizabeth Reed had told. We set up a meeting date.

During lunch, Eugene Hall told me that his wife Dolores began working as a clerk at Emory in 1956, and her career lasted 33 years in the Registrar's Office. At the peak of her career, she served as acting Registrar.

Her husband insisted on saying for the record that his wife would never do anything illegal. "When Dr. Reed told us his story, it took Dolores less than a minute to decide that it was a moral issue, and that's what enabled her to do what she did. I have no idea how long it took her, but at some point," he said, "Dolores turned the data over to Dr. Reed." Mr. Hall was unaware how she accomplished her task. In his mind, it was immaterial.

Reed took the information to Levin, providing him with the essential statistical information his superiors had insisted on. Levin now had sufficient evidence to press charges.

CHAPTER 13

Vicious Infighting

A rmed with the statistical evidence the ADL national office insisted was critical, Art Levin met with community leaders. But even now, their immediate support was not forthcoming– the leadership of the community still was not convinced that a strong punch at Emory was the best long-term approach. Community Relations Committee minutes from that time show that only when Levin proposed that highly respected Atlanta attorney Morris Abram be appointed chairman for the wobbly coalition was the Jewish community's leadership willing to align and take action. Abram had gained national attention for his support of Georgia school desegregation and other civil rights cases. Emory would have to take notice if Abram were leading the charge, and if Abram petitioned President Martin for a meeting, there was no way the request would be denied.

The Committee agreed that Art Levin would present the statistics. Others selected to attend the meeting were William Schwartz, Jr., chairman of the Atlanta Community Relations Committee, Dr. Irving Greenberg, president of the Atlanta Jewish Community Council, and William Breman, active community leader. (I read the minutes of these Community Relations Committee meetings in my research at the Ida Cuba Archives, housed at the Breman Museum and named in honor and memory of William Breman.)

On December 16, 1960, with Morris Abram taking the lead, the Jewish community met with Emory President S. Walter Martin and Vice

President for Health Affairs Boisfeuillet Jones. Jones was responsible for expanding and combining Emory's dental, medical, and nursing schools, which ultimately led to the creation of the Emory Clinic in 1953. He had a great deal of discretion for decision making regarding the dental school. These two men were the highest-level representatives of the university. This was a high stakes meeting.

Participants at the December 1960 ADL/CRC
meeting with the Emory administration

In a December 19, 1960 letter from Art Levin to Arnold Forster, ADL's national general counsel, Levin summarized the meeting:

1. The President and Vice-President received the group with the utmost cordiality and indicated their very deep concern on behalf of the reputation of Emory University, as well as for the anxiety of the Atlanta Jewish community.

2. While they were aware that these allegations had been abroad for a number of years, and because of complaints of individual students and personal, informal presentations by some of the local dentists here, they had in the past only dealt with individual cases and they were shocked and stunned at the magnitude of the total picture as we presented it to them. Both Dr. Martin and Mr. Jones on several occasions stated that 'the evidence was insurmountable'.

3. Dr. Martin indicated that he had had several discussions with Dean Buhler and the faculty about these allegations, but the assurances of the Jewish dental faculty member, Dr. Marvin Sugarman, that no antisemitism existed in the dental school was the obstacle to pinning down the issue. Also, Dr. Buhler had taken great pains to substantiate each individual case in which Jewish students had suffered difficulties, so that Dr. Buhler was able to counteract by such individual treatment any charges of discrimination against the Jewish group as a whole.

   It was made exceedingly clear by us that Dr. Sugarman was viewed by us as a Jewish apologist for antisemitism, and that he had admitted to the CRC that antisemitism existed but was at the same time telling the opposite story to the administration of Emory University. Furthermore, the entire purpose of the statistical study was to get away from these individual cases and to present a pattern which clearly showed that Jewish students were being disadvantaged out of all proportion to what could be accepted simply on the basis of competence. Here references were also made to the affidavits that we had, and to statements of unnamed faculty members, and I offered to furnish these affidavits and names to Dr. Martin, but he replied that 'this won't be necessary.'

4. When it was pointed out that, irrespective of religion, Emory Dental School had an abnormally high rate of failure and repeat as compared to the other 42 dental schools in the country, Mr.

Jones indicated that he had been concerned with this for a number of years and that he had told Dr. Buhler 'maintaining high standards doesn't mean being a rigid martinet'.

Levin further reported that Martin and Jones didn't try to justify the situation and gave the Jewish delegation reason to feel that they were in no way satisfied with the dental school nor with the conduct of Dean Buhler. Levin noted President Martin's assurances that Emory would "do anything and everything to correct the matter," and that they would hear back from Emory in several weeks. Martin said that he planned to talk to Dean Buhler unofficially, and that Mr. Jones would speak with Buhler officially about the charges and statistics that had been presented at the meeting.

But in the end, Emory stonewalled. Vice President Boisfeuillet Jones was called to Washington, DC in early 1961 to serve in the Kennedy administration as special assistant to the Secretary for Health, Education, and Welfare, and Emory used this as a pretext to delay replying to the charges of antisemitism. Soon thereafter, Morris Abram also was called to Washington to serve in the Kennedy administration as general counsel to the Peace Corps, and the process was paralyzed.

At this point it was time for God to harden Pharaoh's heart.[54] Buhler was withering under the heat. In a desperate attempt to counter the ADL statistics that undoubtedly had been shared with him by the administration, the Dean convened the dental classes separately and circulated an "anonymous" questionnaire eliciting details about discrimination. Though no signature line was included, each student was required in his own handwriting to state whether he had ever encountered any kind of antisemitic discrimination. Students were scared to admit discrimination, and angry for not being able to do so. Dean Buhler also completely redesigned the Emory dental school application form for the upcoming Fall 1961 class, adding a new classification for "RACE" with three choices: "Caucasian, Jew, or Other." Calls came into the ADL, and both forms fell into the hands of Art Levin, who was incensed.

The forms were taken to President Walter Martin, who in December had just assured the Jewish community that he would do "anything and everything"—but apparently had done less than nothing. Fortunately, Dr. Martin, already known for his indecision, was out of town. In his absence, the outrageous forms were taken to Vice President and Dean of the Faculties Judson Ward. Ward was infuriated. According to his own documents, carefully preserved at Emory's Rose Library, Dean Ward immediately confronted Buhler.

The following weeks were both tense and suspenseful. There were clues that Buhler's downfall might occur. On Tuesday, March 14, 1961, Harold Braverman from the national ADL office wrote Art Levin in Atlanta, agreeing with Levin that Buhler was likely going down. On that same day in Atlanta, the Community Relations Committee administrative committee was convened. They reviewed the minutes of the December 16, 1960 meeting with Emory, and Fred Baker, the recording secretary, reported that the dental school matter was under active consideration by Emory. Baker noted in the CRC committee minutes that another meeting had been scheduled for April 3, 1961 by Emory, and that just the previous week, the CRC had presented "additional data that gave direct proof of the anti-Jewish character of the situation at the dental school" to President Martin's assistant, Robert Whitaker, Dean Ward, and Dean Orie Myers. Secretary Baker also noted in the minutes that Art Levin of the ADL had reported on the activities of the American Nazi Party with regard to the showing of the movie *Exodus*. Baker added, "The Chairman of the CRC immediately admonished Levin that the ADL and all other outside groups must defer to the CRC with respect to speaking to reporters. The CRC will remain the central governing body of the community."

Meanwhile over at Emory on that same Tuesday, Dean Orie Myers, dean of the Emory administration, sent a memo to Emory dental school faculty leaders, reminding them about the upcoming April 3, 1961 meeting with the Jewish CRC and other Jewish leaders. The meeting would be hosted by President Martin in Room 406 of the university's Administration Building.

The following Tuesday, March 21, 1961, Dean Buhler and faculty member Dr. James Garland exchanged memos from the perceived safety of their dental school offices. They shared their disgust with the "special interest groups" who were plotting to undermine them, and agreed, "Jews cry anti-Semitism." On that same day, Buhler also wrote President Martin, Dean Myers, and members of the dental school's administrative committee, directing his attack on the NAACP and other minority pressure groups.

On Monday afternoon, April 3, 1961, the meeting at Emory finally convened, with President Martin presiding. All members of the original committee, who had met Dr. Martin on December 16, 1960 had been invited. This included Dr. Irving Greenberg, William B. Schwartz, Jr., William Breman, Ed Kahn, and Art Levin. As Morris Abram had moved to Washington, DC, Abe Goldstein attended in his absence. Also invited were David Goldwasser and Max Rittenbaum, Jewish members of Emory's Board of Visitors. The university was represented by Dr. S. Walter Martin, Dr. Judson Ward, Dean Orie Myers, Robert Whitaker, Dr. John Buhler, and members of the dental school administrative committee. These included Dr. George Moulton, Dr. Ernest Banks, and Dr. James Garland. Also invited were Jewish faculty members of the dental school, Dr. William Weichselbaum of Savannah, and Drs. Marvin Sugarman and Robert Bunnen of Atlanta).

By all accounts, the meeting quickly spun out of control, with personal accusations coming from both sides. Dean Judson Ward's papers reveal that after the meeting, he sent conciliatory letters to Rabbis Harry Epstein of Ahavath Achim Synagogue and Jacob Rothschild of The Temple. Ward expressed his regrets that the meeting couldn't have ended on a positive note.

Ward learned from Dean Buhler's wife that her husband had left for Buffalo, New York, immediately following the meeting. Two days after the contentious April 3, 1961 meeting of Emory and the Atlanta Jewish leaders, Dean Ward wrote a lengthy letter to Dean Buhler complimenting, consoling, and supporting him. The letter was addressed to the Town House hotel in Buffalo, New York.

One must keep in mind that only two weeks before, Dean Ward had scolded Dr. Buhler for forcing the dental students to sign a form asking them if they had ever experienced discrimination in the school. Ward reportedly told William Schwartz afterwards that it was one of the "most stupid things that anybody could have done."

Now Ward was writing Buhler that he couldn't sleep following the April 3 meeting. "The two-and-a-half-hour session late Monday afternoon, April 3rd, was one of the roughest kinds of experiences I have been through. On Tuesday I didn't call you because I was trying to get myself straightened out. I talked with some of the people around the University. And finally, about five o'clock in the afternoon Marvin Sugarman called me, and after his call I began to feel human again. I called your home to learn what I should already have known and that was you were leaving town and I had missed you.

"I am merely writing this letter to say what I would have said to you over the telephone on Tuesday had I been ready to talk to anybody. And that is simply that I was pleased with the presentation that you made on Monday afternoon and thought that all of our people conducted themselves in a very fine fashion. I was pleased, too, that President Martin made the strong statement that he did at the end, and whether or not any good will come of the meeting we still just have to wait and see. Frankly, I cannot help feeling that a great deal of good will come from it.

"I suppose what I am really trying to let you know is that you have certainly been on my mind a great deal in the past hours, and I did not want you to go a whole week without knowing this. I myself will be out of town most of the two weeks after you have returned to Emory so am very likely not to see you. But this does not mean that I am not with you. I hope you have a good meeting, get away from all this, and return in a fine frame of mind. This is probably what I need at this point."

The very next day, April 6, 1961, Ward sent an interoffice memorandum to President Martin:

"Sam Fried, the jovial dry-cleaning man in the Emory community whom all the students and faculty know and love, showed me the attached letter which he has received from John Buhler. Sam is not making any issue of this and neither am I. The only point he made was: 'This man just makes trouble for himself, Dean Ward.' Sam says that he is covered by insurance, that he apologized for the scratch put on Dean Buhler's car, and that there was no trouble at all. Then he received this stiff official letter from Dean Buhler about his car. He is not offended, but just wanted me to know about it."

Dean Ward just wanted President Martin "to know about it," too. In doing so, he provided the weight that tipped the scale. The following week, on April 21, 1961, Dean Buhler "resigned." It is quite likely that Buhler had seen the writing on the wall and was already looking for a new job in Buffalo. Following Buhler's resignation, Emory's President Martin told newspaper reporters that Buhler was leaving to take a position in the private sector. The position, according to the *Atlanta Journal*, was as vice president and general manager with the Hanau Corporation, a dental manufacturing company headquartered in Buffalo, New York.

Buhler, a year later, suggested in a 24-page handwritten letter to his patron, Goodrich C. White, that it was a Jewish conspiracy that lured him away from Emory dental school. In the February 26, 1962, letter, Buhler mused, "I'd likely be at Emory yet today, not out in the business world, where, ironically, the man who is my 'boss' and who dangled the 'bait' is himself a Jew."

Atlanta newspapers jumped on the story. Emory vigorously denied a connection between Buhler's resignation and the ADL/CRC/Alpha Omega charges of antisemitism. President Martin said that Buhler could have stayed if he wanted to. Emory categorically discounted the charges of antisemitism. The press attempted to get a response from the Jewish community, but its leaders felt that the matter was over and there was no need to reply.

Art Levin didn't conceal his feelings. On April 14, he sent a special delivery letter to ADL headquarters, copying all its top officials: "My own attitude is that Emory University—both the president and the Board of Trustees—have gratuitously and viciously castigated the Jewish community in such a way that an answer—I maintain a public answer—is now imperative. I favor releasing the whole story, including the statistical analysis in detail, to the newspapers. As a lesser alternative, for which at the moment I am not sure I am willing to settle, is an official letter from the Jewish Community Council to the Emory president and chairman of the Board of Trustees indicating in the strongest possible terms our disappointment, displeasure and disgust."

The public heard only one side of the story, Emory's defense of the dean and their denial of any discrimination at the dental school, and they responded accordingly. On April 16, 1961, the Jewish Community Relations Committee received this anonymous letter:

"Let us congratulate you on your crucifixion of Dr. Buhler— you started on Christmas and culminated it on Easter! How appropriate. Incidentally—does your anti-defamation mean only against Jews? Does it automatically give you the right to defame others? Just wondering."

On April 17, 1961, Arthur Levin reported again to the ADL New York office that the Jewish leaders felt "great dismay, distress and disappointment" that Emory's president stated to the reporters that the charges of discrimination were just a misunderstanding. Levin concluded, "However, since Dean Buhler did resign, it was felt that the dental school matter is closed, at least for the time being."

During the next several weeks, the Atlanta Jewish community began to feel a relative sense of calm. The 1958 bombing of the Hebrew Benevolent Temple on Peachtree Street in mid-town Atlanta, followed by the prolonged stress of the Emory dental school episode, had taken its emotional toll. There was still a lingering disappointment and dissatisfaction with Emory's deceitful behavior. And there remained a smoldering disagreement between certain factions of the Jewish community. But Dean Buhler was gone, and the wounds appeared to be healing.

On May 9, 1961, Southeastern ADL Board Chairman Simon Weil of Nashville sent a memo to his regional board expressing pride in Art Levin and the ADL for its role in resolving the Emory dental school matter.

"Because of its vital interest, I want to share with you the following report which I received from Art Levin, Director of the Southeastern Office."

Weil then described the December 16, 1960, meeting of the consortium of Jewish leaders with the president and vice president of Emory University.

He explained that the statistical evidence and affidavits presented at the meeting to the Emory officials were developed by the Southeastern region office of ADL, with the assistance of several Atlanta dentists and the Alpha Omega dental fraternity.

Then Weil detailed the events that followed the December 16 meeting, leading to Dean Buhler's resignation on April 12, 1961. He concluded the three-page memo:

"This brief account obviously cannot do justice to the months of investigation by the Southeastern Regional Office required to develop and substantiate the charges of discrimination, the numerous meetings and the enormous amount of time expended by the various committee members, and the differences of opinion within the Jewish community concerning procedures and tactics to be employed in processing the case. But all this is incidental to the main factor of solidarity of the Jewish community leadership, under the chairmanship of William B. Schwartz, Jr., chairman of the Atlanta CRC, who is also an ADL Regional Board member, and with the unfailing wise counsel and guidance of National Vice-Chairman Abe Goldstein, in pursuing this matter to its conclusion with dignity and strength of conviction."

On May 23, 1961, the Atlanta Community Relations Committee held its monthly meeting. Art Levin attended the meeting and described it in a letter written the following day to Arnold Forster, Benjamin Epstein, and Alex Miller at the national headquarters.

"The first item on the agenda was a report from the Chairman, William B. Schwartz, Jr., about the conclusion of the Emory University School of Dentistry matter. Mr. Schwartz read a letter from President Martin and announced that as far as the CRC was concerned, the matter was closed. There followed a round of congratulations among the members of the CRC for a job well done, mutual praise, and general backslapping. The ADL was never mentioned, shape or form as having existed in the situation.

"The chairman then stated that he would make some privileged remarks. I settled back for some kudos. Mr. Schwartz then launched into a severe attack upon me and ADL for having the temerity for having reported the Emory matter to the Southeastern Regional Board. Mr. Schwartz stated that I had no right to report this matter, which was confidential, that I had no right to use the information which ADL turned over to the CRC, which then became CRC property and was privileged for exclusive use of the CRC, and especially condemned me for attaching to the report the statement of the Jewish Community Council to Emory University detailing the evidence of discrimination.
"I couldn't believe my ears and asked the chairman whether he wasn't joking. He answered that he was not only dead serious, but that ADL had betrayed the confidence of the CRC. I then

said a number of things, including facts of how I had to fight with the CRC to even present our case to Emory University after having developed the entire case and presenting it to the CRC. Without going into the gory details, I ended by saying that I had gone out of my way in every step of the matter to furnish utmost cooperation in the best possible sense to the CRC, and if this represented 'a betrayal of the CRC,' then it was impossible to cooperate with the CRC and I would no longer try."

Levin issued an ultimatum: "I have attended my last meeting of the CRC. If it is considered essential that someone represent the ADL office in future CRC meetings, it will have to be someone else than me, I cannot further jeopardize my health or sanity by exposing myself to this type of vituperation."

This was Art Levin's last recorded correspondence in the ADL files. It was his misfortune to be the central figure in a Jewish organizational turf war in Atlanta that was also playing out in other American cities. The local establishment felt that it was their exclusive right to determine political and social strategies, and they deeply resented outside organizations threatening their autonomy.

Levin had served the ADL and his community faithfully and effectively for many years, and was highly regarded by his board, professional coworkers, and local and state law-enforcement officers. Levin had exposed a decades-long travesty at Emory and contributed to the downfall of the principal perpetrator. He resented Emory's failure to take the blame. In openly indicting the university, he crossed over a line that even his strongest supporters weren't prepared to traverse. He misjudged the willingness of his own people to challenge the power structure. One of his superiors counseled him, "Opposing Emory in Atlanta is like going against the Vatican in Boston."

Levin took a formal leave of absence from his Atlanta ADL director's position in the summer of 1961. The ADL in Atlanta hired an interim director, Richard Shapiro, as Levin weighed his options. *The Southern*

Israelite reported that on April 4, 1962, the Atlanta Metropolitan Council of B'nai B'rith, the two women's chapters, and the two men's chapters of B'nai B'rith honored Levin at the Mayfair Club for his 15 years of service to the Atlanta and Southeastern Jewish communities. It was announced that Levin was assuming a position with responsibilities in developing human relations as a consultant in Washington, DC.

Buhler Has Second Thoughts

John Buhler regretted his decision the moment he resigned as dean. In his letters back to friends at Emory, he told them that even though he was making more money, he had to consider his pride. He complained: "I'm a dentist —more than that, I was the dean, and now I'm selling dental equipment. My true calling is in dental education. If I can't be dean, I'll do anything. I'll even be a teacher." Buhler knew that the position had already been offered to Dr. George Moulton, the head of the crown and bridge department, but he hoped that decision could be reversed. He soon learned that the door to his former office was closed.

But Dr. Buhler didn't give up. The University of Iowa dental school was seeking a new dean, and Buhler flew to Des Moines for an interview. On March 8, 1962, Buhler thanked Dr. Goodrich C. White for his strong letter of recommendation for the position and wrote that, at his interview at Iowa, he had been told he was on the short list.

The Omaha office of the Anti-Defamation League was also interested in Buhler's application. They contacted Edward Zerin, rabbi of Temple B'nai Jeshurun of Des Moines, who was an active member of the ADL board. After a thorough briefing, Zerin succeeded in obtaining a meeting with the Iowa dental school selection committee. The chairman of the committee informed Zerin that they were receiving conflicting reports from Atlanta about Dean Buhler. The Emory dental school officials, including a Jewish member of the faculty, were strongly endorsing Dr. Buhler, while the Atlanta ADL officials were vigorously opposing him.

Rabbi Zerin quickly wrote his Atlanta colleague, Jacob Rothschild, the rabbi of the Hebrew Benevolent Temple, the Jewish house of worship that had been bombed four years earlier. Zerin's original letter, dated March 21, 1962, and a copy of Rothschild's letter of reply, can be found in the Rothschild archives at Emory University. Zerin was soliciting Rothschild's knowledge of the controversial events surrounding Dean Buhler.

Rabbi Rothschild replied that he was on the committee that presented the matter to the president of Emory University: "I, for my part am convinced that the statistics compiled by the ADL and presented through the Atlanta Jewish Community Council were conclusive and irrefutable." Additionally, Rothschild stated, "The Jewish dentist who serves as a member of the faculty holds the position that the reason for the large number of flunk outs was because the better Jewish students don't attend Emory dental school. This, he says, is because there has been an undercurrent rumor about the dean and the school and therefore the better men steer clear of the place. This, according to him, explains the inordinate percentage of those who are in school failing or are forced to repeat their work. I was convinced from reading the report prepared by us that there was a definite record of antisemitism at the dental school during the tenure of Dean Buhler. I do not know anything about Buhler personally, but, as the head of the school, he was certainly responsible for the policy which existed." Rabbi Zerin immediately reported his findings to the Iowa special committee.

Less than a week later, Buhler and his wife Ruth arrived in Atlanta for the annual Hinman Dental Society meeting, the third largest dental meeting in the United States. Buhler's new employer, the Hanau Engineering Company, occupied its usual prime location (Booth No. 89) in the Hinman exhibition hall.

This would be the first year that Buhler attended the Hinman meeting, not as a dean, but instead hawking dental products. That alone was embarrassing enough, but during the meeting he would be further humiliated. The March 26th afternoon edition of the Atlanta Journal announced the publication of a new book about antisemitism in America, *Some of My Best Friends*. The 11th chapter was devoted to the alleged discrimination at the Emory dental school from 1948 to 1961, and the resultant resignation of its dean, Dr. John Buhler. The news of the book spread throughout the Hinman exhibition hall and lecture rooms, and even further. On April 2, Russell Weintraub, a prominent Iowa law professor followed up on Rabbi Zerin's earlier visit to the Iowa dental school. Professor Weintraub met with the chairman of the selection committee, Dr. Daniel Waite, and presented Dr. Waite a copy of *Some of My Best Friends*, directing him specifically to the chapter concerning Dr. Buhler and the Emory dental school. Soon afterwards, Dr. Buhler was informed that Iowa had chosen another candidate for the position.

Following the Hinman dental meeting, Buhler told his close friends that the news article had a devastating effect on his wife Ruth, who had accompanied him to the meeting. He wrote Dr. Goodrich White that it had taken Ruth a year to get over their leaving the school, and this had given them both an unmerciful shock. "We are shocked at the cupidity which was involved and the disregard for truth or for morality. But this is the way 'folks'—some folks, that is—seem to work." When Buhler used the term "folks" in his letters to Dr. White, it was often a reference to Jews. White, in turn, adopted the expression when replying to Buhler, occasionally substituting the term "your friends."

Was the relationship between Buhler, the scheming opportunist, and White, the aloof intellectual, genuine? Aristotle would have said no, because of their wicked ways. The highest form of friendship, according to the philosopher's foundational Nicomachean Ethics, is the bond formed when people are mutually drawn to each other's virtue.

Alexander Nehamas, a philosophy professor at Princeton, would disagree. He cites Thelma & Louise, Bonnie and Clyde. Mr. Nehamas proposes that we can certainly experience friendship where there is immorality, because moral values are only one aspect of human life. Equally important are values such as love, friendship, individuality, and beauty. He goes so far as to say that "immorality may sometimes be part and parcel of a good friendship.[55]

Buhler continued his quest to become a dean, only to be rejected, sometimes at the last minute. He enumerated the supposed reasons to his colleague, William C. Fleming, dean of the University of California dental school. "I don't have a college degree. I don't have a graduate degree except dentistry." He also didn't have a specialty in dentistry, and didn't have a research background. At one time he had some connections with the ADA, but most of them were not there anymore. Buhler commented sarcastically: "In the health services these days, you have to be identified with 'test tubes, electron microscopes and experimental animals'."

Buhler's Comeback

Buhler had incessant correspondence with Goodrich White, who was now Chancellor of Emory. Reminiscent of many of his previous letters, Buhler's letter of January 30, 1964, began with "I need you to do something for me, if you will...." This time it was about the proposed new dental school at the University of South Carolina.

Buhler asked for White's help, and Dr. White replied that he would help him again. Buhler told White that his friend, Dr. John Douglass, a graduate of the Atlanta-Southern Dental College and a prosperous cattle breeder, was sponsoring him for the deanship of the new South Carolina dental school. Buhler provided a letter for White to copy verbatim and stipulated that the letter should be sent "To whom it may concern." Buhler further explained, "They told me I have to do it that way. It has to be behind the scenes. They're going to get me through the back door. It has to be secret, hush-hush."

White wrote the "To whom it may concern" letter on February 3, 1964 as he had been instructed. Henry Bowden, chairman of the Emory Board of Trustees, joined forces with White on behalf of Buhler. Bowden agreed to lobby South Carolina Governor Donald Russell on Buhler's behalf.

Bowden and others felt that former President Martin was at fault for the bad publicity Emory had received and for Buhler's forced resignation. They disapproved of the way Martin had responded to the newspapers and the negative publicity that ensued. Bowden, White, and others thought President Martin should have acted more forcefully. He shouldn't have just stonewalled. He shouldn't have allowed the Jewish community leaders into his office in the first place. To make amends, Bowden and White were going to rally around Dr. Buhler and restore his dignity and his title. If they were successful, he would become "Dean Buhler" once again.

By way of brilliant maneuvering, Douglass and his political allies were able to circumvent the usual vetting process, and successfully obtained Buhler's appointment by the Medical Board as the first dean of South Carolina's dental school. The appointment stirred controversy throughout the state. Dr. Joseph E. Wallace, President of the South Carolina Dental Association, told reporters that the dental association had not even been consulted about the appointment.

The Charleston Jewish Community Relations Council was stunned at the announcement, having had no previous warning. They called for an emergency session and released an immediate protest to the appointment, asking that it be rescinded. The Columbia, South Carolina B'nai B'rith chapter convened an emergency meeting, but their response was more subdued. A former Emory dental student, now a lawyer, who attended the meeting wrote, "I recall that the meeting was very heated, but I left because I was angry that the feeling was 'let's not make waves.'" In the end, the Columbia B'nai B'rith lodge joined the Charleston lodge in officially protesting Buhler's appointment.

A year later, the Jewish community of Charleston was still in lively discussion over the Buhler appointment. They reported to the ADL that the South Carolina legislature had appropriated funds for the dental school, but federal funds had not yet been obtained. They wrote, "Dr. Buhler is acting dean of a nonexistent school."

At first exuberant, Buhler soon became despondent. He discovered that the proposed dental school was a political football. The politicians were more concerned about where the school would be built (Columbia or Charleston) than about who would be dean. Buhler complained that he was not being treated respectfully in the planning process. He despaired at his future prospects and began making contingent plans.

In one of his letters to Goodrich White, Buhler writes, "I am hopeful that the Jewish commotion has faded out...at least I have heard nothing for some weeks now. You folks in Atlanta did a masterful job of putting the whole thing in proper perspective and in straightening out some miserable lies. Actually, from what I hear from my dentist friends over there, the 'backlash' from all that stuff was most damaging to the Jews themselves. It sure did show one thing: while they seem to be one's 'dearest friends' and all that, when the time comes to stand up and be counted, somehow they just 'ain't' there. Was a right disappointing thing to witness."

He continued, "All hell broke loose when I did appoint Marvin Sugarman to the faculty...all HELL from both sides. There were a significant number of folks around the school and out among the practicing profession who really gave me a fit for putting a Jew on the faculty...and Sugarman was the first one to ever hold faculty appointment in that school. But if you think the gentiles raised a fuss, you should have heard the commotion the Goldsteins raised...for they thoroughly detested Sugarman.

"Sugarman used to try to entertain us...we did on the few occasions we would permit...they sure gave us a 'big play' for several years and we had to be pretty discreet to avoid getting taken in too much by them and yet not insult them. But when that crowd let loose their 'expert' in agitation, Sugarman, Bunnen, Benveniste, Wenger and Weichselbaum all ran for cover. Oh well, just so it keeps quiet...and I pray it does."

By 1965, the Southeastern ADL office in Atlanta received information of Dr. Buhler's consideration and possible appointment as the first dean of the proposed College of Dentistry of the University of Florida, scheduled to open in 1972. They exchanged numerous letters with Florida alumni, guaranteeing an effective opposition to a Buhler candidacy. Buhler endured multiple obstacles and challenges before finally realizing his goal. After three years of his laying the groundwork, the Medical University of South Carolina College of Dental Medicine was able to matriculate the first class of 24 in temporary facilities in the fall of 1967.

Buhler suffered a heart attack shortly after the school occupied its new facilities in January 1971. He was unable to continue his daily duties as dean but was allowed to present diplomas to the graduating seniors.

Dr. Herbert Butts, a senior faculty member, was appointed interim dean following Buhler's heart attack. I interviewed Dr. Butts in Memphis, Tennessee, on October 25, 2011. Butts, whom I had known during my dental school days at UT, was loyal to his former dean but sat back for three hours recalling the constant infighting at the school during Buhler's tenure as dean.

"Dr. Buhler told me that the internal bickering reminded him of Emory dental school when he arrived there in 1948. He told me that he had to knock heads. I think that he enjoyed exercising his power. John had numerous requests to speak at dental society meetings and community service organizations such as Kiwanis and Rotary. He loved the limelight. But when the Negro dental society asked him to address their group, he wasn't interested. He knew that I was raised in a rural community 70 miles from Nashville and grew up comfortable around all people. So, he designated me to take him off the hook."

On June 21, 1971, Buhler received a letter from his longtime supporter, Dr. John Douglass. "Want you to know that I am grateful for what you have done for all phases of dentistry in South Carolina. However, I do feel a guilt of conscience for my part in bringing you here, resulting in a permanent impairment of your health."

On August 14, 1971, Douglass, responding to Buhler's reply, wrote in a handwritten letter to Buhler from his farm in Douglass, South Carolina. "Thank you for your nice kind letter and for your kind comments and acceptance of facts attributable to you. Read with interest the historical data forwarded to me relating to obstacles and difficulties encountered in creating the school. Don't be the least bit perturbed over any reaction by the

Jews. I have been at war with them since Rosen was president of the coastal society. I attended his meeting while president and saw it dominated by Jews even to the extent of one trying to sell an insurance program.

"My belief has always been that the Jews would work toward self-aggrandizement. They were motivated by an intense desire to hold office. It has been illustrated by Rosen [Jack Rosen from Charleston] and that other loud mouth Jew [presumably referring to Leon Feldman from Charleston] becoming presidents. Up until that time the association never had but one Jewish President, Wineburg [*sic*] from Sumter."

Buhler responded on August 17, 1971. "Many thanks for your welcome letter of the 14th. Ruth and I both enjoyed it a lot and got a big kick about your observations relative to some of the Charleston crowd. I'll bet one thing, however, and that is that the Profession in the State is relieved that most of those characters—the majority by far—are concentrated in Charleston. At least you all don't have to live with them. They are for sure 'something else again.'"

Buhler maintained an office at the school for two more years, but his failing health prevented him from remaining any longer. Buhler died on April 18, 1976, in Charleston. His obituary in the 1976 summer issue of the South Carolina Dental Journal stated that he was laid to rest in the cemetery of the historic St. Philip's Episcopal Church, near the tomb of the immortal John C. Calhoun, whom he greatly admired.

Ruth, Buhler's wife, remarried after her husband died. Their daughter Karen far surpassed her father's expectations. He often wrote to his friends that he was skeptical that she could complete her academic nursing program. In fact, she became a distinguished professor of community health at the University of Pennsylvania School of Nursing, where she taught from 1972 until her death in 2006. It was Karen who donated her father's papers to the Medical University of South Carolina library.

In his letters to friends, Buhler also expressed his concern for his son's indecision in choosing an academic career. Nevertheless, Dr. John E. Buhler Jr. had a notable career in the military followed by many successful years as an oral surgeon in Indiana, his father's birthplace.

CHAPTER 14

A Cold Case Defrosted

B y early 2011, I had collected evidence that convinced me the Emory dental school story, for so long a cold case, should be further defrosted. I had reason to believe that additional archival material was awaiting my discovery. I had already recorded testimony of a sizable number of students who were victimized, and I had acquired ample evidence that they were targeted for antisemitic reasons. I also knew that to reopen the case, I would have to be much more aggressive than my predecessors and risk upsetting the status quo. To me, it was more than a story; it was a crime. But how was it viewed at the time? I would need to understand the past before moving forward. There were two sources of information—recorded documents and live testimony.

News of the dental school controversy was narrowly confined to the leadership of the two principal adversaries, Emory University and the Atlanta office of the Anti-Defamation League. For *shalom bayit* (peace in the family), the ADL was operating under the mantle of the Atlanta Jewish Community Council.

Emory did not publicize the conflict through any of its official organs. For them it was an irritant, a virtual non-issue. The proceedings of Emory's Board of Trustees were confidential and remain so to this day.

Under the leadership of Arthur J. Levin, the Atlanta office of the ADL shared its activities only with its local board, its Southeastern regional board, and its national office in New York. They never leaked news of their inquiry to local newspaper reporters or to sources outside their organization.

The Atlanta Jewish Community Council was the nominal leader of the Jewish coalition and was initially hostile to the ADL's efforts to confront Emory with the dental school issue. Their members were tight-lipped. Even the rabbinic members of their subcommittee, who were privy to the charges of antisemitism, never mentioned the issue in sermons from their pulpits. We will see later that there was outside interest from the National Jewish Community Relations Advisory Council (NCRAC), but they refrained from interfering in local politics.

The attitude and behavior of the leaders of these four cohorts shaped the landscape available for inspection by future historians. The following is a summary of their distinctly different opinions, culled from organizational archives and newspaper accounts.

Historical Summary of Events

ADL's Art Levin, alone, believed the Jewish dental students when they claimed they had been discriminated against at Emory dental school. When Levin presented his statistical findings to his superiors, they told him that, in their opinion, it was prima facie evidence of systemic antisemitism in the Emory dental school. However, they advised him that should Emory go to court, he would need additional data on the non-Jewish students. He obtained that information, and along with community leaders, made a formal presentation to the Emory administration. The ADL certainly believed that a crime had been committed.

Emory disagreed. On December 16, 1960, a delegation from the Jewish community met with Emory President S. Walter Martin, at which time they presented charges of antisemitism at the Emory dental school. Dr. Martin responded that he had found previous charges unwarranted.

On April 3, 1961, President Martin presided over a meeting between the organized Atlanta Jewish community, the Emory administration, and officials and faculty members of the Emory dental school. The

Jewish leaders once again made charges of antisemitism. Following the meeting, Dr. Martin issued a letter stating that the charges were not sufficiently backed by evidence.

After Dean John Buhler offered his resignation on April 12, 1961, President Martin, responding to inquiries from the press, asserted that the charges of antisemitism against Dean Buhler were unfounded. On April 25, 1961, President Martin wrote to William Schwartz, chairman of the Jewish Community Relations Committee: "You brought to our attention a matter that involved principles which are important to all of us. We are hopeful that every member of your group has been reassured of the firm policy of this University to treat all students alike."

Martin disregarded all the statistics that had been provided to the university showing that 65% of Jewish students had been flunked out or had to repeat one or more years over a 10-year period. Instead, he sidestepped years of discrimination and listed only one single violation that he was willing to acknowledge: "We earnestly hope that such embarrassing lapses as the grossly misworded application blank will not recur. We are sincerely sorry for the resentment this sheet has caused."

Thus, it is safe to say that Emory University, with President Martin as its spokesman, was either consistent in their belief, or at least in their action, that no crime had been committed.

Throughout the prolonged controversy, Atlanta's Jewish leaders were measured in their actions, and even compliant. They were willing to let bygones be bygones. But when Emory publicly stiff-armed them, an angry minority threatened to go public with the real story. Responding immediately, two Jewish members of the Emory Board of Visitors were sent to quell the uprising. They left no room for discussion, demanding, "You will accept Emory's position as 'understandable face saving.'" The Jews were left to console themselves with the knowledge that the dean was gone. As described in the ADL publication *Some of My Best Friends*, when the dean was gone, "here the matter rested."

The general Jewish community interpreted the acquiescence of the Jewish leaders as acknowledgement that yet another crisis was averted.

Among the majority of Jews, there was not a strong impression that a major crime had been committed.

The outside Jewish community was certainly aware of the problems in Atlanta. But they had formally distanced themselves from what they considered a local issue. After the dust had settled, Philip Jacobson, chairman of NCRAC, the National Jewish Community Relations Advisory Council, wrote a brief congratulatory letter to William Schwartz Jr., chairman of the Atlanta Community Relations Committee. No mention was made of Schwartz's affiliation with NCRAC, where he subsequently served as a national vice president.

"My colleagues and I at the NCRAC have been following with a great deal of interest—and admiration—the activities of your Community Relations Committee in respect to the problem at Emory University. We want to congratulate you and your colleagues on the truly remarkable result achieved, and equally important, the manner in which that result was reached. We want to commend you particularly for the vigorous and intelligent leadership you provided. If it were not for the very confidential nature of these negotiations, I am sure all of our member agencies would benefit immeasurably from a study of this very difficult and delicate case history." NCRAC did not for a moment consider that a crime had been committed. It was merely "a very difficult and delicate case history." They praised it as a classic example of conflict resolution.

Different Sides of the Story

Arthur J. Levin was 93 years old when my wife Shirley and I met him on Monday afternoon, July 19, 2010. I had called him six days earlier to ask for an interview, and we wasted no time driving to Coral Gables, Florida, when he finally agreed.

I imagined playing the role of the legendary television host Ralph Edwards, the creator and master of ceremonies of *This Is Your Life,* the American reality show on NBC television from 1952 to 1961. In the program, the host would surprise a guest and then take him through a retrospective of his life in front of an audience, including appearances by colleagues, friends, and family.

We set up our recording studio in Levin's attractive 12th-floor apartment, where he allowed us to intrude into a life he had long left behind. From my research, I was able to walk him through his early professional career, reminding him of his numerous accomplishments. He smiled and observed, "You know more about me than I do."

I quickly re-explained to Mr. Levin who I was, and why I was so interested in the story at this late point in my life. He was 15 years older than I, but still amazingly alert. Even so, it was initially difficult for him to accommodate to the time warp. I patiently drew a timeline for him. He narrowed his eyes and took in a deep breath when I told him that I was kicked out of the dental school just three years before he became ADL Southeastern director in the Atlanta office. At a certain point, I could tell that he was just as excited and interested in the story as I was. Whenever facts seemed not to jibe, he would stop, recalculate, and move on. When his memory failed him, he insisted on relying on the chronological accuracy of the documents. I knew that I could rely on Art Levin for an honest account of the dental school controversy.

What I also knew was that Art left behind a host of friends and enemies when he moved out of Atlanta in 1962. Their silence was a testament to the truth he had uncovered. His allies refused to forget, and his detractors conspired to deny.

"When I left Atlanta, I never looked back," Levin told me. "I put the entire experience, satisfying as it was at first and painful as it turned out to be later, behind me."

As we reminisced, I reminded him that he had proved his case by presenting his startling statistical analysis, intentionally avoiding listing the students' names. I reminded him, "When the Emory situation was resolved, the victims were never recognized. We were forgotten. No one from the Jewish community or from the Emory administration sought to reach out to us."

Wistfully, as if it were the first time this idea had ever occurred to him, he replied, "Nor did I."

Levin was silent and composed as I recounted events one year after his departure. I told him that the ADL published *Some of My Best Friends*, a comprehensive exposé of discrimination in America. The 11th chapter was devoted to the scandal at Emory dental school. The authors, Benjamin Epstein and Arnold Forster, used the information Art Levin had compiled, without crediting him by name. When the book was reviewed in the *Atlanta Journal-Constitution* on March 26, 1962, all hell broke loose again. Emory and its friends attacked the ADL for reopening the "false charges" against them. I recounted for Levin how the various articles in local publications were sharp in their condemnation of the Jews.

I told him that, the next day, bold headlines read, "Anti-Jewish Bias At Emory Denied. Emory University President S. Walter Martin said flatly that charges of anti-Semitism on the part of the University are false." The general community criticized the Jewish community. Reeling from the criticism, the Atlanta CRC threatened to expel the ADL from Atlanta for rekindling the dental school story. The fallout was enormous on both sides.

I reminded Art that he sold his home and left Atlanta with his family on April 5, 1962. Soon afterwards, on April 19, having lost support of the Emory Board of Trustees, Emory President S. Walter Martin was pressured to resign.

The Jewish community leaders again felt betrayed by Emory officials, whom they knew to be denying the truth. But they remembered the bitter aftermath of the Leo Frank case (1913-1915) and the 1958 bombing of the Hebrew Benevolent Temple. They decided to fold their tents and allow the conflict to fade away. The silence lasted 50 years.

In a flash, I had brought Art Levin up to date.

After I returned to Atlanta, Levin sent me email updates as past events and dates came to mind. On July 31, 2010, my new friend sent a very sweet note thanking me for all the material I was sending him. "You are resurrecting my life for me—long forgotten events, meetings, reports, articles. What my grandson will make of this ancient history, or even be interested, is questionable. But I am enjoying it."

Our correspondence continued with lengthy phone and email conversations. It didn't take Levin long to roll back the years and focus on the five or six years he dedicated to fighting on behalf of the dental students. "I believed them. Nobody else believed them." Ironically, because he had based his case on statistics, he never developed a personal bond with any particular student.

Levin displayed emotion when speaking of Morris Abram. "He was a bright young lawyer and one of my board members. He got us the appointment with the president of Emory." He fondly remembered Dr. Marvin Goldstein, who spent long hours helping him accumulate the information on the Jewish students. "But he couldn't get the other dentists to agree to help me." Levin had a total distrust of the Jewish establishment. "During our meeting with the president and vice president of Emory, I presented our charges. They told us that they were shocked. The vice president kept repeating that the Jewish member of the faculty had assured him that there wasn't any antisemitism in the school. I told him that we considered the Jewish faculty member an apologist for the dean and that he was talking out of both sides of his mouth. Then the president promised us that he would talk again with Dean Buhler. So, the committee members left the meeting deciding to give the school more time to solve the problem. I said to them, 'Screw that. You're going to give them more time while they're flunking our boys'?"

Reflecting back, Levin displayed some understanding of their position. "I understood that they didn't want an outsider telling them what to do or how to handle things. But I was hired to defend against discrimination no matter where it came from, and I wasn't going to sit back while those poor students were getting slaughtered. It was the same with the 1958 Temple bombing. The Jewish Council wanted to handle it themselves. The FBI and the reporters came to me because I knew what was going on with the KKK. We at the ADL released a statement linking the Klan with the NSRP, the National States Rights Party, and I was criticized for speaking out. The CRC wanted me to clear everything with them before making any statements."

During my lengthy discussions with Art Levin, Dr. Harlan Horner's name never came up. I had to ask Art what he knew about Horner. Levin had never heard of him. He, like everyone else, including his superiors at the ADL in New York, had focused on the situation at Emory and had never considered the situation at Emory as part of a wider conspiracy, one that had been conceived and carried out by Dr. Horner and his cronies. They proceeded apparently unaware that Horner and his committee had already carried out their plan in Atlanta, Philadelphia, Washington, Baltimore, and elsewhere two years before they were exposed in the *New York Times* on February 7, 1945.

I returned to Florida on June 20, 2011, for a follow-up interview with Levin. By then, I had shared my information with the national ADL, and they had already sent their Florida director to reunite with their former colleague. It was a long-overdue meeting and resulted in a positive reconciliation. They were prepared to honor Levin at their national meeting, but Levin's health prevented him from attending. He died on April 3, 2013, 10 days short of his 96th birthday.

******

William B. Schwartz Jr. was a lifelong resident of Atlanta. For most of his business career he was associated with National Service Industries Inc., where he was a board member as well as president of the Zep Manufacturing Company division. His close friends and family called him Billy.

Schwartz was an active supporter of Jimmy Carter's presidential campaign and was appointed ambassador to the Bahamas, where he served from 1977-1981. Younger friends addressed him as "Ambassador." "Call me Bill," he would insist when I interviewed him about his years serving as chairman of the Jewish Community Relations Council.

When I called him from my car in early November 2009, Bill Schwartz and his wife Sonia were preparing to depart for their 40th annual winter stay at their Gulf Coast home in Sarasota, Florida. We had spoken earlier in the month, and he had agreed to talk with me about his tenure on the Community Relations Council back in the late 1950s and early 1960s. He didn't at that time mention that he would soon be leaving town.

I told Schwartz that I had assembled some documents. I was in the vicinity, and I was eager to show them to him. He courteously told me that he could only spend a few minutes with me, but that we could talk later by long-distance. I felt an urgency to see the ambassador, but I knew that a brief visit would be fruitless. I also felt that his wife would not appreciate the last-minute intrusion. So, I agreed to give him a call later in the week.

Then I had another thought.

I drove up to the back entrance of the Schwartz's high-rise Peachtree Road residence and handed over the large package of documents to the concierge stationed just inside the entrance. He assured me that he would personally deliver the package to the ambassador.

As I was driving away, I received a call. "Why didn't you come up?" Schwartz asked. I told him that I didn't want to inconvenience him. "After you get settled," I suggested, "take a good look at the documents and give me a call at your convenience. Then we can get together after you return."

I called my friend Betty Ann Jacobson to get Bill Schwartz's Florida phone number. Betty and her late husband Harvey knew the Schwartzes socially. They were also fellow members of The Temple and had a business connection through the National Linen Company. Betty was known as the consummate community volunteer and offered me valuable insights into the mindset of the men and women serving on the Community Relations Committee and the Jewish Community Council.

Over the winter months, Bill Schwartz and I had several phone conversations. He repeatedly reminded me that his chairmanship of the Jewish Community Relations Committee was just one of many volunteer positions he held, and that he wasn't able to recall specific details of the subjects I was interested in. At the same time, he was able to recall countless details of many other unrelated topics, but he chose to avoid discussing the dental school matter. "That was only one of many things going on at that time," he said. "I was president of The Temple at the time of the bombing in 1958. That was another thing that I was dealing with."

Picking up on that subject, I told Schwartz that Melissa Fay Greene, in her 1996 book *The Temple Bombing*, made a passing reference to the Emory dental school. On page 190, she wrote, referring to Rabbi Jacob Rothschild: "But to his congregants, the rabbi seemed to be out of touch with their quiet daily struggles to keep at bay the pariah status surrounding Jewishness. They might have enjoyed hearing from Rothschild that he was working behind the scenes to end the religious barriers at the golf clubs, the law firms, or at the dental school."

"When I read that," I said to Schwartz, "I wondered who the congregants were that might have given Melissa Fay Greene that insight. I'm sure Greene must have interviewed you when writing her book. Were you one of the congregants she referred to who asked the hypothetical question about the dental school?"

The ambassador deftly avoided my effort to make a connection. He closed off the discussion by replying, "She asked me lots of questions, and she didn't quote me on a single one." (In fact, he is quoted at least twice in *The Temple Bombing* and Melissa told me that his insights informed a number of scenes.)

We spoke one last time soon after his return to Atlanta. Citing medical problems, he canceled a planned meeting but promised to get together with me as soon as his problems were resolved. Unfortunately, that meeting didn't occur. Schwartz died peacefully on May 18, 2010, at Piedmont Hospital. He was 88 years old.

******

In the spring of 2010, Marvin Sugarman, in what would be the last year of his life, asked a friend to invite me to his home, where he was confined to a hospital bed. He had heard that I was researching the dental school story and presumably wanted to tell me his side of the story. This was two years before the Emory University apology on October 10, 2012. I was prepared with a video camera, audio recorder, camera, and note pad. He kept me waiting for some time, as he had numerous attendants, friends, and visitors coming in and out of his room. Charming and cordial, he welcomed me with a scratchy yet hearty voice and a strong handshake.

Sugarman had prepared for the interview by having available numerous scrapbooks of his family and professional life. Even though he was the one who caused our meeting to be delayed, I was only offered an hour of his time, as he would be having lunch in an hour followed by a bridge game. He encouraged me to photograph plaques and certificates of his lifetime accomplishments while he embellished on the particulars of each event.

I managed to direct some of the conversation to the phases of his dental career in which I was most interested. I had prepared an outline for the intended interview, but I soon realized this would have to wait for another day. He rewarded my patience. He agreed to another date at which, he assured me, I would be allowed to conduct a more formal interview. I realized that I would have to assert myself at the next meeting. We mutually agreed to continue the interview two weeks later on May 11, 2010.

The second interview lasted over an hour and a half. There were very few outside interruptions. I was able to ask a broad range of questions, but Marvin Sugarman was determined to control the conversation. He continued to place the antisemitism at the dental school at the doorstep of Dr. Ralph Byrnes, who was dean when he was a dental student. Sugarman insisted that Buhler merely picked up where Byrnes left off. He reiterated that Buhler was too dumb to have an original idea. He repeatedly characterized Buhler as "the dumbest white man I have ever met." He said that, in private, his wife Rose Sugarman always labeled Buhler as a *gornisht*, a Yiddish term for "a nothing."

There were certain thoughts Marvin wanted to convey, or to explain, or perhaps exculpate his activities and behavior regarding the dental school. To dispel any thought that he was complicit in the antisemitism at the school, he repeatedly cited his Jewishness. "I never drank a drop of water on Yom Kippur, and I never ate a piece of bread on Passover." Sugarman's not joining the Alpha Omega (AO) Jewish dental fraternity was obviously a contentious issue. Sugarman described coming home after his first day in school and revealing to his mother that he didn't join Alpha Omega. "I told Momma that I wanted to join Psi Omega. 'Not and live here,' she said. My mother scolded me for not joining the Jewish fraternity. 'You can't go against the Jews,'" she said. Despite his mother's admonition, Sugarman knowingly made his bed and was prepared to sleep in it.

The more he talked, the more it became obvious that Marvin Sugarman resented Dr. Irving Goldstein, and over time had come to intensely dislike him. Goldstein, a native Atlantan, was 12 years his senior. He was the founding member of the Atlanta chapter of the AO national Jewish fraternity and was perceived to be Atlanta's most prominent Jewish dentist. Sugarman decided that he would prefer being independent rather than living under Goldstein's shadow for the rest of his professional and social career. Sugarman disparaged Irving Goldstein personally and professionally. He allowed himself to extend his animosity to Irving's younger brother, Marvin. Both Marvins, Sugarman and Goldstein, graduated from Atlanta-Southern Dental College in 1938. From that point on, their paths diverged. Nevertheless, Sugarman took the time to denigrate his former classmate. At the end of one of his denunciations, he said, "The best part of Marvin was his wife, Rita."

Sugarman said that the Goldsteins were upset because he had received an appointment to the dental school faculty, and they had not. He said that they spread the rumor that Buhler was an antisemite when in fact

Buhler was only continuing the quota begun by the real antisemite, his predecessor, Dr. Ralph Byrnes. Sugarman repeated his mantra: "Buhler was too dumb to be an antisemite."

Continuing his testimony, Sugarman said that the Goldsteins openly encouraged Jewish boys to go to Northern dental schools and urged their fellow Alpha Omegans around the country to do the same. This resulted, he said, in a lower quality of Jewish students at Emory, and this was the cause of the high Jewish failure rate.

Sugarman seemed eager to share a revelation. "I often wondered why Irving Goldstein sent his son Ronny to Emory. His good friend, Myron Aisenberg, was the dean at Maryland. Why didn't he send him there?" Sugarman answered his own question. "I finally figured it out. If Ronny went to Emory and was flunked out, Irving could blame it on antisemitism." He returned to his theme. "Irving and Marvin, both of them, were liars. They would tell you it was Friday and the sun was shining, when you could look out and see that it was Tuesday and it was raining." Sugarman also blamed the ADL for targeting Buhler and for encouraging young men to apply to other schools. "That's when I quit giving money to the ADL." Sugarman claimed that the Jewish acceptance rate increased after he became a faculty member. I showed him the data and the graphs indicating that the Jewish flunk-out rate was astronomical during his time on the faculty. "That's because the best Jewish students went to other dental schools." I asked Sugarman if he socialized with Dean Buhler. "Oh, sure. We ate over at their house. He was self-promoting—only thought of himself. He didn't like his wife and she didn't like him. Actually, the best part of Buhler was his wife. She was a nice lady." I showed Marvin an ADL document explaining how Dr. John Buhler, labeled an antisemite by the Charleston, South Carolina, Jewish community leaders, finally succeeded in 1965 in being appointed dean of the new dental school in South Carolina. The inter-office memo indicated that Dr. Buhler's final hurdle was surmounted when the Jewish faculty member at Emory dental school endorsed Buhler's candidacy. I asked Marvin, "Do you remember that?" "Sure, I remember," he instantly replied. "When Buhler left Emory, they called me from South Carolina and asked me if I thought Buhler was antisemitic. I said no, he's just dumb. They told me they didn't care if he was dumb. They just wanted to be sure he wasn't antisemitic. 'We need someone who is experienced. But we just want you to tell us he's not antisemitic.' I said, 'He's too dumb to be antisemitic.'"

Sugarman summed up the interview: "I think you and I agree on about 99% of the things we talked about," he said. "I agree with you that Buhler probably was an antisemite, but I think he really was anti-almost everything. He never gave anybody credit for anything. He was just interested in promoting himself. Arch McEwen and George Parry were on the faculty. They were about the nicest people you would ever meet. What did Buhler do? He fired them. I told you—he was the dumbest white man I ever met. Now you see what I mean? I just wanted you to hear the other side of the story."

Dr. Marvin Sugarman passed away six months later at age 95.

******

Mrs. Charlotte Rothenberg Wilen was arguably the most important Jewish female community social worker in Atlanta history. Her work began soon after her arrival in Atlanta in 1940 as the 20-year-old wife of Israel (Icky) Wilen. Her accomplishments in the Jewish and the general community are legendary.

I received a phone call from Charlotte a few weeks after the October 10, 2012, public apology by Emory University President James Wagner. She lamented not being able to attend the event. She was no longer able to drive and was unable to get a ride to the event. She wanted to meet with me to share information she insisted should be entered into the public record.

I followed up and received a luncheon invitation to Charlotte's home in Buckhead. Charlotte told me in advance that her information was based on meetings she attended in 1960 as a member of the

Atlanta Jewish Federation's Community Relations Committee (CRC). I checked my scanned records of the CRC and verified that Mrs. I. Wilen was indeed a member. Examining the other names on the list, I suddenly realized that Charlotte Wilen was the last living member. She alone could offer first-hand testimony of what transpired during the CRC meetings.

Charlotte recounted that in 1960 she was president of the Atlanta B'nai B'rith Women. The national organization gave her the go-ahead to begin organizing an effort to integrate the segregated Atlanta schools.

Word of her mandate reached the ears of William Schwartz Jr., chairman of the CRC. Schwartz, a social friend of Charlotte and her husband Icky, told her that Ed Kahn, the Federation executive director, wanted to meet with her. Schwartz told her that Kahn had heard that she was involved in the movement to integrate the Atlanta schools. Schwartz urged her to come to the CRC meeting; he assured Charlotte that he would back her. A few minutes later, she received a call from Rabbi Jacob Rothschild, Charlotte's rabbi at The Temple. The rabbi also assured her that she would receive his backing. She was reluctant but at the same time eager to attend the meeting.

After the meeting with the CRC, Charlotte felt comfortable that she could proceed with her plans but understood that the community leaders wanted to "hold her hand." Soon thereafter, Charlotte was invited to be a member of the CRC. As such, she was privy to the multiple challenges the Jewish community was facing, and how they dealt with them. Relatively young, and somewhat sheltered, she was "mortified" to hear the shocking stories of the dental students at Emory dental school. "One of the failed students killed himself," she said. "I can't remember his name. He was from South Georgia." Regaining her composure, Charlotte continued, "The ADL director, Art Levin, presented irrefutable evidence that two-thirds of the Jewish students were being flunked out or being made to repeat one or more years.

"I was dismayed that there was such a strong faction of the committee that did not want to confront the Emory administration." I reminded Charlotte that her rabbi, Jacob Rothschild, was a subcommittee member of the CRC. He was known for his relentless sermons seeking equal rights for blacks. I asked Charlotte if Rabbi Rothschild ever, from the pulpit, told his congregation about the problem of Jewish dental students at Emory? Charlotte explained, "No, we were told as committee members that it was privileged information."

Charlotte spoke on the record for over an hour about the CRC meetings, with an emphasis on the dental school controversy. "What you have done is so important," she said. "You uncovered and exposed a shameful episode, which has remained hidden for all these years. This long-delayed travesty of justice is due mainly to one person, a Jewish faculty member at the Emory dental school."

"One evening, the Emory dental school was the sole topic of discussion at the CRC meeting. The chairman of the CRC called on the Jewish faculty member for his assessment of Dean John Buhler, who had been labeled an antisemite by ADL's Art Levin.

"Dr. Marvin Sugarman was a childhood friend of my husband. He was known as 'Snookie.' Our families were members of The Temple, and we belonged to the same social crowd. Snookie insisted that not only was Buhler not an antisemite, but in fact was friendly and helpful to the Jewish students. He was charming, as usual, and succeeded in deflecting the ADL charges. I was appalled at his testimony," she added.

"The dean resigned a year or so later, and the matter was allowed to disappear. Apparently, Snookie could not forget. Every time he would see me at a social gathering, he would say, 'Charlotte, have you ever forgiven me for what I said at the meetings?' This happened over and over again. I finally told him that *I* had forgiven him but reminded him each time that what he did was awful. Until the day he died, he never stopped soliciting my forgiveness."

Two years after I interviewed her, on March 27, 2015, Charlotte Wilen passed away at the age of 93. I arrived at the funeral service early and looked out at an already overflowing crowd of mourners. The expansive eulogies came from all segments of the community. The scope of her volunteer work was inspiring. I reflected on the unique sensitivity of this awesome woman, who near the end of her life, a life of multiple accomplishments, summoned me because she wanted a long-suppressed truth revealed.

In a sense, Charlotte Wilen had forgiven, but she had not forgotten. As the lone survivor of the 1960 CRC dental school hearings, she felt the need to set the record straight, even if it was 53 years later.

CHAPTER 15

A Few Good Men

S ifting through the murky evidence of an increasingly disturbing case, there emerged a steady and deliberate pattern of credible evidence. I quickly reminded myself of Art Levin's deep disappointment when his superiors in New York told him that he needed additional evidence to prove his case. With that in mind, I felt the need to identify and personally interview every Jewish student who had attended Emory dental school over the course of Dean Buhler's tenure. Using the yearbooks from 1948-1961, I created a digital composite photograph of the Jewish students who attended Emory during those years. I started my search in Atlanta.

Composite of Emory's Jewish dental students during Buhler's regime

Six of the 11 Atlanta men, including myself, were still alive. I had already interviewed Ron Goldstein, and his willingness to express himself strongly influenced the decision of two more within this group to agree to a video interview from their homes. One man reluctantly agreed to a phone interview. The remaining two, my very close friends, refused to be interviewed at all. The wife of one even forbade him to discuss it. The wife of another was unaware of that part of his life, and he didn't want her or their children to find out. The subject was too close to home. But eventually they validated my work.

Irving Shulman, Jack Rousso, Morris Benveniste, Coleman Socoloff, and Sam Goodrich had all passed away prior to my investigation. But there were those who could tell their stories. The widow and brother of Irving (I.J.) Shulman, Dean Buhler's first casualty, recalled the indignities Irving experienced. Marshall Benveniste, Morris Benveniste's son, and Morris' former dental partner, Bob Triff, provided valuable insights into issues Morris faced when he returned as an instructor while Buhler was still dean. Coleman Socoloff's brother and classmates shared memories of Coleman's travails. Sam Goodrich's former classmates, as well as his uncle and sister-in-law, tearfully described the brutal treatment Sam received from his instructors. Jack Rousso's nephew, Sidney Tourial, was previously unaware that his uncle was forced to repeat his second year at Emory. Sidney's mother later confirmed that it was a well-guarded family secret.

It was snowing on December 24, 2010, when I arrived to interview Jay Paulen at his northwest Atlanta home. Jay, still practicing dentistry after 52 years, was taking a few days off for the winter holidays. Rosalie, Jay's wife, welcomed me to their lovely home. She led me to the room she had set up for the recording session. Before she left, I showed her the 1958 Emory yearbook in which she appeared as the sponsor of the Alpha Omega fraternity. Rosalie was painfully aware of the story Jay was about to tell me.

Jay Paulen was one of only 12 Jewish students during the Buhler era who was able to graduate in four years. Yet, in my opinion, Jay suffered more than any of the other men I interviewed. Instructors constantly taunted Jay in front of his classmates, and he was wrongfully accused by the dean of cheating from the day he arrived until the very last week of his senior year. He was even told two weeks before graduating not to send out graduation invitations.

Jay was a convenient target. Almost six and a half feet tall, he towered over diminutive instructor William Ashendorf, who constantly badgered him and frequently asked him how long he thought he could hang in there. "I told him that my ass was callused, and that I wasn't going to give up. He eventually left me alone."

L. Berry Brown, chief of prosthetics, tried to wear Jay down, constantly refusing to check his work. "One day, I was sitting all by myself on the bench in the lab during lunchtime. I guess I had tears in my eyes. Marvin Sugarman came by and asked me what was wrong, and I told him. An hour later I was called into the dean's office. The dean said to me: 'Do you think you can get special treatment by crying on another Jew's shoulder? Well, I can tell you that you won't.'"

Students were seated alphabetically in the labs. Jay Paulen was seated next to George Patterson. They became fast friends and studied their notes together almost every night. "I quizzed George on a certain amount of questions from my notes, and George in turn quizzed me from his notes. When we had exams, we would get identical scores. Buhler called me into his office and accused me of cheating. 'What do you have to say for yourself,' the dean asked me. He was ready to kick me out of school."

"I suggested that the dean put George and me in two rooms and give us the same exam. He did, and we answered the questions exactly the same. Buhler gave George an A and gave me a B. I was always downgraded. Two weeks before graduation, I received a note telling me to report to the dean's office. I knocked on his door and walked in. There they were, it was like the Supreme Court. Every head of a department was seated around the table. And they went around one by one telling me how bad I was, and that I wasn't going to graduate. Then, before dismissing me, the dean told me not to send out graduation invitations.

"I was halfway down the hall," Jay told me, "when one of the instructors came running after me. He said, 'Jay, you know you're one of my best students, but I've got a wife and two kids, and I have to play on the team.' So, I knew then exactly how it was."

Reliving that horrible episode, Jay unsuccessfully fought back the tears in his eyes. He paused, unable to fully control his trembling voice, and stared into the video camera. I tried to break the tension. "What happened?" I asked.

"I just hung around my house, and a week later I got a letter telling me that I was going to graduate."

Jay was a Florida resident and hoped to practice in South Florida. "I signed a contract to rent office space north of Miami Beach. It was contingent on my passing the Florida Boards. I took the boards and thought I did okay. But I got a letter telling me that I didn't pass. I came back to Atlanta, and word got around that I hadn't passed. Marvin Goldstein told me that the word on the street was that Berry Brown, my old nemesis at the school, had called a former classmate of his who was on the Florida Board. Marvin told me that I didn't have a chance of passing. Rosalie was an Atlanta girl, so I set up practice here."

Jay was visibly relieved as we concluded the interview. He and Rosalie had raised a wonderful family. One of their children, Brenda, Jay proudly told me, was a graduate of the University of Pennsylvania dental school. "She heard too many of my stories to consider going to Emory. I still see some of my classmates and even some of my former instructors at local dental meetings. But we enjoy much more going to the local and national Alpha Omega meetings. We have been very active in our support of the Israeli dental schools in Jerusalem and Tel Aviv, each built with the financial support of Alpha Omega."

The Atlantans Who Didn't Attend Emory Dental School
I thought it would be instructive to interview the Atlanta Jewish dentists who did not attend Emory dental school. Their stories were almost identical. Each of them did his pre-dental work at Emory. Three of them

actually earned their undergraduate degree at Emory. They all intended to remain in Atlanta, but at the last minute they and their families heard disturbing rumors about the Emory dental school. And, for the record, the negative news didn't come from the Goldsteins.

Malcolm Rosenbloom's uncle, Arnold Hoffman, an Emory alumnus, wrote to the American Dental Association on July 23, 1956, expressing his deep concern about the extreme failure rate of Jewish students at Emory dental school. After receiving no answer from the ADA, Hoffman insisted that his nephew apply to the Maryland dental school, where he graduated in 1960. Rosenbloom told me that he had planned to go to Emory, but his uncle vetoed that plan.

Alvin Siegel was born and raised in Atlanta. Alvin was a senior in the college at Emory in 1956 and planned to attend the Emory dental school. Siegel's uncle, Dr. Ed Reisman, was serving on the Atlanta Jewish Community Council in the 1950s. He heard reports about the anti-semitism at Emory dental school. Reisman also held a part-time position teaching anatomy at Emory medical school, where he began to hear similar rumors. Reisman convinced his sister and brother-in-law that their son Alvin should not attend Emory dental school. After receiving his undergraduate degree at Emory in 1956, Siegel was accepted to the University of Pittsburgh where he graduated dental school in 1960.

Joel Adler hailed from Hattiesburg, Mississippi. He thrived at Emory and in 1956, after only two years of pre-dental education, was ready to transition to dental school. Although confident that Emory would accept him, he hedged his bets by also applying to Northwestern dental school in Chicago and Maryland dental school in Baltimore. On July 30, 2010, Adler, a retired Atlanta oral surgeon, recalled with precision an important turning point in his life.

"I, by chance, ran into a fellow who had been my dormitory counselor when I was a freshman. I was already living in the fraternity house and hadn't seen him for a year. He asked me how things were going, and I told him that I was planning on going to dental school at Emory. And he then asked me, 'Do you have interviews at any other schools?' And I said,

'Yes, I've got a scheduled interview at Northwestern and at Maryland, but I'm not going to bother to go since I've been accepted at Emory.' And he advised me to go ahead and take those interviews and if I were accepted, to go there. And so I asked him, 'Why are you saying this?' He said, 'Well, you're Jewish, aren't you?' And I said, 'Yes. What does that have to do with it?' Now this fellow was a graduate student, and I think in orthodontics. And he wasn't Jewish. He had had a friend in his class in dental school—a Jewish guy—who was a very good student, but they had flunked him on attitude, and my former counselor felt that that was just an excuse to get rid of him. He said he was a very good student and he thought would have made a good dentist and that he had transferred to the University of Miami, where he was in medical school doing very well. And he said, 'I sort of see you in that same light, and if I were you, I would not put myself in that position.' And so, I thanked him. I did not investigate to see if that was true or not, but I went and had an interview at the University of Maryland, with which I was impressed—it was the first dental school in the country, and the dean at the time happened to be Jewish—his name was Aisenberg—and they seemed like they wanted me, so they accepted me, and I went to the University of Maryland. But I wish I knew who the graduate student was so I could thank him because I think he did me a real favor."

Joel continued his story. "When I came back to Atlanta after my first year at Maryland, I talked to Lester Breen, who had been a TEP fraternity brother of mine at Emory. I convinced Lester and his family that he too should come to Maryland. Later I talked to Charles Rosenberg. By then, Charles had already made up his mind to come to Maryland. I remember another fraternity brother from Augusta, Georgia. One of the older Jewish dentists in Atlanta, also a TEP, was trying to convince him to go to Emory, but I advised him otherwise. He followed my advice."

Lester Breen, an Atlanta native, did his pre-dental work at Emory, but chose to join his friends at Maryland in 1957. He graduated from the University of Maryland with honors in 1961 and returned to Atlanta that same year. He practiced dentistry in Atlanta from 1961 until he retired with a medical disability in 1994. His second career was as a financial planner, and he was as successful in this field as he was in his specialty of endodontics.

By the time Charles Rosenberg, an Atlanta native, began his senior year at Emory University in 1960, word was out that the failure rate of Jewish students at Emory dental school was astronomical. It was disappointing, because Charles had truly enjoyed his undergraduate experience in the college. Now he was certain that he shouldn't even apply to the Emory dental school. His friends Lester Breen and Joel Adler convinced him to enroll at Maryland. The same year Charles finished his freshman year in Baltimore, Dean Buhler's 12-year reign at Emory came to an end. Charles graduated with honors from Maryland in 1964. After a two-year stint in the Navy, Charles took three years of oral surgery training. He returned to Atlanta with his wife Bunny and his two sons and joined Ed Green and me as a third partner in our practice. Charles had no knowledge of my Emory experience until I interviewed him on July 30, 2010.

A Stop Off in Savannah

On our way to Florida for additional scheduled interviews, Shirley and I stopped in Savannah, Georgia, to visit Harold Black and his wife Charlotte. Harold graduated Emory dental school in 1959, one of the few Jewish students who graduated without having to repeat a year.

Black, born and raised in Savannah, was one of the few remaining locals who had maintained his distinctive native accent. A popular lecturer on the dental circuit, he was widely known for his unique style of storytelling. Black joined us after a full day in his office. I was impressed with the seriousness with which he prepared for his interview. He had doffed his dental jacket, and out of respect for the subject, came dressed in a starched white shirt, coat, and tie. He had given considerable thought to the subject at hand.

"You had to be careful with every step you took, every word you said. The best thing was to stay out of their way as much as you could.

Even then, you never knew from moment to moment what was going to happen. I lived in dread. We were harassed every day. I never told my parents how much I feared that I would be failed out like so many of my fraternity brothers. They worked so hard to send me through school. They couldn't have stood it. We had to turn in our wax *cah-vins*. Every tooth in the *ahch*, set up in wax in a typodont. They's no *weh* anybody *evah gahrded* anything *mo-ah* than we *gahrded* those wax *cah-vins*. I felt proud when I turned them in to Dr. Bartholomew. He was known as 'Black Bart.'

"The next day, Dr. Bartholomew, who made a point of calling me his 'Black Sheep,' called me over. 'Black,' he said, 'I've got bad news. One of your teeth is missing.'

"'Oh, no, Dr. Bartholomew, I know I turned them all in.'

"'*Ah you callin' me a liah?*' he said. 'No, *suh*, Dr. Bartholomew.' But I was thinking, there's no *weh* that tooth is lost.

"I went back to my fraternity house and looked all over for that first bicuspid tooth. About two in the morning, I went to the lab and *cahved* another tooth. I finished about the time the rest of the guys were waking up for breakfast. I held it in the palm of my hand and approached Dr. Bartholomew. Before I had time to say anything, he said, 'Uh-hmm, uh-hmm, Black, we found that tooth.'

"I was so relieved, and I said, 'Oh, thank you, Dr. Bartholomew,' and I went back and sat down." Black paused and lowered his voice. "That son-of-a-bitch."

Black told me that years later, long after Dean Buhler was gone, he was in Atlanta for the Hinman dental meeting. "I decided to go over to the dental school. I had a difficult case I was working on, and I decided to ask Dr. George Moulton, who was now dean, for some advice. The school was still on Forrest Avenue. Stanley Krugman went over with me. So we were sitting out in that little waiting area where the patients used to sit. There was an aura around you when you were in that building. And I'm sitting next to Stan Krugman. And I look at him, and he looks at me, and we both started smiling. And he said, 'It's still here, isn't it, Harold? Harold, it's still here.' I said to Stan, 'Stan, it's still here.'"

The following day, we met with Bucky and Joan Bloom at their retirement home on Skidaway Island, a half-hour drive from downtown Savannah. The distressing and heart-rending interview is described in Chapter 10.

Next Stop—Florida

Our next stop was Brooksville, Florida, the county seat of Hernando County. Brooksville is located in Central Florida, 300 miles southwest of Savannah and an hour north of Tampa. This outwardly placid, nondescript community specializes in breeding Andalusian and Arabian horses.

I asked our host, George Marholin, who met his wife Eleanor Nodvin in Atlanta while a student at Emory dental school, how they settled in such an unpredictable location. George spent a few minutes describing his multiple business interests following his early retirement from dentistry. But it became clear that George was waiting to talk about a different topic, and it didn't involve horses.

George Marholin was raised in South Florida by a single mother and had worked all his life to help his mom make ends meet. He attended the University of Florida on a football scholarship. He decided to study dentistry after suffering several concussions. "The State of Florida didn't have a dental school at that time, so they paid Emory a generous subsidy to accept Florida residents. So, I came to Emory."

Unlike the majority of his Jewish classmates, George graduated Emory dental school in four years, one of the top men in his class. But he had nothing good to say about his experience there.

"One day, during lunch break, two of my non-Jewish classmates and I were sitting on a bench in the student locker room. The door opens, and in walks Dr. Bartholomew. He starts screaming at me. He called me a 'goddammed Jew.' I got up, ready to go at him. My two friends tackled me and held on until Bartholomew turned around and left. They saved my career. I would have killed him."

Marholin concluded his interview by proudly declaring, "In our wills, my wife and I are going to give 25% of our assets to the University of Florida."

"What," I asked, "are you giving to Emory?" He paused, narrowed his eyes, and issued an angry one-word response. "Zip."

The following day, June 6, 2010, I finally reconnected with my old fraternity brother Larry Fall. Larry and his wife were living in a trailer park in Valrico, Florida, a small town 35 miles east of Tampa. Larry entered Emory dental school in 1950, one year before I did. He passed his first two years but was forced to repeat his junior year. During the repetition of the junior year (his fourth year in school), he was called into the dean's office and dismissed from school. Four years. No degree. He returned to college, earned his bachelor's degree, and entered the computer science field when it was in its infancy. He told me that he had enjoyed a satisfying and successful career. He had long ago reconciled his fate but was still hopeful that Emory would acknowledge the injustice he and others had experienced. As we drove away, Larry urged me to keep in touch.

We met with Dick Arnold in Miami and Stanley Krugman in Coral Gables. Dick and Stanley had to repeat a year, which was for both an emotional and financial burden. Arnold was defiant and resentful. "They said I didn't have it in my hands. That was ridiculous. To get in school, I took the same digital dexterity test as everyone else. I had it in my hands then, and I still have it in my hands." He had completely adjusted but still held Emory accountable for their actions. "I still go back for my class reunions. My classmates know exactly how I feel, and they know I am right."

Krugman was more phlegmatic. After five years at Emory, he set up practice in Columbia, South Carolina. After relocating to Florida, he never discussed the matter with anyone. Once affable and outgoing, Stan had become withdrawn, even melancholy. What he confided to me, he wished to remain confidential. Later, after deciding to share his dental school experience with his two daughters, his exuberant nature slowly returned. I was pleased when Stan called me and released me from our agreement of silence.

Jack Berne and his wife Helen invited us to their home in Aventura, Florida. Jack was widely loved and praised as a skillful children's dentist. Jack and Helen's experience at Emory dental school was the single blemish in their otherwise blissful lives. After making it through the first two years of dental school, Jack was forced to repeat his third year.

"None of us minded working hard, but they made it unreasonably difficult for the Jewish boys. We had all spent two or three or four years in college. We had already spent an equal amount of time in dental school, and they were ready to 'cut us loose.' You looked around and saw the favorites getting help from the instructors. No one helped us. There was one Jewish instructor, Sugarman, and he never lifted a finger to help us. I'll never forgive him. He was Buhler's Jew."

Jack finally smiled. "Helen told me that when I was in school, I clenched my teeth in my sleep. When I graduated, I didn't clench anymore."

Our next stop was Boca Raton to visit with Shep Masarek and his wife Rhoda. Shep came to Emory dental school in 1954 from the University of Miami. While there, he had excelled in his pre-dental studies. He was flunked out in 1956 after two years at Emory dental school. Shep had a deep desire to practice dentistry and intensely sought to be allowed to repeat his sophomore year. He had glowing letters of recommendation. Letters in the Buhler archives show that Dean Buhler had an equal desire not to allow Masarek to return.

Shep still harbored bitter recollections of his treatment by Dean Buhler and the Emory faculty. After his dismissal from school, he rebounded and created a company that sold dental and medical supplies. But success in business was not his main goal. His wife Rhoda said that her husband would come home after a busy day, having never gotten over his Emory experience, and say, "They should be selling me dental supplies instead of the other way around." Shirley and I drove in a northwesterly direction from Boca Raton to Longwood, Florida, to visit Hank Greenberg and his wife Norma. Hank's experience at the Emory dental school was a low moment in his life, and he had decided to erase that time from his memory. It was Norma who convinced Hank to hear what I had to say.

Harold "Hank" Greenberg loved his undergraduate days at Emory. In 1961, after two years in Emory dental school, he was not given the opportunity to return. Like Bucky Bloom, he was accepted to the University of Miami medical school, where he graduated in 1966 with high honors. He practiced cardiology in Central Florida for 35 years. He was past president of the Orange County Medical Society. In his interview, he stated, "When I first heard what you told me in your letter, my first action was disbelief. Then the concrete realization set in that this had happened not only to me, but also to other dental students primarily based on their religious background. It happened because we were Jewish."

Now the moment I had waited for. We arrived in Jacksonville on August 16, 2010. Finally, after months of soul-searching and contemplation, my former classmate Art Burns was ready to talk. Art's lovely wife Olly and Shirley left Art and me alone in Art's study. Art, a self-described type A control freak, was meticulous in his preparation. He was seated behind his large mahogany desk upon which lay numerous dental artifacts, plaques, and certificates. A huge original painting, surrounded on all sides by handsome bookcases, served as a backdrop. Art had already approved a three-page outline of my proposed protocol for our interview. I stood next to Art and introduced myself to the video camera:

SPB: Hello, I'm Perry Brickman, and I'm pleased and honored to be here in Jacksonville, Florida, on August 17th, 2010, guest of Olly and Art Burns, and this is really emotional for both of us because it has been 57 years since we've seen each other. We've talked only a couple of times. We've communicated, but 57 years since I was invited to go someplace else other than Emory dental school, and it's been actually longer than that that we first met each other. So, what I want to say is that I was a young fellow from Chattanooga, Tennessee. It was September of 1949 that I came to Emory University College as a freshman at exactly the same time Art came from Jacksonville, Florida, and we were classmates together at Emory University in 1949. We went to school for two years and were accepted to dental school. At that time there were two other friends of ours who were also accepted from Emory College at that time too. So, four of us Jewish boys were in the class of 1951. I only lasted a year. At the end of 1952, I was told not to return. So, 1952 is when I left, and then you were there for another year, and in 1953 you were invited not to come back. So, we are sort of unique in a way for several reasons, one of which we started school together. We knew each other in school and we entered the same class dental school together, but more than that, we are really, I think, unique insomuch as we were the only two guys who were later—we were very fortunate to be able to get accepted to other dental schools, and so I'm proud to say that I'm a 1956 graduate of The University of Tennessee in Memphis, and Art later, after having served two years in the service—and maybe we'll talk more about that— he was accepted to Temple University, had to start all the way at the beginning just like I did, and finished in 1959, correct?

AB: Correct.

SPB: And then you did great in school. We'll hear about that. You got into orthodontic graduate training, two more years, and then came back here to practice orthodontics in Jacksonville. What I'm going to ask you to do is, after we're through, I want you to orally grant me permission to use and reproduce any recorded interviews, photographs, and documents that we share with each other.

AB: I grant you permission to use what you mentioned.

SPB: [laughs] Okay, great. And then you can sign this later on. Okay. I want you to give us a little background on—your educational background, where you were born, the schools that you went to prior to coming to

Emory. A little bit about your background, your family and so on, and tell us how you made the decision to come to Emory.

Art's transcribed remarks occupy 28 single-spaced pages. Although he had prepared index cards, he spoke without referring to them.

AB: My Emory undergraduate experience was wonderful. The ambience of the dental school was totally different. The mood was different. There was a mood of growing uneasiness. Unlike the college, I knew very few of my classmates, and I knew nobody in any of the other three classes. At the end of the year, like everyone else, I struggled to finish my work. A lot of it was hurried work. It was pressurized work. My anatomy, my polished gold, and the rest of my work—as I remember it——I thought I finished my work. No one ever called me in and said, "If you don't finish this, you're out of here." I do not seem to remember ever an instructor calling me in and saying, "This is your status before year end." I did not know that I was dismissed from the school until I received the letter from Dr. Buhler, from the dean.

SPB: Did you get the letter, or did your parents get the letter?

AB: The letter was addressed to Mr. Arthur Stanton Burns at my address on Lakewood Road in Jacksonville, Florida. That was a letter which, when opened and read—the dreaded letter. And with the kind of parents that I had, to go to my parents and say, "Hey, guess what I just got in the mail?" And I will tell you that taking the letter up to my mother in particular, who, another certified obsessive, who I characterize as, if I came home in my earlier days of schooling and told her I made a 100 on a test, she would say, "Why didn't you make a 103?" So that was a very difficult time, and their reaction at the time was, "What is this?" I've never told them anything about school. I may have told them I was uneasy. I may have given them some warning. I do not remember how badly I characterized how I felt in school, but that was an extremely difficult time because you have nothing to back you up. You have absolutely nothing but a letter.

I went back to school at the University of Florida where I took a few courses, with the idea of possibly getting into another dental school. That couldn't happen overnight, so I decided to get my military obligation behind me.

Art described his basic training in subfreezing weather, followed by two years as a dental lab technician in the Army.

AB: One morning his commanding officer pulled him aside to give him a warning. "Your former dean, Dr. Buhler, is part of a team who will be inspecting our facility. Don't be concerned. I've got your back." My back stiffened as I heard the door to the lab open, and I recognized a familiar officious voice from the back of the room. When the dean, who was wearing a military uniform, approached my lab desk, he peered over my shoulder, stared at me, and said, 'Burns—I would recognize that nose anywhere.' Out of respect for my commanding officer or perhaps out of fear, I didn't reply. And then the miracle of being accepted as a freshman student at Temple University dental school. Emory considered me as trash. Buhler told me I was the worst in my class. At the end of my four years at Temple, I was at the top of my class. Worst to first. I guess I finally redeemed myself in my mother's eyes.

Art was accepted to the prestigious orthodontic program at the University of Washington in Seattle. He returned to Jacksonville where he enjoyed a storied career as a modern innovative orthodontist and a pioneer in the field of forensic dentistry. He was summoned to New York in 2001 by Dr. Jeff Burkes, chief forensic dentist for OCME (Office of the Chief Medical Examiner, New York City) to help in the identification of the victims of the Twin Towers catastrophe.

I uploaded all my recordings, backed up my records, and returned home. Art Levin's statistics were now live human beings, and they were prepared to speak out.

CHAPTER 16

Long-Overdue Recognition

L eaving Jacksonville and heading home to Atlanta brought back vivid memories of the 1956 Florida Dental Board examination. Fifty-four years had passed, and circumstances had changed remarkably. This time I was not alone in my car. Shirley was with me, and, thankfully, her new car was air-conditioned. I did have one selfish regret. The modern interstate highway, convenient as it was, denied me the previous enjoyment of navigating the town squares of rural South Georgia. Back in Atlanta, I reshuffled my priorities. Art Levin, still alive, was in his 94th year and, in my opinion, deserved proper recognition.

That coming December of 2010 would mark the 50th anniversary of Alpha Omega's official declaration of appreciation to Art Levin and the ADL. The original resolution, dated December 29, 1960, praised Arthur Levin and the ADL, and acknowledged the aid and cooperation of the Anti-Defamation League of B'nai B'rith in addressing *certain mutual problems.* "The League lent considerable aid to our Fraternity in solving these problems."

No one had openly discussed the issue of the Emory dental school in 50 years. It was time to define the mysterious "problems" alluded to 50 years before and give proper recognition to Art Levin and the Anti-Defamation League. Alpha Omega stepped up. Understanding my suggestion, the following proposal was made at the national meeting in San Diego, California, on December 29, 2010:

"Therefore, be it resolved that this Convention assembled in San Diego, California on December 29, 2010 offer its specific thanks to the National officers of the Anti-Defamation League and especially commend Arthur Levin, the Southeastern Regional Director of A.D.L for recognizing and successfully bringing to an end the antisemitism which prevailed at the Emory University School of Dentistry during the years 1948-1961. Be it further resolved that a copy of this resolution be placed in our minutes and a copy be sent to the national office of the A.D.L., its Southeastern regional office and to Mr. Arthur Levin. Moved by Sidney R. Tourial, seconded by Richard Shapiro that the above resolution be approved. December 29, 2010."

The resolution was approved by unanimous vote. Of course, Art Levin was extremely pleased to receive the long-overdue recognition. I suspected that current ADL leadership would be unfamiliar with the 50-year-old controversy and require context. Dale Schwartz, a longtime ADL activist, was most helpful to me in identifying the current regional and national ADL leaders who should receive the resolution, along with pertinent historical background information. Shortly afterwards, national ADL recognized Levin and honored him with the Centennial Champion Award at their national meeting.

AO Atlanta Chapter

Michael and Ellen Chalef are one of my favorite dental school student couples. We remained in close touch after Michael graduated Emory dental school in 1982 and opened his practice in Atlanta. Michael was president of the Atlanta Alpha Omega Alumni chapter at the time I returned from Florida in 2010 after meeting Art Levin, and he had already received news of the Alpha Omega resolution approved in San Diego.

Michael was captivated by the story I shared with him. He was certain that, like himself, few of our members were aware of Emory's past. Most of them had graduated from Emory after Dean Buhler and had never experienced antisemitism at the school. Michael asked if I would be willing to present a program at one of the chapter's upcoming meetings.

On May 18, 2011, the Atlanta Alpha Omega Dental Fraternity hosted a dinner at Wildfire Restaurant in Sandy Springs. There was an overflow crowd, and the logistics of following a dinner with a PowerPoint presentation were challenging. After the tables were cleared and the waiters dismissed, I presented *The Buhler Years—1948-1961*. There was total silence, even in the crowded restaurant. Many of the younger dentists were shocked and angered when they learned what had transpired at the dental school during the Buhler era. David Hochberg, a 1979 Emory graduate, expressed the sentiment of many of his colleagues: "We want our tuition money back." The buzz following the presentation continued for weeks, providing me additional encouragement to continue my work. The recorded interviews and the gigabytes of information needed to be digitally organized into a format that would enable me to share my story with a wider audience. To this end, I committed myself to a serious schedule of one-to-one instruction at the Apple store at Lenox Square in Atlanta. My Apple instructors urged me to produce a DVD documentary which, they assured me, could be "easily" produced on my laptop computer. On Sunday afternoon, September 25, 2011, author Melissa Fay Greene was scheduled to speak on her newest book at the Breman Museum in midtown Atlanta. Greene's plane from Columbus, Georgia was delayed, and the disappointed crowd was taken to the Breman auditorium to see a movie. Miles Alexander and I had been sitting together since we first arrived, and Miles suggested that we remain where we were sitting and continue our conversation while the others went inside to see the movie.

Miles was noticeably pleased to hear about the Alpha Omega presentation and insisted on a follow-up meeting at his office as soon as possible to see my nearly completed documentary. In the meantime, he said: "I'm going to send you a questionnaire. I'm going to ask you to document your sources."

Shortly after our chance meeting at the Breman, I received a list of subjects and related questions from Miles Alexander regarding the Emory University School of Dentistry problem. He posed the following subjects and questions:

1. Each student and treatment
2. Post-Emory experience
3. Perry Brickman
4. Impact on families/trauma
5. Dean Buhler
6. Who else participated on the faculty? Hard for the dean to do it alone.
7. What was the general quota for Jewish applicants?
8. Stories of Jews having lab work turned down—giving the same work to a Christian and having it accepted by the same instructor
9. Stipends for students from Florida and South Carolina
10. When were the first non-Southern students accepted after 1961?
11. What percentage of the class was not Southern?
12. How did the Massell Clinic fit into the discrimination controversy? When was it first confronted or challenged?
13. Who at Emory denied discrimination?
14. Comparison of the quotas and attitude in the dental school to the medical school
15. Buhler's papers at South Carolina?
16. John E. Buhler (1908-1976—pre-Emory [Indiana and Temple]; post-Emory [South Carolina])
17. Early Jewish supporters of raising the Emory dental school issue
18. Proponents of "don't rock the boat" versus confronting the university
19. Effect of the controversy on the cost to Emory—alumni contributions
20. Why did this whole incident happen?

21. Compare academic qualifications of dental to medical admissions
22. Percent of admissions who were Emory undergrads (two, three, or four years)
23. Who at Emory has been contacted already and their responses?

I quickly complied with his request as I had most of the information close at hand. When I requested additional time to complete the questionnaire, Miles responded that I could take a breath, for I had provided sufficient information to allow him to move forward. Apparently, he was working on something important, and I was very pleased and excited. Having now completed my documentary, I dropped off a copy of the DVD at Miles's law office.

Simultaneously, I distributed copies of the DVD to close friends, former dental classmates, and Emory faculty members, including Dr. Eric Goldstein, Dr. David Blumenthal, and Dr. Deborah Lipstadt. On December 10, 2011, I received a late Saturday evening email from Emory professor and distinguished Holocaust scholar Deborah Lipstadt. Due to a delay in grading papers, she had finally viewed the DVD. She wrote:

Dear Perry:
Shavuah Tov.
Tonight, I finally got to watch the video. First of all my apologies for taking so long. It is the end of semester craziness and I have been up to my ears in all sorts of work, which needs doing. However, I am also sorry I waited a week because I found the material you presented and the manner in which you presented it so very compelling. You are low keyed, judicious, and yet devastating in your assessment of the school, the dean, and the university. It is an important piece of work and I think your research and the DVD are the beginning not the end of this story.

*I am thinking about what should be the next step?
Publication? A movie? If so, where and in what form? Is it
necessary to do more research? What is the wider context,
e.g. the record at other dental schools, etc.? I know that
Ginger Cain wrote to you asking for a copy and I saw Vice
President Gary Hauk and told him how pleased I was that
you were meeting with him. Has the date for that been
finalized? He was not sure that it had.
In friendship and deep appreciation for this important
work,*

Deborah

On December 20, 2011, Miles Alexander wrote Chairman of the
Emory Board of Trustees Ben Johnson requesting a luncheon meeting.

*Sent: Tuesday, December 20, 2011 1:01 PM
To: Johnson, Ben
Subject: Emory*

*Ben,
After Christmas if you have time, I would like to discuss,
and get your thoughts on, a very sensitive Emory issue.
Please let me know if your schedule permits a breakfast
or lunch meeting, and if you are available please give me
a couple of alternative dates. I would like to discuss some
ideas, before trying to set up an appointment with President
Wagner and others.
It involves bringing to closure some historic anti-
Semitism that as you know occurred decades ago at the
Emory dental school. It devastated the lives of many of
my contemporaries. I have now seen the interviews of
some of the survivors who are in their 70s and 80s. I also*

anticipate a book and TV coverage (which I believe it will be a very accurate, well documented, and a fair portrayal), undertaken by a distinguished retired Emory alumnus, who has devoted his full time to researching this project. He wishes Emory no harm but believes that Emory's acknowledgment has been late and fallen short of the mark, and that the destructive impact it had on the individual victims and their families has never been appreciated. In reviewing the compelling material he has collected, it would be difficult to disagree. Because we are dealing with 1948 - 1961 and Emory has already made public this unfortunate chapter in its history I believe the issues are not essentially legal in nature but involve morality questions and Emory's image. I have some win-win thoughts on ways to ameliorate any negative impact on what is now a very different environment at Emory.

Miles

On January 23, 2012, Chairman of the Board Ben Johnson and Chief Counsel Steve Sencer met for lunch at Miles Alexander's office. Miles showed them my 56-minute documentary *The Buhler Years*. Miles's strategy obviously worked. According to Miles, his two guests were visibly moved. They responded by saying that the film should be presented to Emory Vice President Gary Hauk.

I would soon be sitting in the Candler Library/Jewish Studies Building with Professor Eric Goldstein of Emory's Tam Institute and Vice President and Deputy to the President Gary Hauk. The purpose of the meeting was to show my documentary DVD to Dr. Hauk. My belief is that several people spoke to the vice president, urging him to view the documentary. These would include Chairman of the Board Ben Johnson, Chief Counsel Steve Sencer, Professor Deborah Lipstadt, Professor David Blumenthal, and of course Professor Eric Goldstein.

Dr. Hauk was one of the most polite, diplomatic, and genuinely caring persons I have ever met. As he sat watching and listening to my documentary, I felt almost sorry for him that he was the one having to singularly bear the brunt of the case I was making against Emory.

Of course, it had never entered my mind to seek legal action against Emory. The court of public opinion was where we had always intended to rest our case. But circumstances had brought us to the top level of the university, and suddenly we were presenting our closing argument to the high court.

The documentary was long—almost an hour. But really, it could have been longer as lots of equally important material was left on the screening room floor. I was generally pleased with the content. Furthermore, Deborah Lipstadt had graciously observed that I had presented the information in a respectful way. Still, I wondered: what would be Dr. Hauk's impression?

Eric Goldstein turned on the lights and removed the DVD from the projector. Dr. Hauk's response was declarative, but not defensive. "But that's not Emory now," he stated in his deep, cultured radio-announcer's voice.

My response was strong, but not combative. "But it was," I replied.

Without hesitation, Dr. Hauk inquired, "What would you like us to do?" A moment passed before I responded. "I'm going to leave that up to you," was my answer.

Professor Lipstadt later commented that she has never seen a high-level decision at Emory implemented as quickly as this one. Dr. Hauk called me a week later. He had spoken with President James Wagner, and a decision had been made, subject to our approval. A public acknowledgement of the wrongdoing was going to be made by President Wagner. They had in mind a time in the coming fall that would accommodate everyone's schedules.

Several layers of protocol needed to be navigated, but Dr. Hauk and Emory were committed to the task. To maximize the impact of the event and all that would follow, Dr. Hauk explained the need to keep the plans under wraps. He reminded us that Emory had its own media and public relations departments, and they would begin immediately coordinating their plans. We were assured that the outside media would be notified in due time. Dr. Hauk cautioned us, however, that to ensure the event would receive the importance it deserved, we had to preserve the secret until the proper time. It was clear from the beginning that, at the highest level, Emory considered this a moral issue, fully deserving its highest attention. It was much more than a mere gesture; it was an unprecedented acknowledgement of long-term institutional misbehavior that had to be dismissed for all time.

Ducks in a Row

Early on, Hauk solicited Eric Goldstein's assistance in planning a series of events leading up to the event, as well as the event itself. Eric turned to a team of close friends and associates to develop a shared vision of what the program might look like.

Eric submitted to Vice President Hauk a basic outline suggesting:

A large public event to be held in the fall of 2012, which would include the showing of an edited version of Perry's documentary. This would be followed by a panel discussion in which Dr. Goldstein would contextualize the dental school incident within the larger history of Emory and its Jewish presence. A second panelist would link this history with Emory's contemporary efforts to address issues of difference and diversity. Eric further discussed the possibility of inviting an outside speaker to address the larger history of anti-Jewish discrimination in higher education.

In conjunction with this public program, Emory could invite all identifiable individuals who were affected by the dental school incident and who would be greeted by President Wagner and other Emory officials at a reception of some sort preceding the public event. President Wagner could then make some sort of acknowledgement of the incident at the public gathering, perhaps sharing some of his inner actions with these men; that would be very significant. This could be the basis for a statement that might later be adopted by the Board of Trustees and published.

In order to create discussion and awareness of this commemoration leading up to the public program, we would like to do two things:

Pursue the opportunity you mentioned to have an article in the *Emory Magazine* about these events and

We would like to convene a number of small groups such as the Campus ministers, members of the Race and Difference initiative, members of the President's Commission On Race and Ethnicity, the Jewish Studies faculty, etc., and show them Perry's documentary. This way there will be a greater interest in and knowledge about these events when the public program is announced in the fall.

There was a suggestion by Dean Leslie Harris that this discussion be made a part of Founder's Week next year. Perhaps Perry and other former dental students could share their experience with the students and answer questions.

Emory could assist with funding and/or resources to have the documentary edited and made more professional. That would help strengthen the program and assure that it can be completed in a reasonable period of time.

Eric completed his memorandum by asking Gary Hauk for his thoughts about the suggestions. Taking into account the Jewish calendar and President Wagner's personal schedule, they chose Wednesday, October 10, 2012, as a target date for the event.

Art Burns notified me that he and his wife Olly would be in Atlanta for a professional meeting the week of February 22, 2012. Bucky Bloom and his wife Joan were also planning to visit Atlanta that same week. I considered that to be an ideal opportunity to reunite Art and Bucky with their former college and dental school friends. I would also present them to younger colleagues and introduce them to the faculty members who were working on our behalf. The dining facilities at Emory Hillel served as a perfect location for an informal dinner meeting, which attracted a large and enthusiastic crowd. Professor Deborah Lipstadt later commented, "I have spent the major part of my professional career writing on discrimination and antisemitism. But never have I had the opportunity to observe it so up close."

Brickman, Burns, and Shaw: the three classmates who, after being kicked out of Emory, made it back into dental school

Miles Alexander was in a unique position to guide the plans and proceedings for the proposed October event. Miles was a distinguished Emory alumnus. His motives to remove the stain on Emory's reputation were unquestioned by all sides. Miles was unwavering in emphasizing that we, the "victims," would have to be satisfied with how the story was presented. He did remind us, however, that Emory is a different institution today, and this undertaking shouldn't taint its current reputation.

Bucky Bloom summed up the feeling of the majority of the former students. "I am amazed that your efforts have gone so far. I would return to Emory for an apology if it materializes. I am personally happy knowing what I have done with my life, and I don't need Emory to list my accomplishments. Your excellent DVD represents accurately the personal 'victims' statements and does not have to be reiterated.

"An acknowledgement by Emory of their failure to recognize the discrimination and injustice done to a particular segment of their student population, their failure to act on it, a global apology to the public and that segment of student population, and a concerted effort by the school to ensure nothing like that will ever again tarnish Emory's name will do just fine as far as I am concerned."

On May 4, 2012, Eric shared with me an email indicating that Gary Hauk wished to meet with him soon to discuss the *Emory Magazine* article and what should be accomplished in the production of the Emory film.

On this same subject Miles Alexander emailed that Gary Hauk and President Wagner had four proposed dates in October for the big event. "They are mentioning producing a documentary for the event. At present, they are considering the Woodruff Special Collections Library as the venue for the private meeting and the Jones Room for the public event, with Cox Hall as an alternate if necessary." They would ultimately realize that the Jones Room was barely sufficient to contain the private meeting, and the Cox Hall backup location was absolutely necessary to accommodate the standing-room-only audience for the public event.

I met with David Hughes Duke and his son John on May 30, 2012. Emory engaged their company, Duke and Associates, to produce the documentary that would have its premier showing on October 10, 2012. I listed an inventory of my files, including audio and video recordings, documents, a general summary of my findings, and a general idea of what I would like the documentary to express.

I emailed my list of dental students on June 25, 2012, the following: "It's official- a public apology will be given by Emory President Dr. James Wagner on October 10th, 2012," and attached the following letter:

June 25th, 2012
Dear _____,
I met this past Wednesday with Dr. Gary Hauk, Senior Vice President of Emory University. We were joined by Professor Eric Goldstein of the History Department at

Emory and Mr. David Hughes Duke, President of Duke Associates and Living Stories TV. http://www.livingstories. tv/about-2/

It's official. At 5:00 pm on October 10, 2012, Emory President James Wagner will meet privately with the Jewish students who attended the Emory dental school during the deanship of Dr. John Buhler. Dr. Wagner will formally apologize for Emory's role in the discriminatory practices that led to sixty-five per-cent of the Jewish students being failed out of school or having to repeat one or more years. Immediately following the private meeting, Emory will host a public meeting that will be open to the general community. A documentary movie, which will become a permanent part of the Emory archives, will detail the events that occurred during the years 1948-1961. David Duke, a renowned award-winning television producer, has been selected to produce the documentary. Emory officials, educators, community leaders and former students will be featured. The meeting will be held on the Emory campus at a site suitable to accommodate the public gathering. I encourage you to attend, and to bring your family and friends.

Thanks to all of you who spoke out, breaking a sixty-year period of silence. Thanks to the institutions, librarians and archivists who shared their long dormant records. And, a sincere expression of gratitude to Emory University for its unparalleled courage and honesty.

More details will be sent as the final plans develop. In the meantime, please mark your calendar for Wednesday, October 10th, 2012

Sincerely,
S. Perry Brickman, DDS

On June 27, 2012, Gary Hauk wrote Deborah Lipstadt and me to bring us up to date on what President Wagner and he were discussing about the nature of the apology. He requested a full list of those we expected would attend the event on October 10, 2012. Dr. Hauk was truly amazed to learn how many people we expected to attend. Surviving students, wives, widows, children, and grandchildren from as many as 15 states had indicated their intention to attend.

Dr. Hauk asked that I contact the organizations and publications with which we had a close affiliation, ask them to refrain from leaking the news, and assure them that Emory would welcome all publicity after the event. Deborah Lauter and Abraham Foxman of national ADL, and Bill Nigut, director of the Southeastern region of ADL, were among the dignitaries invited to the event, and they agreed to honor the request.

On August 9, 2012, Gary Hauk asked Eric, Miles, and me to check a draft he had prepared to send to my list of former dental students and families, inviting them to return to the school. The invitation would give the recipients two months lead-time to arrange travel.

On August 10, 2012, we placed the October 10, 2012 date on the Jewish community calendar. The wording was vague in deference to Emory.

On August 28, 2012, Dr. Hauk issued the following letter:

Dear _____,

Thanks to the initiative of a former student of Emory College and the Emory University School of Dentistry, Dr. Perry Brickman, the current administration of Emory has become aware of a set of unfortunate circumstances that have gone unacknowledged for decades.

It is clear from documents and oral testimonies collected by Dr. Brickman that between 1948 and 1961, Jewish students in Emory's dental school were failed out or forced to repeat courses—even entire years of their dental education—at a rate disproportionate to their numbers.

Although data revealing these practices were presented by the Anti-Defamation League more than five decades ago, the Emory administration at the time denied that this unusually high rate of failures and repeats was the result of discrimination by the Dental School's dean and faculty. This refusal to recognize the discrimination only worsened its emotional and professional impact on former dental students struggling to get their lives and careers back on track.

From conversations I have had with Dr. Brickman, I am given to understand that you may have been affected by these circumstances. The university is planning an event for the evening of October 10, 2012, to bring this history to greater awareness and to issue a statement of regret for this chapter in its past.

I am inviting you and a guest to attend a special reception for former Jewish dental students at 5:00 p.m., October 10, in the Jones Room of the Woodruff Library, to be followed by the premiere of a special video in the Cox Hall Ballroom at 6:00 p.m., with comments by President Jim Wagner and Dr. Brickman. If you would be so kind as to let me know whether you can attend, I would be grateful.

Emory is proud that today Jewish students, faculty, and administrators—along with colleagues of every religious, ethnic, and national background—work together in carrying out the university's mission. Emory can never totally repair the impact of that discrimination more than a half-century ago, but we can use the opportunity provided by Dr. Brickman's research to reflect on those events in ways that create a more hopeful and open future for all.

I hope that you will be able to join us. You can contact me directly by calling 404-727-6021 or by emailing to gary. hauk@emory.edu. I look forward to hearing from you.

This comes with my personal best wishes and on behalf of President Wagner and the university.

Sincerely,
Gary S. Hauk Vice-President and Deputy to the President
August 28, 2012

The letters flowed into Vice President Hauk's office.
Phil Nathan, who was flunked out in 1954 after two years at Emory school, wrote from California:

September 7th, 2012
Dr. Gary S. Hauk
Vice President and Deputy to the President
Emory University
410 Administration Building
Atlanta GA 30322

Dear Dr. Hauk,
Thank you for the invitation to the event scheduled for October 10, 2012, sixty years and one month after I entered Emory University Dental School. Unfortunately, my wife's health will not permit us to make that cross-country trip to Atlanta. Since I will not be able to meet you in person, I hope you will allow me to share some recollections.

I was pleasantly surprised to be accepted to the Emory dental school after only two years of undergraduate studies. I had just turned nineteen and was very naive. During my two years in the dental school, I was never counseled or given warning that I was in grave difficulty. I had passed the first year at which time one might have perhaps expected a discussion of my future at the school. I only learned of my dismissal with a curt letter while I was in Connecticut earning my tuition and fees as a waiter in a summer resort. I was stunned. I didn't know what to do or how to explain it to my parents. No one had explained it to me. I was summarily dismissed with not even an opportunity to repeat any subjects in which they believed me to be deficient. Fortunately, I was still young, resilient and while my confidence and self-esteem had been very badly injured, thank G_d they were not destroyed.

During my time at Emory, my parents had moved from Miami, FL to Chicago, IL. My father had developed a debilitating illness that was best treated at Northwestern Medical School's hospital. That September 1954, I was fortunate to be accepted to the University of Illinois and was graduated two years later with a B.A. major in chemistry with Honors. And I never looked back. It was too painful.

Fortunately, my life changed after my purgatory at Emory. Hired directly out of college by General Tire, Akron, OH, I was the first "technical" trainee the Company had ever hired for their fledgling Chemical Division. I went on to study polymer chemistry at the University of Akron, and, at my company's suggestion, also studied business and, in 1961, was granted an M.B.A. from the University of Akron. I was soon asked to join the Corporate Marketing staff as its chemical specialist. After ten years with the company, I received an offer from a Chicago chemical company to manage the marketing for one of its divisions, and later became the company's Corporate Director of Planning.

From those experiences I went on to manage a $20 million division of an NYSE company, ran several private companies and finally became a Managing Director and President of a private investment banking firm from which I retired in 1965. I stayed active in consulting and in 2004, to keep my mind challenged and at the urging of a C.P.A.

son-in-law, became an income tax practitioner earning an Enrolled Agent classification with the Internal Revenue Service. I'm also proud of my professional activities as a builder of organizations such as: election as international vice president of the American Marketing Association, where I later had to decline their request to run for president since it was a full time volunteer position; appointment as the first Director of Economic Development for the city of Brea, CA, and several offices in the South Orange Regional Chamber of Commerce including helping to organize and run a Toastmasters chapter to enable young professionals to learn the art of public speaking.

My wife, Paula, and I have been married for 53 years. We are blessed to have three daughters, eight brilliant and beautiful grandchildren and earlier this year, our first great grandson.

My point is not to brag about my career and life, but to affirm that I wasn't the flunk out Dr. Buhler and the Emory administration attempted to make me. If they were trying to "put me in my place," they certainly failed. The only sad points are that had I been allowed to continue my dental studies, I very humbly believe I could have also made a significant contribution to the dental profession and would have been a proud alumnus of Emory.

While I could never allow myself to look back, I have always carried in my heart a great affection for my fellow classmates and friends particularly Perry Brickman, Allen Shaw and Ed Zwig ז"ל. Dr. Brickman has performed an amazing mitzva to have finally forced the Emory University administration to confront the heinous acts their predecessors perpetrated on innocent young men simply because of their faith.

Your evening program appears to be a sincere gesture by the current administration. However, a positive action such as creating a specific "educational crisis intervention" counseling activity to assist young students of all backgrounds when they or their educators are concerned about the individual student's academic well-being would certainly indicate the school's effort to put good works behind their good gesture.

This is the first time in sixty years I have been able to speak to this issue. I would like to thank your administration and the uncommon effort of Dr. Brickman for giving me the courage to address this period of my life and allowing me to share it.

Sincerely,
Phil Nathan

On September 5, Norman Trieger, a Phi Beta graduate of Emory, wrote from New York:

Dr. Gary Hauk
Vice President and Deputy to the President
Emory University
Dear Sir,
I was pleased to receive your invitation to attend Emory's acknowledgement of wrongdoing of almost a half century ago. I was tangentially involved as a senior student when I applied to Emory's Dental School and sat for the examination best described as "the chalk carving test". I was shocked to learn that my faculty "adviser" felt that I should go elsewhere because of my almost total lack of "manual dexterity". He claimed that I had scored only in the 9th percentile! Subsequently, I did the same exam

at NYU and was accepted; Interviewed at Columbia and accepted; but elected to go to Harvard. I must interpret my experience as a feature of "good luck." I then went on to graduate with honors, selected for an Internship and Residency at the Massachusetts General Hospital where after 4 years received a faculty appointment.

A few years later, I passed my Boards in Oral Surgery. My former associate dean at Harvard had moved on to become the Dean at the new Dental School at UCLA. He invited me to join him as the founding Chair and Professor of Surgery at UCLA. After 5 years in Los Angeles I decided to remain in academia and felt that completing my medical qualification would be helpful. Montefiore Hospital in New York, then affiliated with the Albert Einstein College of Medicine, offered me the Chairmanship of Dentistry and Oral Surgery. Because of their financial crunch they could not provide a full-time salary and I was granted a half-time chairmanship and a tuition-paid opportunity to complete my last two years at the medical school. Over the next two years I worked 16 hours a day and then assumed my full time Chairmanship at Montefiore Medical Center. Several years later unification of the two departments of dentistry merged and I was selected to be Chair of the integrated departments and Chairman of the Department of Dentistry. When I arrived at Montefiore, in 1970, I inherited 3 general practice residents; when I left 32 years later, in 2002, the program included 72 postgraduates in training in 5 fully approved specialties of Dentistry.

I authored almost 80 publications in subjects on hematology, oral cancer, anesthesiology, hospital dentistry, education, periodontal surgery and served as Editor of Anesthesia Progress (J. of the American Dental Society of Anesthesia) and wrote 2 books entitled "Pain Control." I had a wonderful career and even steered my son Michael to attend Emory where he met and married his wife. I do appreciate Emory's present action. It is never too late to recognize bad behavior and fix it. Thank you very much. I plan to attend this event.

Norman Trieger, AB, DMD, MD

Emory made public their plans through a Samuel Freedman essay in the October 6 (Saturday) issue of the *New York Times*.[56] Friends and neighbors responded with obvious surprise and pleasure.

Dear Perry (and Shirley)
Shavua Tov. An Emory friend of mine just sent this to me. Wow! The NY Times. We are so happy for you that all of your hard work is now formally validated. We plan to be there on Wednesday night.

Roberta Scher

The story was finally out. I was on a cloud. I just wished my parents could have lived to see the day.

CHAPTER 17

Memory Lane

here is a saying that it's easier to get a PhD degree at Emory than it is to find a parking place. The event planners were determined that Wednesday, October 10, 2012, would be an exception to that rule. Shuttle buses were provided to and from designated parking lots for all pre- and post-reception guests. They reserved a special parking lot for the general public. Mobile TV and cable crews mobilized at strategic locations, and reporters were stationed along the walkways to interview passers-by.

Shirley and I drove the familiar route down Houston Mill Road and parked at the Gatewood Road parking garage, just a block away from the shuttle pick-up spot. The weather was perfect: 73 degrees, an almost cloudless sky with endless visibility.

We arrived early and were excited to see so many people already seated in the buses. Our special guest, Norman Trieger, accompanied us. Norman, a 1951 Phi Beta Kappa Emory alumnus and a Harvard dental school graduate, attended as a representative of the long list of qualified Jewish students who had been denied entrance to the Emory dental school. Norm was visibly moved by the applause that greeted him as he entered the van. He was a distinguished figure in dental education and was returning to the only institution that had ever rejected him. He called from the van to his adult children in New York to tell them how happy he was.

The familiar marble buildings along Clifton Road were sufficient to transport the white-haired visitors back a half-century to their fond undergraduate days. The scene changed as we approached our destination, the relatively new Joseph W. Jones Room of the Woodruff Library, a popular venue for important university events.

A large crowd had already arrived a quarter-hour before the announced time. Food stations were aligned along a wood-paneled wall, and the young people were enjoying the refreshments. In contrast, the veterans, with broad smiles on their faces, were shaking hands and embracing one another. They put aside their canes and stood tall as they greeted their comrades of years past. Some faces were unfamiliar, as many of the men were separated by more than a decade. Nametags and dates bridged the gap. They were finally meeting fellow survivors of a shared past. They introduced their spouses, adult children, and grandchildren.

President Wagner and Vice President Gary Hauk mingled with the crowd and soon became friends with previously unknown individuals. The atmosphere was spontaneous and unrehearsed. It was magical.

Former dental students and families at the Special Reception[57]

Children and grandchildren at the Special Reception[58]

President Wagner and guests at the Special Reception[59]

Finally, we were asked to take seats at tables that were previously unnoticed. The room was fully occupied. There were an estimated 250 special guests and dignitaries. My close friend, Mickey Steinberg, drew me close and whispered, "If they call on you, keep it short."

Vice President Hauk took the podium and formally greeted the crowd. He had already made many new friends and expressed his appreciation for the outpouring of friendship and respect that he felt. He thanked all for coming to this historic gathering on behalf of the university, especially those who had traveled so far. He invited the crowd, at the end of the hour, to follow him and the president from the library to Cox Hall, just a block away, for the public ceremony. This was scheduled to begin promptly at 6 p.m.

Hauk called me to the podium before introducing President Wagner. Heeding my friend Mickey's advice, I began reciting the 2000-year-old Hebrew prayer, the *Shehecheyanu*. Before I had finished the introduction to the prayer, the entire crowd, totally impromptu, joined me in Hebrew: "*shehecheyanu vekiymanu vehigi'anu lazman hazeh.*" I turned to Drs. Hauk and Wagner and translated: "Blessed are You, Lord our God, King of the Universe, Who has granted us life, sustained us, and enabled us to reach this occasion." They seemed to be awed that the crowd, in so many ways diverse, was able to respond in unison in the ancient Hebrew tongue.

President Wagner recognized the sudden shift of tone from excitement to one of solemnity. He knew that the audience would be listening carefully and with great expectation for his long-awaited words. In his remarks to the assembled students who had been treated so badly, he said all the right things. Yet, his words of regret at this meeting, though humble and sincere, fell short of what I had expected. Deborah Lipstadt confided to me later that she was "clearly distressed by the rather corporate and impersonal nature of his comments." I suspect the president sensed our disappointment. On the walk from the Jones Room to Cox Hall, with his aides at his side, he recalibrated his message.

As soon as we exited the library, we were face-to-face with reporters. They knew we were on the way to another gathering, but they wanted teasers for the evening news. When we arrived at the Cox Hall auditorium, we were amazed to see a capacity audience, with people lined up against the walls. Many of the attendees had received an email notice from Professor Deborah Lipstadt earlier in the week, urging them to attend. It read in part:

"This event has—and I do not believe I am speaking hyperbolically—tremendous significance in, not just the history of Emory, but the history of American higher education. The attached press release will give you the background. The reason I say that it has such significance is that this is the first time that I know of in which a university is acknowledging its past history of antisemitic wrongs directly to some of the people who were most impacted by them. Universities have apologized in the past for their history of racism and antisemitism [e.g. Dartmouth] but never *directly* to those who suffered as a result.

Public gathering at Cox Hall to hear President Wagner's apology

There was a hush as the program began. Vice President Hauk introduced Professor Eric Goldstein, who presented the events of the dental school matter in historical perspective.

Then, with simple formality, Hauk announced, "The President of Emory University, James Wagner."

When the president stood before the packed Cox auditorium to deliver the same message we had recently heard, something remarkable had been added. He began, "On behalf of Emory University, serving as its present president, I hereby express in the deepest, strongest terms, Emory's regret for the antisemitic practices of the dental school during those years," He continued, "We at Emory also regret that it has taken this long for those events to be properly acknowledged." Then, everything changed when he looked up from his prepared remarks and with a slight quiver in his voice said: "I am sorry; we are sorry." With that, the burden of pain so many of us still bore was immeasurably eased.

Then, to my complete surprise, President Wagner asked me to join him at the podium for a second time.

"Stanley Perry Brickman, distinguished oral surgeon, community leader, and maker of Emory history. By your example of intellectual engagement and ethical integrity, you have extended the reach of the enabling power of an excellent mind and a generous heart. By your association with Emory University, you have made its heritage shine more brightly, and have made its name more worthy of renown.

"By your courage and creativity, you have helped open the way for other wise hearts to seek knowledge. By your leadership you have enhanced the common good and enlarged the circle of light that shines in the world. You represent the fulfilled promise of a liberal arts university in a world needing greater humanity. You add to the reservoir of trust so essential to the just and effective workings of civil society. You set a high standard for a new generation of Emory men and women who aim to achieve their own good work in the world. For these and all the ways you exhibit the aspirations of Emory, a grateful university pays tribute to you by spreading your name in the Emory historical record."

Then President Wagner awarded me the "Maker of History Award," the 176th such presentation in Emory's 175 years. I accepted the award on behalf of all my fellow students. "The truth, in a situation like this, is never really validated until the perpetrator says he's sorry. We all owe a great debt of gratitude to Emory University. It's unparalleled what they have done. No other university has ever done anything like this. I am happy that we have been fortunate enough to have lived long enough to see this happen. Thank you very much."

As the crowd filed out, there was a palpable feeling of relief and a collective sense of gratitude to President Wagner and to Emory University. In the following days, there were scores of responses and commentaries in the local and national media. Bill Nigut of the ADL said in a statement:

"We are grateful to President Wagner for his forthright leadership in acknowledging and apologizing for a policy that has haunted many of the Jewish students throughout their long lives. We are now hearing powerful, painful stories of how they came to doubt their own abilities, were viewed as failures by parents and friends, and had to rethink careers—all because the dental school dean at the time was an anti-Semite, and other administrators and faculty either ignored or abetted his prejudice."

SorryWatch.com, a blog dedicated to exposing faux apologies, cited Emory University's apology as "an excellent apology." Titled "I've graphed my bad behavior for you," it was posted on October 12, 2012,[60] and included the following language:

When he saw the graph, Perry Brickman realized that his secret shame wasn't his alone. In 1951 Brickman enrolled in Emory University's dental school. He thought he was doing well. But after his first year he got a letter from John Buhler, dean of the dental school, telling him he had flunked out. Goodbye! No one believed him when he said he'd been doing well. His parents said he hadn't studied enough. Three other students in the dental school had also flunked out. Oddly, like Brickman, they were Jewish. Their parents thought they hadn't studied enough. Ejected from Emory, Brickman went to dental school in Tennessee. He graduated with honors and became a successful dentist. No one knew about his earlier disgrace. He didn't want to talk about it. In 2006, at Emory's library, Brickman saw an exhibit about "Jews at Emory." There was a section about anti-Semitism at the dental school when John Buhler was its dean. Articles, a chapter in a book—and a graph. An eloquent graph. The graph showed the failure rate of Jewish students at the dental school—low in the 30s and 40s, and booming from 1948 to 1961, when Buhler was dean. Under Buhler, 65% of Jewish students failed or had to repeat entire years. Somehow none of the Emory faculty or administrators of the time had the heart to interfere with Buhler's system. Emory had a Jewish quota in those days, but apparently that still meant too many Jews for Buhler's taste. Oh Lord, some of them were persistent— they took those "failed" years over again. In 1961 Buhler changed the dental school application so students had to say whether they were "Caucasian, Jew or Other." Oh, subtle. Not too subtle for the Anti-Defamation League to notice, however, and they complained to the school. Something happened. Buhler resigned. No one would say it was because of the new question or what it showed about prejudice at the dental school. Nobody wanted to talk about it. Years passed. (In 1992 the dental school closed.) But that graph—the more Brickman thought about what it showed and what that meant—it wasn't just him, and he had been a good student, and he wasn't the only one with a humiliating secret—the more he did want to talk about it. He videotaped interviews with dozens of other Jewish students from the dental program in the Buhler regime. For years they'd been too ashamed to talk about it. Now they did. One quoted Buhler saying, "Why do you Jews want to go into dentistry? You don't have it in the hands." Brickman took the interviews to Gary Hauk, Emory's vice-president. "It's shameful, a blot on the institution's history" Hauk has said. Instead of glossing over the ancient blot, Emory, remarkably, hired filmmakers to make a documentary of it, using some of Brickman's videos, and adding interviews with Emory staff. The documentary premiered in an Emory ballroom October 10, 2012, at a public ceremony to which the surviving students were invited. James Wagner, the university president, officially apologized to them. "I hereby express in the deepest, strongest terms Emory's regret for the anti-Semitic practices of the dental school during those years. We at Emory also regret that it has taken this long for those events to be properly acknowledged. I am sorry. We are sorry." (Buhler died in 1976. He probably wouldn't have been sorry.) It's an excellent apology. The school let Buhler get away with bigotry until he got so outrageous (and put it in print) they were forced to act. Then they ignored the matter for decades until it seemed forgotten. But when Brickman brought them the videotaped testimony, words that showed what the graph's figures really meant in people's lives, they acted decisively. The documentary showed specifically what the apology was for. The apology was an emotional vindication for the former students. One former student said he had never believed Emory would let the story come out in his lifetime. "The truth in a situation like this is never really validated until the perpetrator says sorry," Brickman said. I love a story that shows the power of a good apology, not to mention the power of a nice, clear graph.

On October 13, 2012, the following article was posted on CNN, written by Jessica Ravitz.

Shining light on Emory school's past anti-Semitism prompts healing—and, for one man, questions

Atlanta (CNN)—Sixteen years after Susan Shulman Tessel lost her father, she sat on a Southern college campus Wednesday night and couldn't stop thinking about him. Surrounded by hundreds in a packed ballroom, she cried because he was missing. He should have been there with her and her mother. He deserved to be.

The late Irving Shulman was the only Jewish man to enter Emory University's School of Dentistry in 1948. That was the same year someone else came to the school: the newly appointed dean, John E. Buhler.

After one academic year, Shulman flunked out. Buhler stayed on for 13 years, leading what some Jewish students would refer to as a "reign of terror." Between 1948 and 1961, when Buhler left, 65% of Jewish students either failed out or were forced to repeat up to two years of coursework in the four-year program.

Those who lasted often paid. There were insults from professors such as "dirty Jew," accusations by faculty of cheating and questions from the dean like, "Why do you Jews want to be dentists? You don't have it in your hands." Tessel's dad earned the distinction of being the first who failed.

Irving Shulman's widow, Irma Shulman-Weiner, and daughter Susan Shulman Tessel came to Emory last week because he couldn't.

His daughter, who lives in New York, heard him tell stories about the constant reminders of how awful he was. His molds of teeth—which he was so proud of—would either get crushed by hands or grades. Convinced he wasn't being treated fairly, a non-Jewish classmate agreed to turn in one of Shulman's molds under his name. Shulman's handiwork earned that student an A-minus.

"At least he knew he didn't make it up," Tessel said. Her late father gave up his dentistry dream and moved on to pharmacy school. But, she said, being at Emory last week would have helped him make sense of what had transpired. That's when 19 former Jewish dental students who had experienced that era came together and finally received the apology and recognition they had never thought possible. "He didn't have the benefit of knowing he wasn't alone."

'A fraternity of silence'

Three years after Shulman was dubbed a failure at the end of his first academic year, Perry Brickman got his surprise letter from the dean telling him the same. Unlike Shulman, though, he had never been told he wasn't doing well.

Stunned. Embarrassed. Brickman was both. But he wasn't beaten down enough to give up on dentistry and was accepted to the dental school at The University of Tennessee, where he graduated fourth in his class. He would go on to have a 43-year career as a respected oral surgeon in Atlanta. He knew he was no failure. He also knew he wasn't alone. He was one of four Jewish men who entered the school in 1951; two years later they were all gone. Brickman, 79, wasn't one to bring up the past. In 2000, he went to a reunion of his Jewish fraternity brothers from their Emory undergrad days. It turned out eight of the men in the room had been scarred by the same dental program, but it's not something they talked about. Brickman's wife, Shirley, would later start calling the former dental students "a fraternity of silence."

It would be years before that would change.

In 2006, Emory University celebrated its 30th anniversary of Jewish studies. Eric Goldstein, a Jewish history professor, set up the exhibit to coincide with the event. He called it, "Jews of Emory: Faces of a Changing University." Most of the exhibit was a celebration of the campus' Jewish life, Goldstein said, but a small section jumped out at Brickman. He stared at statistics, a bar graph that illustrated what happened at the dental school between 1948 and 1961. The image had been featured in a chapter of "Some of My Best Friends...," a book published by the Anti-Defamation League in the early 1960s. Like a skyscraper among short buildings, he said, the bar showing the numbers of Jews who failed out of the school or repeated coursework towered above all others. He couldn't believe what he was seeing.

The visual highlighted what Brickman always suspected about the dental school leadership and how that period was handled at Emory: "I wasn't a failure. They were a failure."

He knew there were stories behind those numbers—not just of those who hadn't made it but also of those who did. Between the statistics and a conversation with a still-burdened classmate, Brickman set out on a path to find them all.

Making waves

A month before one man got his degree, he was forced to stand before the dean and assembled faculty for an hourlong dressing down. Later, one of the professors pulled the student aside and apologized, saying he had a wife and children to think about and had no choice but to play along.

Another said the day he got his diploma he felt like he'd been released from prison. A third repeated what a professor used to call him, "my little black sheep," and then, bothered by the memory, muttered under his breath, "son of a bitch."

These men said they were the "lucky" ones; the ones who actually made it through to earn degrees from the school. The 39 Jews who Brickman said enrolled during the Buhler era were all men; few women attended the school back then. Of that bunch, a dozen flunked out. Only three of those 12 became dentists. At least 15 of the Jewish dental students who lasted were forced to repeat coursework—and in some cases a year or two of study.

Art Burns, 80, of Jacksonville, Florida, flunked out in 1953 but went on to be first in his class at Temple University's dental school. The retired orthodontist recalled later bumping into the Emory dean in an Army base dental lab. Buhler looked at him and said, "Burns, I'd recognize that nose anywhere."

Another who didn't fail—but who Buhler insisted didn't have the hands for dentistry—found himself being asked to treat dental school faculty throughout his senior year. Crowns, restorations, fillings. You name it, Ronald Goldstein did it.

"I must have had good enough hands for them," said Goldstein, 78, of Atlanta, who lectures around the world, is considered a pioneer in his field and wrote the first comprehensive textbook on cosmetic dentistry.

The men were accepted to the school because admissions were handled by the broader University, not the dental school alone, said history professor Goldstein (no relation to Ronald). While quotas worked against Jews in many institutions at the time, the Emory dental school story was unique in that these students faced discrimination after they arrived.

The issues were talked about in small circles, but they weren't discussed loudly. What student would announce he'd flunked? What parents would talk about such news, especially in a community that put such emphasis on academic achievement? And this was Emory, a hometown, liberal arts jewel many local Jews attended; who would criticize—or believe criticism about—such a place?

Beyond these hangups was the worry about backlash that permeated Atlanta's Jewish community. It was rooted in fears born of history and reality—Atlanta's infamous lynching of Leo Frank in 1913, the ongoing activity of the Ku Klux Klan, the 1958 bombing of the city's most prominent synagogue. Israel was still a fledgling nation. This was also the immediate post-Holocaust era, a time when Jewish people in America were just starting to understand the magnitude of what had happened abroad, said Deborah Lauter, the Anti-Defamation League's civil rights director.

"It was a real period of insecurity for the Jewish community, and that didn't really shift 'til 1967," after the Six-Day War between Israel and its neighbors, she said. "With a war victory came a newfound confidence of Jewish people."

But a small handful of Atlanta Jews refused to let go of what was happening at the dental school.

Art Levin paid attention to every snippet. Then the Southeast regional director of the ADL, Levin was determined to make Emory own up to and deal with the dental school's anti-Jewish bias. He collected graduation programs, which included lists of students in all four years, and studied how the Jewish surnames disappeared or were held back while their classmates moved ahead. He nurtured contacts who helped get him inside information from the registrar's office to back up his calculations. He wanted to make the case not by outing any victims but by presenting irrefutable facts.

When the local Jewish Community Relations Council wanted to tone down pressure on the university, Levin's response, as he stated in an Emory-commissioned documentary that premiered Wednesday evening: "Screw that. This guy has been torturing students for 10 years."

Levin, at the time, was "villified" by segments of the Jewish community for making waves, said ADL's Lauter, a former Atlanta resident who, like Levin, did a stint as the organization's Southeast regional director. "But that's why we're here for people who face discrimination. Sometimes ADL has to be the tough guy. We take no prisoners in the fight against anti-Semitism."

While Levin takes great satisfaction in knowing the story is finally getting public acknowledgement, Lauter said it's "bittersweet" for him. "He did feel stung by the whole experience." In 1962, after nine years in his position, he left the world of Jewish community work. Levin, who now lives in Florida and is hard of hearing, was not able to be interviewed for this story.

A form devised by Buhler, which at the top asked students to check a box—Caucasian, Jewish or other (Emory was not racially integrated at the time)—ended up being his downfall, many say. The university president, S. Walter Martin, had been dismissive of the concerns Levin and some others raised. So, when Martin was out of town, Levin brought a copy of the form to Judson "Jake" Ward, the dean of faculty, and Ward grew incensed. He marched down to see Buhler, who resigned soon after.

Emory's president still refused to acknowledge what had been going on and wrote off Buhler's resignation as coincidental. Martin even insisted to local press, Goldstein said, that Buhler could have stayed at the dental school as long as he wanted.

With the dean gone, Atlanta's Jewish community essentially closed the book and put it away.

Not the man he knew
That book only recently opened for the former dean's son. A sister-in-law sent John E. Buhler Jr., 65, a copy of a recent story in The New York Times about the episode. What he read "caught me completely off guard," he said. "I was completely unaware of that situation." He was a kid when his father landed at Emory and always believed politics in academia prompted his departure, nothing more. Everything he ever knew about his father, who died on Easter Sunday in 1976, belied what is being discussed now.

The former dean of Emory's dental school, John E. Buhler, was a different man to Jewish students than he was to his son.

The younger Buhler, a retired oral surgeon living in Huntington, Indiana, said he grew up with a man who cared about "helping kids stay in school and not throwing *them out of school." When he got into the field himself, he proudly watched how former students sought out his father at conferences, showering him with gratitude. One even boasted that he had named his child after Buhler.*

"It just sort of blows me away...He did so many positive things for dentistry and students," the younger Buhler said. "It's hard to believe." Trying to make sense of it all, Buhler Jr.'s daughter sent her father an article that appeared in The Spartanburg Herald in South Carolina in 1964. It was written soon after the older Buhler assumed the dean's post at the new dental school of what was then known as the Medical College of South Carolina—and after the Jewish community there weighed in with concerns about past anti-Semitism, demanding his appointment be rescinded.

The 1964 article quoted the chairman of the Medical College's board of trustees defending Buhler, saying he was recommended for the new position after a committee concluded the Emory charges were "not as serious as painted at one time."

The former dean's namesake doesn't remember his father ever saying a derogatory word about Jewish people. In fact, he's quick to point out that when the family lived in Atlanta, some of his parents' closest friends were Jewish.

These sorts of claims get former students like Brickman, who led the charge to humanize the dental school's history, riled up. He has collected too many stories and seen too many documents, including incriminating notes written by Buhler himself, to call the former dean anything but an antisemite.

But for Buhler Jr., none of this adds up. Really, how can it? "If this situation did exist, it was certainly out of character of the man I knew," he wrote CNN the morning after the Emory event. "If indeed these events did occur, I feel badly for the individuals involved. Last night's event might have made them feel better but didn't compensate for their injury."

'I am sorry. We are sorry.'

Facing its history is something Emory isn't afraid to do. In 2011, it issued a statement of regret for the school's involvement with slavery. The Southern institution once had slave laborers on campus and faculty members who owned slaves. Earlier this year, Emory fessed up to fudging data to boost its ranking.

Meantime, the university boasts a Center for Ethics, campus dialogues on matters like race, sexuality and gender, and has long-proven its support for Jewish studies and community. It has 20 full-time faculty members dedicated to the field, including world-renowned Holocaust scholar Deborah Lipstadt.

The school seemed ripe for the resurfacing of the dental school's history, which is why Goldstein, the Jewish history professor, placed a call last spring to Gary Hauk, Emory's vice president and deputy to the president. He said he had a friend Hauk needed to meet. With testimonies he had recorded with his Flip camera, Brickman showed Hauk videos of men in their 70s and 80s, their negative Emory dental school experience still etched in their faces and emotions. Hauk didn't need convincing that something needed to be done.

A documentary incorporating Brickman's footage was commissioned, resulting in "From Silence to Recognition: Confronting Discrimination in Emory's Dental School History." A plan was developed to invite the former students, their families and their widows to come together on campus for an apology that was half a century overdue. What had happened to them at the dental school, which closed in the early 1990s for unrelated reasons, had never been formally acknowledged. It was time.

Blue ribbons were strung along aisles to reserve seats for the special guests, who first met privately with Emory President James W. Wagner. The men, some of whom hadn't returned to Emory since the day they left, arrived with family members from all over the country. Many went on to become great successes in dentistry. Those who gave up that dream excelled as physicians, lawyers, CPAs and computer experts. One man who flunked out tried his hand at painting, wanting to prove he had the manual skills the dean said he lacked; he won art show awards.

The experience had been a guarded secret for some—a chapter in life they hid from parents, friends, future spouses and their children. One woman in attendance said she had only learned the day before that her father failed out of Emory. For other former students, their time at Emory haunted them. One of their daughters—who refused even years later to apply to Emory when she went to dental school—dubbed herself and others like her "children of survivors," a term often linked to the Holocaust. An 18-year-old man, who is gay and faced plenty of bullying, realized he could relate to the grandfather sitting next to him in new ways.

Widows and children of deceased former students showed up for those who didn't live long enough to see this day. One man, who was young when his father died, came to hear stories no one else in his life could tell.

All around them, as they took their seats, the ballroom filled. A standing-room-only crowd of hundreds came out to recognize them. Here, any shame from the past was lifted. Instead, these men were the picture of courage and worthy of respect—and that long-awaited apology.

"Institutions—universities—are as fallible as the human beings who populate them, and like individuals, universities need to remind themselves frequently of the principles they want to live by," President Wagner said. "The discrimination against Jewish dental students undermined the academic integrity of the dental school and ultimately of Emory. I am sorry. We are sorry."

The night, which would end with a special dinner for this no-longer-silent fraternity, included a tribute to Brickman, who was called to the stage.

His wife, surrounded by family, clung to a tissue and dabbed her eyes. A daughter clutched her mother's hand. A son looked up at his dad and beamed. Brickman never did this for the Emory History Maker medal Wagner strung around his neck. Nor did he do this for the citation read to honor his work. For him, this was a journey of discovery— one he took with the faces behind the numbers. With him that night were these men and their families, as well as the university he still loved. Throughout the evening, and long after dinner ended, he saw tears, camaraderie, even laughter from some of the very men he feared were no longer capable of smiling.

All of this, he hoped, signaled what mattered most: Healing.

CHAPTER 18

A Story of Survival

F or three weeks, the New York Times October 6, 2012, article on Emory ranked #2 in articles most frequently emailed by NYTimes. com readers. Thanks to my children and their Facebook friends, the story stayed viral for even longer. My fellow students and I were overwhelmed with congratulatory notes and phone calls from friends who were previously unaware of our long-held secret.

The Jewish Telegraphic Agency, through its worldwide distribution, selected Nobel scientists Haroche and Lefkowitz, actress/singer Barbra Streisand, securities trader Larry Greenfield, Hungarian activist András Kerényi and Perry Brickman as its "Friday Five."

There was extensive newspaper, radio, and television coverage throughout Georgia and the Southeast, and educational circles also offered the story wide national attention. *The University World News, The Chronicle of Higher Education,* NewsLibrary.com, The Ivy Coach, USA Education News, and the Weekly News Digest published lengthy news articles and editorials.

The news quickly traversed geographic boundaries, reaching readers in Argentina, Canada, Great Britain, Israel, Japan, Mexico, and New Zealand. Surprisingly, the story even appeared in the Al Jazeera English edition and the Iran Herald. The story resonated to members of all faiths: *Aish Ha-Torah, Real-Clear Religion, Smokerise Baptist Church, The Christian Century, Theology and Society, The Jewish Forward,* and *Huffington Post Religion.*

293

The bloggers' diverse audience included Straightdope.com, Creative Loafing, Elkhorn Denture Blog, insidehighered.com, Mike's Meandering Mind, Muckrake Tweets, Sorry Watch.com, Pro-Israel Bay Bloggers, and Openhealthblog. The majority of the observers praised Emory's stand even if it was late in coming.

Rabbi Wendi Geffen, an Emory alumna, told the readers in her blog *Pri HaGeffen*: "As you likely know, a horrible period in the university's history was recently brought to the surface by the work of Emory professor Dr. Eric Goldstein and one of the former dental students, now Dr. Perry Brickman. In some respects, the revelation of a university's anti-Semitic past is nothing new. But for Emory, which has such deep ties to the Jewish community and leaders in its region (of which many of my own relatives are a part), no less my deep personal connection to the school, this news cut particularly deep. It is why it is hard for me to put into words just how proud I felt when I learned how Emory's administration chose to respond to this history. I could not be prouder to say I went to Emory University."

"Bloodthirsty Liberal" disagreed. "Let's see... 1951. The Holocaust officially ended in 1945, and these little Nazi sympathizers in academia still hadn't learned. Perhaps it was because the NY Times hadn't bothered to inform the elite public that most of those killed in the concentration camps were Jewish until 1950? Could it be that news traveled slowly in those days? No, because the East Coast elite universities were also shunning Jews. (Aside: NYU and MIT developed great math departments because they accepted Jews). Now they're sorry at Emory? Now when these guys are in their 70s and 80s? You think it's never too late? I disagree. It's too late."

"Insightful Riot" was also doubtful. It observed, "More than their heartfelt apology, Emory needs to step up and contribute more tangibly to the war against anti-Semitism. As an institution of higher learning, it is their moral and ethical obligation to take a pittance of their $5.4 billion endowment and put their money where their 'I'm sorry' is."

The Jewish press found the story noteworthy, as did their readers who responded with long-suppressed stories of similar mistreatment. Feature articles appeared in the *Atlanta Jewish Times, Birmingham (AL) Jewish Life Magazine, The Cleveland (Ohio) Jewish News,* the *Hartford (CT) Jewish Ledger, Jewish News of Greater Phoenix, Jewish Press of Tampa, Omaha Jewish Press, Hebrew University Newsletter (Ma Nishma), Southern Jewish Life,* and *The Jewish Georgian.*

There were multiple requests to share the story locally. The audiences ranged from high school students at the Atlanta Jewish Academy, Weber School, Marist Academy, and Temple Sinai to senior citizens at Huntcliff Summit, Marcus Jewish Community Center, Jewish War Veterans, and Emory Osher Institute. The Southeast ADL board, the Hebrew Order of David, and Alpha Omega Atlanta held special meetings to view the documentary and discuss the historical impact on Jewish Atlanta and Emory University.

Emory University totally embraced the dissemination of the story. There were feature articles in the October 8, 2012 *Emory Wheel* and the 2013 *Emory Magazine.* When they scheduled out-of-town events, Katie Busch and Robin Harpak from the Emory Development and Alumni Relations Department actively encouraged Emory alumni to attend. They traveled thousands of miles with me to gatherings in Boston, New York, Cleveland, Chicago, Washington, DC, Baltimore, Tampa/St. Petersburg, Dallas, Toronto, Orlando, Miami, Birmingham, Memphis, Ann Arbor, Tulsa, and Chattanooga. They were also present at the Savannah, Georgia, and Hartford, Connecticut Jewish Film Festivals, where we screened the Emory documentary.

I was asked to give the keynote address in December 2012 at the 78th Annual Meeting of the Alpha Omega International Dental Fraternity convention in Scottsdale, Arizona, which brought together 160 fraters and their families from eight countries and students representing 12 dental schools. My former classmate Art Burns flew from Jacksonville to Phoenix to join me in this historic celebration. At the meeting, I received the Presidential Citation for my work "in exposing the antisemitism that pervaded the Emory University School of Dentistry throughout the 1950s, which included the unjust failing and/or expulsion of numerous Jewish dental students." I reminded the audience that in December 1960, International Alpha Omega was the first organization to join the ADL in publicly calling attention to the discrimination at Emory. And it was Alpha Omega, in December 2010, that cited Art Levin and the ADL for exposing the antisemitism at Emory dental school.

At each of these meetings, I was approached by physicians and dentists who stood in line to relate personal accounts of discrimination they had encountered in schools all over the United States and Canada. In Orlando, Florida, a 99-year-old retired cardiologist related how, as a Jew, he found it very difficult to find housing at the University of Pennsylvania. After his acceptance to Penn medical school, he realized that he and the other Jewish students were singled out and assigned the same cadaver. After reading about Emory, he wrote a letter to the president of the University of Pennsylvania recounting his experience 70 years ago. He wanted me to have copies of his letter and President Amy Gutmann's reply assuring him that it is no longer that way at Penn and she hoped it never would be again.

As I continued my travels, again and again I was told about quotas at dental schools, proprietary and public, private and university-affiliated. At Ann Arbor, Michigan, during a panel discussion, a faculty administrator who identified herself as a minority (female and black) denied any history of Jewish quotas at Michigan. Two other panel members who provided times, dates, and numbers to refute her statement immediately challenged her.

There were a few places where the discussion fell on disbelieving ears. In Boston, Harvard dental students were shocked to hear my presentation and found it difficult to accept. Their dean stood up and corroborated my account. "It wasn't always like it is now," he told them. I added, "The quotas you are familiar with are minority preference quotas. They were imposed to increase enrollment of minorities. The quotas we experienced were set in place to keep us out."

Just about everywhere, members of the audience arose to take the microphone to tell their personal stories. Everyone remembered the Jewish quotas. The numbers varied, but the discrimination existed throughout the country. There were various theories of how it started, when it started, and how it was imposed. There were stories of how "Uncle so and so" changed his name or disguised his identity to "pass," but efforts to avoid the quota rarely worked.

On the plane rides home, I had time to digest all the verbal information I was accumulating at the various meetings. Because the stories were often based on personal accounts rather than hard facts or research, their certitude might be challenged by some as simply anecdotal. But the testimonies came from first-hand sources who seemed reliable. The situation seemed so widespread and pervasive that it appeared that the discrimination had to have been orchestrated from a central source. Having a scientific background, I was trained to discount wild speculation. Yet it appeared that antisemitism at the Emory dental school was not an isolated incident. As bad as the Emory episode was, there were strong indications that Emory was just the tip of the iceberg. Obviously, that didn't in any way soften the long-term effect of the Emory experience on me and my fellow students. It did, however, provide a broader understanding of the destructive nature of antisemitism in higher education in the entire United States during the 20th century.

The Darkest Corners of Society

In our American History classes, we were taught that the Pilgrims came to America to escape persecution and practice their beliefs freely. But from the fact that they came here to practice their beliefs, it doesn't follow that they believed others had the same right. In fact, the Puritans did not have this belief. Just as they had been persecuted, they in turn made it difficult for those who had differing views.

298 | Etracted

That didn't stop other religious denominations, including Jews, from seeking shelter and prosperity in the New World. By the time of the first census in 1790, there were about 2,000 Jews in the United States. The American Jewish population of about 4,500 in 1830 rose to 40,000 in 1845 and leaped to 150,000 by the time of the Civil War. From this figure, the number increased to about 250,000 in 1880. Many of these immigrants made the transition from peddler to prosperous merchant with extraordinary swiftness.

For Jews in America, the thrust of restrictive provisions and antisemitic attitudes was clear. The young nation thought of itself as Christian. Judaism was perceived as a backward religion and, to many, presented a direct and serious challenge to the American spirit and character. Newspapers and magazines streamed abusive stereotypes about Jews. Christian ministers disparaged their character and faith. Even with these negative perceptions, America was so much better than Europe, and Jews continued to flock to the "goldene medina," the Golden Land.

On the eve of the Civil War, antisemitic charges erupted on both sides of the Mason-Dixon line. Even so, this did not deter Jews from serving in the Southern and Northern armies. When the war ended, Jews shared in the growth and prosperity of the Industrial Revolution and the Gilded Age, even as they were banned from exclusive resorts, gentlemen's clubs, and fancy prep schools.

No matter what Jews did or said, they were always regarded as a group apart. But that didn't stop them from being loyal Americans. They knew that America was still the safest land that Jews had ever lived in. From 1881 to 1914, more than 2.5 million Jews migrated from Eastern Europe; 2 million of them reached the United States.

The well-established white Christian community despised the masses of poor immigrants who flocked to the United States, including the Eastern European Jews, and regarded them as a threat to the American way of life and mode of government. The success of the German Jews, on the other hand, aroused envy and antagonism. A prolonged propaganda campaign with strong antisemitic undertones led to the 1921-1924 legislation that drastically limited immigration and revealed an explicit preference for the "Nordic race."

As described in earlier chapters, at precisely the same time the nationwide movement to restrict immigration was gaining momentum, dramatic cuts were being made in Jewish student admissions to Columbia University, followed by Harvard and other Ivy League schools. The most common method to identify the "desirable" (native born, white, Protestant) applicants was to add questions to the application form about religious preferences, race, and nationality. This method was employed by 90% of American universities and colleges at the time. More subtle references included restrictions on subsidies and preferences for alumni sons and daughters.

At Yale University medical school, Dean Milton Winternitz's instructions to the admissions office regarding ethnic quotas were very specific: "Never admit more than five Jews, take only two Italian Catholics, and take no blacks at all." Most of the other medical schools were subtler, but most of them fell in line with a form of numerus clausus.[61]

In a 1938 Roper poll, approximately 60% of the respondents held a low opinion of Jews, labeling them "greedy," "dishonest," and "pushy"; 41% of respondents agreed that Jews had "too much power in the United States," and this figure rose to 58% by 1945. In 1939, a Roper poll found that only 39% of Americans felt that Jews should be treated like other people. Some 53% believed that "Jews are different and should be restricted" and 10% believed that Jews should be deported. Several surveys taken from 1940 to 1946 found that Jews were seen as a greater threat to the welfare of the United States than any other national, religious, or racial group.[62]

We have learned in previous chapters how the nine members of the Council on Dental Education of the American Dental Association and their Executive Secretary, Harlan H. Horner, formalized a plan to impose a "racial quota" on each of the 39 American dental schools. In thinly veiled terms, Horner stated that the dental schools had accepted too many Jews. The nine members of the Council were the elite of dentistry—highly educated, aristocratic, virtuous, and talented. They were "sons of the Mayflower." They were not disposed to handing over their profession to foreigners.

Would it be fair to say that all the above actions, which seem to have the common thread of limiting Jewish progress, constitute antisemitism? The charges against Jews are varied to such an extent that they defy rational discussion. Jews have been labeled capitalist, but they have also been labeled socialist. To some, Jews are cosmopolitans and operate outside borders; others say they are clannish and self-segregate in ghettos.

Antisemitism frequently charges Jews with conspiring to harm humanity, and it is often used to blame Jews for "why things go wrong." It is expressed in speech, writing, visual forms, and action, and employs sinister stereotypes and negative character traits. It would appear that antisemitism, from the time of our nation's founding through the 1960s, was commonplace in American society. It was undisguised and acceptable even in polite society. Yet, despite its evil and threatening nature, it did not deprive Jews of voting rights or loss of property, nor did it succeed in preventing Jewish citizens from climbing the ladder of success. It blocked access to education at certain levels and at certain times, and it prevented access to certain social venues. However, with a few notable exceptions, it did not cause destruction and death as it did in other countries over the past centuries.

Following the establishment of the State of Israel in 1948 and its rapid development into a "startup nation," the public image of the Jews and the Jewish people was thought to have improved. But in 2014, the Anti-Defamation League released the results of a global survey of antisemitism. Abraham Foxman, ADL executive director, stated that negative attitudes toward Jews are "persistent and pervasive in the U.S. and around the world." The poll determined that 34% of respondents are deeply infected with antisemitic attitudes.

Antisemitism is alive and well. We still must rely on law enforcement agencies and "Jewish defense" organizations, e.g., ADL, CAMERA, SWC, ZOA to monitor the traffic and keep us informed. Their role remains to stop the defamation of the Jewish people, and secure justice and fair treatment for all. Until the disease is eradicated, continued advocacy, strategic alliances, and education are our best weapons to cure the world's "oldest hatred."

The Road Less Traveled

It often takes a generation or more before the real truth percolates to the surface, and by then many history stories have already been told. To publicly expose and relate the Emory dental school story is to reveal the incredible naiveté or perhaps willful ignorance of an entire generation. My fellow students and I didn't know what we were getting into, we didn't comprehend what was happening when it happened, and we didn't know what happened even 60 years after it happened. It was only later that we learned we were not alone. The stark reality is that for the better part of the 20th century, higher education throughout the United States discriminated against Jews.

It occurred in a different way than our people had customarily experienced it over the millennia. In America, there were no expulsions as had occurred in Spain, Portugal, and England. There were no pogroms such as our people experienced in Poland and Russia. There were no imposed ghettos, no Nuremberg laws. Jewish men and women proudly served in all of America's battles and wars.

My immigrant parents and grandparents had barriers to overcome, but they never considered themselves anything less than full and equal citizens of our great country. I was born and raised American, educated in public and private schools, served as an officer in the United States Air Force, and enjoyed a full career in dentistry. I knew full well of serious racial inequities that had occurred in my lifetime—internment of Japanese/Americans during WWII and denial of basic civil rights to blacks until the 1960s. I was fully aware of barriers that made it difficult if not impossible for other than white Protestants to participate in certain social circles. So, yes, I knew that in certain ways I was not fully welcome. But those minor impediments never really cramped my style. We learned to rationalize: "That's just the way things are. At times, people like to associate with their own."

In Sunday School, I learned to be proud of my Jewish and American heritage. My teacher taught us that in 1790, a year before the Bill of Rights was ratified, George Washington, the first president of the United States, wrote to the members of Touro Synagogue in Newport, Rhode Island: "...May the children of the Stock of Abraham who dwell in this land continue to merit and enjoy the good will of the other inhabitants— while every one shall sit in safety under his own vine and fig tree and there shall be none to make him afraid."[63]

I learned in history classes alongside my fellow students that, with the discovery of America and the founding of a new country, unbounded opportunities existed for all in "this beacon shining out across the sea." In *Democracy in America*, published in 1835, Alexis de Tocqueville wrote of the New World and its burgeoning democratic order. Observing from the perspective of a detached social scientist, de Tocqueville described his travels through America in the early 19th century when the market revolution, Western expansion, and Jacksonian democracy were radically transforming the fabric of American life.

"Among a democratic people," de Tocqueville wrote, "where there is no hereditary wealth, every man works to earn a living.... Labor is held in honor; the prejudice is not against but in its favor."[64] That's the feeling I had growing up in Chattanooga, Tennessee. That is what I felt I was promised as a citizen of the United States. In this spirit, and after all the interviews and talks I gave throughout the country about antisemitism, I wanted to do something positive to help prevent this in the future. The tireless work of the Emory Development and Alumni Relations Department following the university's apology culminated in numerous gifts from private donors and, in 2014, the Brickman-Levin Fund was established. This fund, a joint effort of the Tam Institute of Jewish

Studies and the Laney Graduate School, supports annual endowments to graduate students in Jewish Studies at Emory. "In this way," Emory's announcement stated, "the fund will provide a meaningful response to the antisemitism of the past by ensuring that Jewish studies remains a permanent part of the graduate curriculum in the future."

There Shall Be None To Make Him Afraid

Six and a half years have now passed since the Emory apology, and we have lost a third of our original group of students. Those remaining stay in touch and share the accomplishments of our children and grandchildren. Many of our offspring are Emory alumni.

While we may have been the target of rabid antisemitism, we are also a symbol of survival, hope, and the generational grit that builds a lasting legacy and impression on society. In God's eyes, we are equal to the next man or woman. It is our oppressors who choose to single us out as stains on this world, and in doing so, besmirch themselves.

They labeled us as failures. But we know that they were the ones who failed. They failed their profession, they failed their institutions, and in doing so, they disgraced themselves.

Antisemitism continues as an evil force. The darkness of that evil gives our light meaning and purpose. Our task, according to the biblical injunction, is to dispel darkness and shine the light of goodness throughout the world.

As a historical note, it is important to record that the antisemitism we encountered at Emory was complex and even unique. The original brand of antisemitism, the religious contempt of Jews, is evident in many of the letters and documents we discovered in the various archives mentioned in previous chapters. We were also targeted by the mutant version of antisemitism, the race-based brand of Jewish hatred exemplified in the American Dental Association Horner report, which criticized the excess of one "racial" group in US dental schools. This also appeared in Dr. Buhler's application form, which under the RACE category asked if you were Caucasian, Jew, or other. If that wasn't sufficient, Emory added a unique twist to their perverted brand of antisemitism. What made Emory dental school unique from all other institutions was not just that it had a Jewish quota. Emory didn't stop there. They rejected 65% of the Jews they accepted. Other schools also had Jewish quotas, but at least once they accepted you, you were "their Jew," and in most cases they treated you as they did all their other students.

In telling my story, I feel that I have faithfully represented the feelings of my schoolmates. We long ago reconciled the hurtful experiences we shared and the inconvenient detours we were forced to take. For the most part, we all rebounded with determination and courage. We changed direction and found alternative ways to continue our lives and contribute to society. As a bonus, we discovered each other and found happiness and fulfillment in our extended family.

We extend our appreciation to Emory University for their public acknowledgement of the indignities we were forced to experience during the Buhler era, and for their unprecedented apology. We deeply regret that our parents were deprived of the satisfaction of hearing the apology. But we are comfortable with the knowledge that the full story has been told and we have been redeemed.

ABOUT THE AUTHOR

After Perry Brickman retired from the practice of oral surgery, a second career as an investigative journalist was thrust upon him. He had long suppressed a painful episode of his life, his ejection from Emory University School of Dentistry. Suddenly, in 2006, he discovered that he was one of dozens of fellow dental students who shared the same dark secret. Their children, neighbors, and friends were totally unaware of the humiliation they had experienced. Brickman's wife labeled them a "fraternity of silence."

Brickman's story was first reported in the New York Times and CNN in October 2012. When he was invited to speak at book fairs and film festivals throughout the country, he learned from audience feed-back that he had only scratched the surface. The antisemitism he and his cohorts encountered at Emory was only part of a nationwide conspiracy to prevent Jewish students from being accepted into the dental profession.

Extracted is Brickman's first book. Although much vital information hit the cutting room floor, it will be preserved in the archives of the Breman Jewish Heritage Museum and the Emory University archives.

INDEX

Bloom, Eugene (Bucky), 124, 136, 144, 173, 243, 246, 260–261
Bloom, Joan, 173, 243, 260
Blumenthal (Wolff), Elly, 86, 108
Blumenthal, David, xvii, 2, 144, 255, 257
B'nai B'rith
calm before the storm, 54
a cold case defrosted, 231
a happy wife is a happy life, 144
long-overdue recognition, 251
out of the frying pan, into the fire, 68
the real world, 150, 153
a tale of two men, 179–180
vicious infighting, 209, 213
B'nai B'rith Women, 209, 231
B'nai Zion Synagogue, 86, 101
Bolton, Virgil, 107
Book, William, 14–15
Botnick, Marvin, iv
Bowden, Henry, 212–213
Bradenton, Florida, 135
Brahmins (New England), 23
Brandeis University, xiii
Braverman, Harold, 201
Breen, Lester, 240–241
Breman, William, 197, 202
Breman Jewish Museum
back home, 91
a glimpse into the past, 3
hurry up and wait, 162, 164, 167
long-overdue recognition, 253–254
a tale of two men, 193

vicious infighting, 197
Brickman (Finer), Teresa, xviii, 132, 138, 142–143, 146, 151–152
Brickman (Freeman), Lori, xviii, 128–132, 138, 142–143, 146, 151–152
Brickman, Ida, 135
Brickman, Jeff, xviii, 138, 142–143, 146, 151–152
Brickman, Joseph, xviii
Brickman, Joseph Herschel, 138
Brickman, Paul Myer (P.M.), ix
Brickman, Perry
2009 letter to fellow dental students, 169–172
2012 letter to fellow dental students, 262–263
advance praise, i–iv
in the beginning, 51
a few good men, 246–248
foreword, xiv–xvi
hurry up and wait, 169–172
long-overdue recognition, 254–255, 259–260, 262–265, 268–269, 271
memory lane, 278–281, 283–285, 289–290, 292
photos, *45, 112, 261*
smooth sailing, 129
a story of survival, 293–294
Brickman, Rita, 44–45, 45, 83, 94, 98, 109, 128
Brickman, Shirley Berkowitz
acknowledgments, xviii
advance praise, ii

ENDNOTES

1   Photograph of Ralph R. Byrnes courtesy of Stuart A. Rose Manuscript, Archives, and Rare Book Library, Emory University.

2   Photograph of Goodrich C. White courtesy of Stuart A. Rose Manuscript, Archives, and Rare Book Library, Emory University.

3   Photograph of John E. Buhler courtesy of Stuart A. Rose Manuscript, Archives, and Rare Book Library, Emory University

4   *The Pittsburgh Courier,* February 10, 1945, p. 5.

5   Harlan H. Horner, "The Needs of Dentistry," *Journal of Dental Education,* December 1945, p.95.

6   Barbara Miller Solomon, *Ancestors and Immigrants: A Changing New England Tradition,* (John Wiley and Sons, Inc., New York), July 1956.

7   Michael N. Dobkowski, *The Tarnished Dream: The Basis of American Anti-Semitism,* (Greenwood Press, Westport, Connecticut,1979), p. 114.

8   Ibid., p.3.

9   David A. Gerber, *Anti-Semitism in American History,* (University of Illinois Press, 1986), p. 5.

10 Oscar Handlin, *Adventure in Freedom: 300 Years of Jewish Life in America* (McGraw-Hill, New York, 1954) pp.197-98.

11 David A. Gerber, *Anti-Semitism in American History,* (University of Illinois Press, 1986), p. 5.

12 Leonard Dinnerstein, *Anti-Semitism in America,* (Oxford University Press, 1994), pp.329-354.

13 Dobkowski, pp.243-291.

14 Dinnerstein, p. xiii

15 William Nichols, *Christian Antisemitism,* (Jason Aronson, Inc.,1993), pp. xix, xxiv, 385

16 Hannah Adams, *The History of the Jews From the Destruction of*

337

Jerusalem to the 19th Century (John Eliot, Jr.,   Boston 1812), vol. 2, pp. 325-26.

17   J. Kitto, *An Illustrated History of the Holy Bible,* (Henry Bill, Norwich, Connecticut, 1868) pp. 496-97, 556, 560, 574, 631-32.

18   John Huston Finley, *The Jew in Modern History*, (Unpublished address, 1886, John Huston Finley Papers, *Speeches* file, New York Public Library, New York.

19   James K. Hosmer, *The Story of the Jews* (New York: G.P. Putnam's Sons, 1893), p. 215.

20   Michael N. Dobkowski, *The Tarnished Dream*, Isaac M. Wise *Reminiscences*, trans. David Philipson (Cincinnati, L. Wise, 1901), p. 272.

21   Ibid., *The Tarnished Dream*, p. 6-7.

22   Carey McWilliams, *A Mask for Privilege: Anti-Semitism In America,* (*Little, Brown and Company*, Boston, 1948), pp. 18-19.

23   Dinnerstein, quoting Bertram W. Korn, *Lincoln and the Jews*, (Journal of the Illinois State Historical Society, Vol. 48, No. 2, Summer 1955), p.186.

24   McWilliams, p.8.

25   Ibid., pp.18,19.

26   Ernest Volkman, *Hate, A Legacy of Anti-Semitism in America*, (Franklin Watts, 1982), p. 26.

27   Stephen H. Norwood, *The Third Reich in the Ivory Tower*, (Cambridge University Press, 2011), p.38.

28   Dinnerstein, p. 44.

29   Ibid., p. 47.

30   Ibid., p. 51.

31   Ibid., pp. 56-57.

32   Ibid., p. 57.

33   Abraham Flexner, *Medical Education In The United States and Canada: A Report To The Carnegie Foundation For The Advancement of Teaching*, 1910.

34   Theodor Billroth, MD, *The Medical Sciences in the German Universities*, 1876, Translation by Dr. William H Welch, (The McMillan Company, New York, 1924), pp.105-110.

35   Abraham Flexner, *The American College: A Criticism*, (The Century Co.,

1908), pp. 10-11.

36 Newsletter, American College of Dentists (ACD) Spring 2017, p.1, p.6.

37 Newsletter, American College of Dentists (ACD) Spring 2018, p.1, p.9.

38 William J. Gies, *The Gies Report*, Journal of the American Dental Association (JADA) April 1984, issue 4, page 522, volume 108.

39 Brooklyn Eagle, December 3, 1917, p.18.

40 Jonathan Zimmerman, *Harold Wechsler and the Myth of Meritocracy*, The Chronicle of Higher Education, February 24, 2017.

41 Jerome Karabel, *The Chosen: The Hidden History of Admission and Exclusion at Harvard, Yale, and Princeton*, (Houghton Mifflin Company 2005), p. 96.
Marcia Graham Synnott, *The Half-Opened Door*, (Greenwood Press 1979), p.107.

42 *The Journal of the American Dental Association* (JADA), May 1939, Volume 26, Issue 5, p. 798.

43 Photograph of John E. Buhler courtesy of Stuart A. Rose Manuscript, Archives, and Rare Book Library, Emory University.

44 Photograph of Harlan H. Horner reprinted from The Journal of the American Dental Association (JADA), "A Full Time Secretary For the Council On Dental Education," Volume 27, Issue 8, page 1295, August 1940, with permission of Elselvier.

45 Photograph of Gerald D. Timmons reprinted from The Journal of the American Dental Association (JADA), "Gerald D. Timmons installed as president, James P. Hollers named president-elect," Volume 65, Issue 6, page 828, December 1962, with permission from Elselvier.

46 Heywood Broun and George Britt, *Christians Only*, (The Vanguard Press 1931), p.145.

47 Lawrence Bloomgarden, Commentary Magazine, *Medical School Quotas and National Health: Discrimination that Hurts Us All*, January 1953.

48 Edward C. Halperin, *The Jewish Problem in U.S. Medical Education*, 1920-1955, (Journal of the History of Medicine and Allied Sciences, Volume 56, Number 2, April 2001), pp.140-167.

49 Robert S. Wistrich, *Antisemitism, The Longest Hatred*, (Pantheon Books, 1991), p.118.

50 Thomas Carlyle. *Signs of the Times*, Edinburgh Review, Volume 3, 1829.

51 Kent Nerburn, https://www.inspiringquotes.us/author/1395-kent-nerburn.

52 Thomas H. English, Emory University 1915–1965: *A Semi-centennial History. Atlanta:* (Emory University, 1966), p. 175

53 New Georgia Encyclopedia, https://www.georgiaencyclopedia.org/articles/history-archaeology/leo-frank-case.

54 Old Testament, Exodus 7:3-4.

55 Alexander Nehamas, *On Friendship*, (Basic Books, 2016), p.6.

56 Samuel G. Freedman, New York Times, *Emory Confronts a Legacy of Bias Against Jews*, October 6, 2012.

57 Emory University event photo (October 10, 2012) with permission of Emory Photo/Video

58 Emory University event photo (October 10, 2012) with permission of Emory Photo/Video

59 Emory University event photo (October 10, 2012) with permission of Emory Photo/Video

60 Susan McCarthy, SorryWatch.com, *I've graphed my bad behavior for you*, October12, 2012.

61 Dan A. Oren, *Joining The Club: A History of Jews and Yale*, (Yale University Press, 1985), p.148.

62 Frederic Cople Jaher, *The Jews and the Nation: Revolution, Emancipation, State Formation, and the Liberal Paradigm in America and France*, (Princeton University Press, 2002), p. 230

63 *George Washington: A Collection*, ed. W.B. Allen (Liberty Fund, Indianapolis, 1988)

64 Alexis de Tocqueville, *Democracy In America*, (Alfred A. Knopf, New York, 1980), p.52, Volume 2, Chapter 18.

Printed in the USA
CPSIA information can be obtained
at www.ICGtesting.com
JSHW022206140824
68134JS00018B/888

9 781642 792942